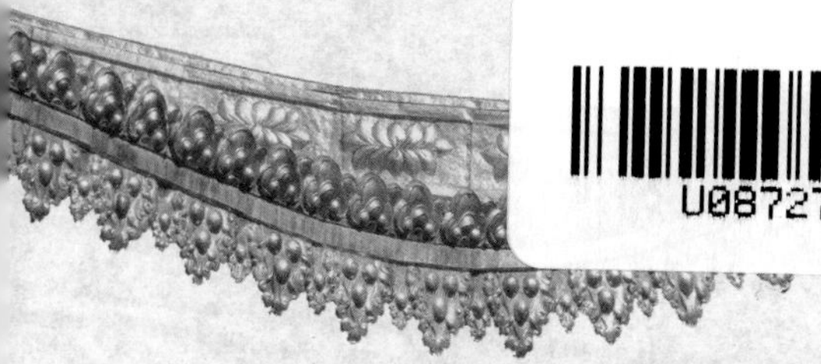

沿途导游掌中宝

英语导游文化讲解资料库

杨天庆　编著
（美）Spencer Brainard 审校

旅游教育出版社
·北　京·

出版说明

近年来,中国入境游进一步蓬勃发展,英语导游的素质也在不断提高,但是外国游客对英语导游的期望值也越来越高。他们不仅希望英语导游可以介绍中国美丽的风景和悠久的古迹,也希望通过英语导游更多地了解中国的文化和风土人情。英语导游一般对中国文化都有一定程度的了解,但是外国友人的提问有时会是他们没有特别留意的地方;或者有些内容他们也很熟悉,但是一时不知道怎么用英语表达才好。为了提高英语导游的综合文化素养,我们精心策划了这套"英语导游文化讲解资料库",以满足英语导游的知识需求。

综合看来,本丛书主要有以下特色:第一,作者权威。本丛书作者均具备丰富的英语导游教学与实践经验,熟悉中国文化内容,了解英语导游工作的实际需要。第二,选材丰富,内容实用。本丛书所选内容都是老外感兴趣的话题,涉及中国文化和导游工作的方方面面,具有较强的知识性和趣味性。第三,语言地道、简练。我们专门聘请外国专家审校,确保本丛书语言符合英语习惯,容易被外国游客理解;另外本丛书尽量避免使用晦涩难懂的生词和繁复的句式,而是选用常用词和简练的语句,使其口语化,适合讲解。

本丛书既是英语导游的好帮手,也是广大英语爱好者不可多得的知识读本。书中若有不足之处,敬请读者批评指正。

旅游教育出版社

2007.1

目录
Contents

传统节日 /158
Traditional Festivals

家训集览 /301
Traditional Family Instructions

前 言
Preface

沿途英语导游工作是旅游工作的重要组成部分，也是英语导游工作的难点。在英语导游队伍不断壮大的同时，也出现了英语导游沿途讲解文化性不强，话题乏味，甚至“游而不导”的现象。本人根据自己多年的教学与实践，针对外国游客经常提出的问题，编写了这本《沿途导游掌中宝》，旨在提高英语导游的讲解水平。

本书正文部分涵盖了中国文化的很多方面，包括历史与地理、天文与时令、汉字的产生与演变、姓名的由来、古代婚姻、传统服饰、饮食、传统酒文化、品茶、风俗习惯、传统节日、古代科举、不同朝代的文化发展、古建筑风格和道教与佛教共15个专题，117个常见话题。采取了中英文提问，英文回答的形式，目的是让读者翻开书，就能从中文提问中知道书的内容，便于检索。

本书的一个亮点在于附录部分增加了购物、部分景点细节描述范例、家训集览和古代寓言的内容。购物部分模拟了导购的现场讲解词，非常实用。景点细节描述范例一改以往英文景点描述翻译痕迹明显的弊病，展示了一种新的讲解词写作模式，既达到了讲解的目的，又避免了语言生硬。在沿途讲解中插入有趣的故事，既可以提高文化讲解的趣味性，又可以让游客忘记旅途疲劳。本书从家训集览和古代寓言中各选出20个流传较广的有趣小故事，供导游选择使用。

本书的一大特色在于语言简短，朗朗上口。本人在编写过程中，特意选择了常用的英语单词、词组和句型，使所有的译文通顺简洁，口语化，使英语导游的讲解更加自然，而不会让人觉得像是在背书。英语和旅游专业的学生也可利用此书学习如何用英语讲解中国文化，用中国文化的内容来练习英语口语。

本人在编写过程中，承蒙执教于四川师范大学的 Spencer Brainard 先生的积极支持，他对全书进行了审校，在此表示感谢。

由于水平有限，书中难免有疏漏之处，敬请读者批评指正。

编者

2006.6

历史与地理
History and Geography

1 在中国的文化史上有哪四大发现?

What four great discoveries have been made in the course of Chinese civilization?

In Chinese history, there have been extraordinary breakthrough discoveries that have shed light on the customs and ways of life of later dynasties. Below are four great discoveries that have greatly influenced the historical understanding of Chinese civilization.

The first discovery occurred towards the end of the period of Emperor Wu Di of the Han Dynasty(汉武帝)(c. 92 BC). During this time, many Confucian classics were uncovered, including *The Classic of History* (《书经》), *The Analects* (《论语》), *The Classic of Rites* (《礼记》), *The Classic of Filial Duty* (《孝经》), among other important books. These works were written in an ancient pre-Qin-script, and they are called "the Old Script" texts.

The second discovery took place in the beginning of the Western Jin Dynasty (265 – 317) when a large amount of bamboo annals were unearthed in the tomb of King Xiang Wang of the State of Wei(魏襄王). There were 75 volumes in total. These annals are commonly referred to as *The Bamboo Books of Ji's Tomb*(《汲冢竹书》).

The third discovery are ancient inscriptions on bones or tortoise shells known as the "Tortoise Shell Characters(龟板文字)." These inscriptions were used for divination during the Shang and Zhou dynasties (1600 BC –256 BC). Toward the end of the Qing Dynasty (c. 1911), peasants continually found fragments of these bones and shells while ploughing their fields, thinking that these artifacts were in fact "dragon bones" which could be used for medical treatment. Through careful study, scholars came to realize that the symbols engraved on the bones were scripts used before the Qin Dynasty(221 BC – 2006 BC), leading to insight into the socio-political, economical, and cultural aspects of the Shang and Zhou dynasties.

The fourth discovery came about in 1899 with the unearthing of the Dunhuang precious deposits(敦煌宝藏), previously hidden in the unknown caves of the Dunhuang Grottos. The books totaled 20,000 bound volumes, mostly Buddhist and Daoist scriptures, and also many other kinds of works of history, poetry, folk literature, local chronicles, medicine and almanac recordings. Unfortunately foreign thieves made off with most of these works causing great loss to China's cultural heritage.

Notes: ①breakthrough 突破 ②civilization 文明 ③analects 论集 ④rite 仪式 ⑤filial duty 孝道 ⑥script 书写体 ⑦annals 历史记载 ⑧inscription 铭刻 ⑨insight into 深刻的理解 ⑩unearthing(从地下)发掘 ⑪chronicle 编年史 ⑫almanac 历书 ⑬make off with 偷走 ⑭cultural heritage 文化遗产

2 什么是"九州"?

What is *jiuzhou*?

Jiuzhou means "the nine states," the denomination of administrative areas in ancient China. Before the Han Dynasty(206 BC – 220 AD), historians thought that the *jiuzhou* administrative areas were divided after Yu the Great drained the flood waters and built canals. Until the Eastern Han Dynasty (25 – 220), some thought that *jiuzhou* was divided in the Zhou or Yin Dynasty. *The Classic of Documents*(《尚书》) says that *jiuzhou* includes *Ji*(冀), *Yan*(兖), *Qing*(青), *Xu*(徐), *Yang*(扬), *Jing*(荆), *Yu*(豫), *Liang*(梁) and *Yong*(雍).

Notes: ①denomination 名称 ②administrative 行政的

3 什么是“郡、县”？

What is *jun* and *xian*?

The *jun* (prefecture, 郡) and the *xian* (county, 县) were a system of local administration. During the Spring and Autumn Period (722 BC – 476 BC), the county administration held more power than the prefecture. Throughout the Qin Dynasty (221 BC – 206 BC), however, the prefecture became more dominant. When Qin Shihuang, the first Emperor of the Qin Dynasty, founded his empire, he divided the country into more than 36 prefectures. Each prefecture administratively managed several counties. During the Han Dynasty (206 BC – 220 AD), the first emperor divided his country into 63 prefectures. The size of each prefecture was smaller than that of the Qin Dynasty. During the Sui and Tang dynasties (581 – 907), the name of *jun* had been replaced by *zhou* (州) or *fu* (府), and since then the county has been under the jurisdiction of the prefecture.

Notes: ① administration 行政机构 ② centralized 集中的 ③ jurisdiction 管辖权

4 什么是"国"?

What is *guo*?

Guo in the Zhou Dynasty (1046 BC – 256 BC) refers to the lord state. During the Western Zhou Dynasty (1046 BC – 256 BC), the king distributed territory to his nobility, and each lord or prince set up his state accordingly. With the arrival of the Qin Dynasty (221 BC – 206 BC), the Qin emperor temporarily put an end to the Zhou enfeoffment system (分封制). Later on in the Western Han Dynasty (1046 BC – 771 BC), *guo* (the state) and *jun* (the prefecture) co-existed, of the same territorial size. The Western Han (206 BC – 25 AD) feudal princes and lords governed the state and prefecture as administrative areas.

Notes: ①nobility 贵族 ②enfeoffment 赐以封地 ③temporarily 暂时地

5 什么是"道"?

What is *dao*?

The *dao* (道) refers to an administrative district in

ancient China. During the Tang Dynasty (618 – 907), the whole empire was divided into 15 *daos*. The size of each *dao* was almost the same as that of the *zhou* (the prefecture, 州) of the Han Dynasty (206 BC – 220 AD). Until the beginning of the Northern Song Dynasty (960 – 1127), the country was divided into thirteen *daos*, but soon this system was abolished, replaced instead by the *lu* (路) system. In the Qing Dynasty (1616 – 1911), the *dao* system was brought back, given more administrative power than the prefecture *zhou*, but was still under the control of the province.

Notes: ①empire 帝国

6 什么是“路”？

What is *lu*?

The *lu* replaced the *dao* in the Northern Song Dynasty (960 – 1127). Originally 15 *lus* were set up to levy taxes and transport grains to the capital along rivers or canals. The *lu* gradually gained regional administrative and military power. Throughout the Southern Song Dynasty (1127 – 1279), there were 16 *lus*, which included Fujian Lu(福建路), Guangdong Lu(广东路),

Guangxi Lu(广西路) and Hunan Lu(湖南路). The regional size of each *lu* was almost the same as that of a province. During the Yuan Dynasty (1206 – 1368), *lu*'s size shrank to that of a prefecture.

Notes: ① levy 征收 ②transport 运输

7 什么是"省"?

What is *sheng*?

Sheng means "province." How did *sheng* evolve? Originally *sheng* referred to the forbidden area where emperors and imperial families resided. Throughout the Wei and Jin dynasties (220 – 420), *sheng* defined one of the departments under the central government. During the Tang Dynasty (618 – 907), the central government consisted of three departments: the *shang shu sheng*(Department of State Affairs, 尚书省), *zhong shu sheng* (the Secretariat, 中书省) and *men xia sheng*(the Chancellery, 门下省). The latter two departments handled the huge flow of governmental documents. In the period of the Yuan Dynasty (1206 – 1368), the central government was known as *zhong shu sheng*(中书省). Meanwhile the Yuan central government set up its field administrative agencies in *lu* prefectures. The government agency *xing sheng* (literally meaning "the field secretariat",行省), had state power, representing the central government in local areas. The term *xing sheng* was later shortened to *sheng* (province).

Notes: ①secretariat 秘书处 ②chancellery 总理(或大臣;大法官)之职

8 中国有哪十大风景名胜?

What are the ten major scenic sights in China?

Traditionally there are ten major scenic sights(十大风景名胜)in China that are well worth making a trip to see: the Great Wall(万里长城), the Scenery in Guilin(桂林山水), the West Lake in Hangzhou(杭州西湖), the Palace Museum in Beijing(北京故宫), Gardens in Suzhou(苏州园林), Mt. Huangshan in Anhui(安徽黄山), the Three Gorges on the Yangtze River(长江三峡), the Sun Moon Lake in Taiwan(台湾日月潭), the Imperial Summer Villa in Chengde(承德避暑山庄)and the Terracotta Warriors in Xi'an(西安兵马俑).

Notes: ①scenery 风景 ②terracotta 赤陶

9 人们对中国的部分景点有哪些赞美之词？
What are some popular sayings praising some of China's scenic sights?

No place under Heaven is as beautiful as Mt. Emei.（峨眉天下秀）

Mt. Qingcheng is commonly known for its solitary tranquility under Heaven.（青城天下幽）

Leshan Giant Buddha, the largest Buddha statue in the world（乐山大佛——天下第一大佛）

Mt. Putuo, the first mountain on the sea（普陀山——海山第一）

The misty rain on the West Lake, famous through ancient dynasties to the present（西湖烟雨誉古今）

The landscape in Guilin, unsurpassed in its beauty（桂林山水甲天下）

Mt. Jiuhuashan, the first mountain in Southeast China（九华山——东南第一山）

The beauty of Mt. Lushan, unmatched in the world（匡庐奇秀甲天下）

One will not visit any other mountain after having climbed Mt. Huangshan（黄山归来不看岳）

Dongting Lake holds all the waters under Heaven (洞庭天下水)

Mt. Songshan Shaolin Temple, the first Buddhist temple under Heaven (嵩山少林寺——天下第一刹)

Shanhaiguan Pass, the first pass of mountains and sea under Heaven (山海关——天下第一关)

Baotu Spring (Jet Spring) in Jinan, the first spring under Heaven (济南趵突泉——天下第一泉)

Notes: ①unsurpassed 卓越的 ②unmatched 无与伦比的

10 中国名山的名称是怎样得来的？

What are the origins of the names of famous mountains in China?

Himalayas(喜马拉雅山)

This mountain range has two names. One name is Himalayas(喜马拉雅山), which means "Abode of Snow (雪之家)" in Sanskrit. The other is Mt. Qomolangma(珠穆朗玛峰), which means "Goddess Peak (后妃神女)" in Tibetan. Mt. Tanggula(唐古拉山) refers to "the Mountain on the Plateau(高原上的山)," and Mt. Gangdise (冈底斯山) to "Master of all Mountains(众山之主)" in Tibetan.

Mt. Huashan(华山)

It is said that during the Taikang Period (280 - 290)(太康年间) of the Jin Dynasty "a thousand-leaf-stone-lotus flower(千叶石莲花) grew on Mt. Huashan (华山)." In ancient Chinese language, *hua* (华) stands for "flower," thus giving this mountain its namesake. According to another legend, the mountain is named after its five peaks, and each peak resembles a petal of a flower.

Mt. Emei(峨眉山)

Mt. Emei has four peaks. The first peak(万佛顶, the Ten Thousand Buddha Summit) and the second peak(金顶, the Golden Summit) stand facing each other, resembling *emei*(娥眉), the delicate eyebrows of a Chinese woman.

Mt. Lushan (庐山)

Originally known as Mt. Kuangshan(匡山) after the Kuang brothers, who during the Zhou Dynasty (1046 BC - 256 BC), secluded themselves there, this mountain was later renamed after the ancient state of Luzi(庐子国) of the Spring and Autumn Period (770 BC - 476 BC) whose people used it as a former base.

Mt. Huangshan(黄山)

Mt. Huangshan(黄山) is known in English as the Yellow Mountains. According to legend, the Yellow Emperor(黄帝)(c. 3000 BC - c. 2100 BC) used to go to these mountains where he would prepare herbal medicine with famous alchemists of the time.

Notes: ①abode 住所 ②plateau 高原 ③namesake 同名的人；同名物 ④alchemist 炼金术士

11 中国以前有哪些主要朝代？

What are the major dynasties of ancient China?

(1) Shang Dynasty (1550 BC – 1030 BC): City states emerge, writing developed and society divided into classes made up of peasants, merchants, the military, scholars and aristocracy.

(2) Zhou Dynasty (1030 BC – 256 BC): Feudal states emerge, salt and iron industries developed; wealthy merchant class emerges. Age of Confucius and Daoism.

(3) Qin Dynasty (221 BC – 207 BC): Feudal states merged into unified China; uniform legal code created; written language, weights and measures, length of cart axles standardized.

(4) Han Dynasty (206 BC – 220 AD): Government becomes feudalistic; civil service instituted to run

government; Buddhism introduced from India; Confucianism becomes state religion.

(5) Three Kingdoms, Southern and Northern Dynasties (221 – 581): Social, political discontent; revolts against feudal government; Buddhism spreads.

(6) Sui Dynasty (581 – 618): Empire reunified; north and south joined by the Grand Canal.

(7) Tang Dynasty (618 – 907): Empire continues to expand; trading vessels penetrate Indian Ocean; art, music and scholarship flourish among the rich and ruling classes.

(8) Five Dynasties (907 – 960): Period of turmoil and short-lived dynasties.

(9) Song Dynasty (960 – 1127): Northern tribes become serious threat, forcing capital to move south; paper money in use; size and sophistication of cities grow.

(10) Southern Song Dynasty (1127 – 1279): Song rulers move south; new dynasty set up in the north.

(11) Yuan Dynasty (1280 – 1368): Empire reunified under the Yuan; the empire attracts Western travelers, including Marco Polo; novel published, and opera developed.

(12) Ming and Qing dynasties (1368 – 1911): The gradual decline of feudalism in ancient China; agriculture and handicrafts make progress and rudiments of

capitalism appears by the end of the Ming; China becomes already a united multi-national country; a large fleet under the command of Zheng He has made seven long ocean voyages over three decades.

Notes: ①merchants 商人 ②aristocracy 贵族 ③emerge 出现 ④axle 车轴 ⑤feudalistic 封建制度的 ⑥civil service 文职 ⑦discontent 不满的 ⑧vessel 船 ⑨penetrate 穿过 ⑩turmoil 骚动 ⑪sophistication 复杂 ⑫handicraft 手工艺 ⑬rudiment 雏形;萌芽 ⑭multi-national 多民族的

12 怎样简述中国领土和行政区域?

Will you give us a brief introduction of the Chinese territory and administrative divisions?

China is situated in the eastern part of Asia, on the west coast of the Pacific Ocean. China has a total land area of 9.6 million square kilometers. It stretches from the central line of the main navigation channel of the Heilongjiang River(黑龙江)to the north of Mohe River(漠河)in the north to the Zengmu Reef(曾母暗沙)of the Nansha Islands in the south, and from the Pamirs(帕米尔高原)to the west of Wuqia County(乌恰县)in the Xinjiang Uygur Autonomous Region in the west to the confluence of the Heilongjiang River(黑龙江) and Wusuli River(乌苏里江)in the east. China is bordered by the Democratic People's Republic of Korea to the east; the People's Republic of Mongolia to the north; Russia to the northeast; Kazakhstan, Kirghizstan, Tajikistan to the northwest; Afghanistan, Pakistan, India, Nepal, Sikkim and Bhutan to the west and southwest; and Myanmar, Laos and Vietnam to the south.

The Chinese mainland is bordered by the Bohai Sea, the Yellow Sea, the East China Sea and the South China Sea in the east and south. Across the East China Sea to the east and the South China Sea to the southeast, are Japan, the Philippines, Malaysia and Brunei. More than 5,000 islands are scattered over China's vast territorial seas, the largest being Taiwan and the next largest, Hainan.

For administrative purposes, China is divided into 23 provinces, 5 autonomous regions, 4 municipalities directly under the Central Government and 2 special administrative regions. The administrative units under a province or an autonomous region include cities, autonomous prefectures, counties, and autonomous counties. Under a county or autonomous county are township, nationality townships and towns. Beijing is the capital of China.

Notes: ①navigation 航海 ②latitude 纬度 ③longitude 经度 ④Kazakhstan 哈萨克斯坦 ⑤Kirghizstan 吉尔吉斯斯坦 ⑥Tajikistan 塔吉克斯坦 ⑦Afghanistan 阿富汗 ⑧Pakistan 巴基斯坦 ⑨Nepal 尼泊尔 ⑩Sikkim 锡金 ⑪Bhutan 不丹 ⑫Myanmar 缅甸 ⑬Laos 老挝 ⑭Brunei 文莱 ⑮Municipality 自治市

天文与时令
Astronomy and Seasons

1 中国古代早期的天文发展是什么样的情况？

What is the early history of ancient Chinese astronomy?

Astronomy in ancient China started during the Neolithic Period. At this time, people began to observe how the sun rose and set, and especially the moon's different phases. They even painted the sun, the moon, and stars on pottery. It was during the Xia Dynasty (2070 BC – 1600 BC), about three or four thousand years ago, that the lunar calendar came into existence. In China, many traditional festivities in a year are usually calculated according to this calendar. The present lunar calendar is still named "Xia calendar" (夏历). In accordance with the records written on the Oracle Bone Scripts (甲骨文), a year was divided into spring and autumn during the Xia Dynasty (2070 BC – 1600 BC); there were 12 months a year, and 13 months a leap year(闰年); 30 days a solar month and 29days a lunar month. The Oracle Bone Scripts also record solar and lunar eclipses that took place during the Shang Dynasty(1600 BC – 1046 BC). In the period of the Western Zhou Dynasty (1046 BC – 771 BC), political officials were appointed to take charge of observing and recording the changes of the sky. During the Spring and Autumn Period (770 BC – 476 BC), according to the position of the moon each month, people were able to trace the movement of the sun, thus establishing the 28-*xiu*(lunar mansions, 宿) system. *Xiu* is also translated as zodiac constellations. *The Spring and Autumn Annals*(《春秋》), one of the "Four Books and Five Classics" (四书五经), records the historical development of the State of Lu from 722 BC to 479 BC. This book recounts how a year was divided by the four seasons during this period.

Notes: ①astronomy 天文学 ②Neolithic 新石器时代的 ③phase(月球的)位相 ④oracle 神谕 ⑤eclipse 蚀 ⑥mansion 宅第 ⑦zodiac 黄道带 ⑧constellation 星宿

2 中国古代人们一般怎样看待天文？

How popular was astronomy in ancient China?

In ancient China, astronomers believed that the movements of the stars were related closely to the destiny of the country and its rulers, and therefore cataloged every observable star. A constellation was called "a palace", with the major star being the emperor star and lesser stars princes. When a wise prince occupied the throne, the moon followed the right way. When the prince was not wise and the ministers abused power, the moon lost its way. From the 16th century BC to the end of the 19th century AD, almost every dynasty appointed officials to take charge of observing and recording the changes in the sky.

The Chinese believed planetary phenomena could reveal if life was out of balance. For example, if the sun or the moon was to inexplicably lose brightness, early Chinese believed light may never return, and the world would end. A solar eclipse provoked even more anxiety, for astronomers imagined that a dragon was devouring the sun. Precisely because of this and many other fears, the ancient Chinese began to observe solar and lunar eclipses, recording the time and size of the event, and searching for the reasons behind the eclipses.

Notes: ①astronomer 天文学家 ②catalog 记载 ③observable 看得见的 ④planetary 行星的 ⑤phenomena(phenomenon 的复数)现象 ⑥inexplicably 无法说明地 ⑦provoke 激起 ⑧devour 吞没

3 什么是三垣、四象、二十八宿？

What are 3 *yuan*, 4 *xiang* and 28 *xiu*?

Ancient astronomers divided the astral regions around the North Pole into 3 *yuan* and 28 *xiu*. Yuan means "wall," so the 3 *yuan* means "the Three Walls" which consist of the Ziwei Wall(紫微垣), the Taiwei Wall(太微垣) and the Tianshi Wall(天市垣).

When the earth completes a rotation around the sun, direct sunlight falls inside the North-South Tropic that is regarded by ancient astronomers as the lucky ecliptic(黄道吉). Astronomers divided the stars around the ecliptic into four quarters; the east, the south, the west and the north. Each quarter relates to a lucky supernatural beast. The Qinglong (the green dragon, 青龙) represents the east, the Zhuque (the phoenix-like bird, 朱雀) the south, the Baihu (the white tiger, 白虎)

the west and the Xuanwu (the tortoise-like creature with a snake winding round it, 玄武) the north. These supernatural creatures represent the images of stars, and therefore they are called "the Four Images."

Ancient astronomers also placed 28 *xiu*s on the different images, each image having seven *xiu*s. These *xiu*s are situated along the moon's path as it rotates around the earth each month. They are called "mansions" or "lodges" because they were once understood to be resting places for the moon during its journey.

Notes: ①North Pole 北极 ②supernatural 神的 ③phoenix 凤凰 ④rotate 转动

4 什么是上古、中古、三古?

What are the Remote Ancient Times, the Middle Ancient Times and the Three Ancient Times?

The Remote Ancient Times refer to the age before written language, and therefore time was recorded by tying knots with a rope.

The Middle Ancient Times refer to the age between the Shang and Zhou dynasties (1600 BC - 256 BC). However, historians hold different opinions about when these two ages began and ended. According to the book *Han Feizi*(《韩非子》), "During the Middle Ancient Times, heavy waters flooded the whole country, and Yu, the Great, is believed to have been in charge of draining the flood waters and building canals(中古之世,天下大水,而鲧禹决渎)." These times refer to the legendary Yuxia Period(虞夏时期).

The Three Ancient Times refer to the remote, the middle and the age after the middle. As told by *The Book of the Earlier Han Dynasty*(《汉书》), Fu Xi (伏羲) lived during the Remote Ancient Times; King Wen of the Zhou Dynasty(周文王) during the Middle Ancient Times, and Confucius during the Ancient Times after the middle ones. Fu Xi was the first of the three noble emperors in Chinese mythology. King Wen was the father of King Wu(武王), the founder of the Zhou Dynasty, and one of the sage rulers regarded by Confucian historians as a model king.

Notes: ①knot(绳等的)结 ②mythology 神话 ③sage 贤明的

5 什么是阴历?

What is the Chinese lunar calendar?

Yinli is the lunar or agricultural calendar, which

contains a mixture of solar and lunar elements. The lunar calendar is derived from astronomical observations of the longitude of the sun and the phases of the moon. Its beginnings can trace back to the 14th century BC. Legend has it that the Yellow Emperor (黄帝) invented the calendar in 2637 BC. The Chinese calendar's years coincide with the tropical years, and its months coincide with the synodic months. An ordinary year has 12 months while a leap year has 13 months. An ordinary year has 353, 354, or 355 days, and a leap year has 383, 384, or 385 days. The Chinese calendar does not use a continuous year count, but instead uses a 60 – year cycle and a system of regional years (starting with each emperor). In 1582 Jesuit missionaries introduced the Gregorian calendar to China, but not until 1912 was it adopted. With the adoption of the Western calendar, the *yin-yang* calendar lost its primary importance in Chinese society. Currently Chinese use the lunar calendar for the scheduling of holidays such as Chinese New Year (Spring Festival), the Mid-Autumn Festival, and for divination, including choosing the most auspicious date for a wedding or the grand opening of an important building.

Notes: ①coincide with 相符；巧合 ②tropical year 回归年；太阳年 ③synodic 相合的 ④continuous 连续的 ⑤Jesuit 耶稣会信徒 ⑥Gregorian calendar 格列高利历；公历

6 什么是“黄历”和“皇历”？

What are the “Huang Di Almanac” and the “Imperial Calendar?”

Before the Western Han Dynasty (206 BC – 25 AD), there were six different ancient lunar calendars: the Huang Di Calendar (黄历, Almanac), the Xia Calendar (夏历, the Lunar Calendar), the Yin Calendar (殷历) among others. Legend has it that Huang Di, the Yellow Emperor who reined from 2698 BC to 2599 BC, invented the first Chinese calendar called “Huang Di Calendar,” or the “Huang Calendar.” After omens, superstitions, and taboos were added, the name of the calendar became a general term referring to any ancient almanac.

In the early 9th century, the imperial government of the Tang Dynasty gave an order that calendars or almanacs should not be printed until after the emperor examined them. The order also declared that only official printing shops were permitted to print out calendars. From then on, calendars were called “the Imperial Calendar (皇历).”

There exist other explanations of the origins of the Imperial Calendar. For example, towards the end of every lunar year, Emperor Tai Zong of the Song Dynasty (宋太宗) (976 – 998) would present calendars to his civil officials and generals. These calendar contained information related to the dates of lunar festivals and seasons, and basic knowledge of farming and planting. A calendar from then on was known as the "Imperial Calendar" because the Emperor would grant it to his subjects.

Notes: ①almanac 历书 ②omen 预兆 ③superstition 迷信 ④taboo 忌讳 ⑤grant 赐予

7 什么是节气？

What is *jieqi*?

Jieqi means "solar period" or "solar term." The solar-based agricultural calendar is divided into 24 solar periods, each period being marked by three climatic signs. These climatic signs occur when the sun reaches one of twenty-four equally spaced points along the ecliptic, positioned at fifteen-degree intervals. These periods are measured in the standard astronomical convention of the ecliptic longitude, with zero degrees positioned at the vernal equinox point.

Even though the solar-based periods fall around the same date every year in the solar calendar, they do not form any obvious pattern in the Chinese calendar. These solar periods primarily work as seasonal markers to help farmers decide when to plant and harvest crops. The 24 periods are published each year in the farmers' calendar, with each calendar month containing the designated periods. These periods begin at the equinox in February, known in Chinese as the "Beginning of Spring (立春)." In the same month, the second period is called "Rain Water (雨水)," which means "Starting at this point, the temperature makes rain more likely than snow." The third period in March is called "Awakening of Insects(惊蛰)," which means "all the hibernating insects will awaken."

Notes: ①solar period 节气 ②climatic sign 症候 ③convention 惯例 ④vernal equinox point 春分 ⑤hibernate 冬眠

8 什么是天干、地支？

What are *tiangan* and *dizhi*?

The Chinese calendar uses the terminology *tiangan* (Heavenly Stems) and *dizhi* (Earthly Branches). The

10 Heavenly Stems are *jia*(甲), *yi*(乙), *bing*(丙), *ding*(丁), *wu*(戊), *ji*(己), *geng*(庚), *xin*(辛), *ren*(壬) and *gui*(癸). The 12 Earthly Branches are *zi*(子), *chou*(丑), *yin*(寅), *mao*(卯), *chen*(辰), *si*(巳), *wu*(午), *wei*(未), *shen*(申), *you*(酉), *xu*(戌) *and hai*(亥).

Initially the ten stems were invented to record the days. *Jia* referred to the first day, *yi* to the second day, *bing* to the third day, etc. The twelve branches were invented to record the months. *Zi* referred to the first month, *chou* to the second month, *yin* to the third month, etc. Ancient people used the Ten Heavenly Stems and the Twelve Earthly Branches to formulate a sixty-year cycle. Beginning in the Han Dynasty (206 BC – 220 AD), however, the sixty-year cycle began to be used in both official and unofficial ways. These sixty combinations have been applied widely—to days, months and any variety of other items that can be counted in a cycle. Before the 1911 revolution, years were always counted starting from the date a new emperor came to power.

So how does one count years? Within each 60 – year cycle, each year is assigned a name consisting of two components. The first component is a Heavenly Stem, and the second component is an Earthly Branch. Each of the two components is used sequentially. For example, the first year of the 60-year cycle is called *jia-zi*(甲子), the second year *yi-chou*(乙丑), the third year *bing-yin*(丙寅), etc. When we arrive at *gui*(癸), the last one of the Heavenly Stems, we call the 10th year as *gui-you*(癸酉). Then we restart with *jia*, the first Heavenly Stem, and call the 11th year as *jia-xu*(甲戌). After we arrive at *hai*(亥), the last of the Earthly Branches, we will restart with *zi*. Such a process goes on until we arrive at the 60th year that is called *gui-hai*(癸亥).

Notes: ①terminology 术语 ②Heavenly Stem 天干 ③Earthly Branch 地支 ④component 成分 ⑤sequentially 相继地

9 什么是生肖?

How does the Chinese Zodiac work?

The Chinese zodiac or *shengxiao*, is composed of 12 animals in the following order: Mouse, Ox, Tiger, Rabbit, Dragon, Snake, Horse, Sheep (or Goat), Monkey, Cock, Dog, and Pig. Although, the zodiac is an important part of traditional Chinese culture, its origins are unknown. Each of these twelve animal signs symbolizes a lunar year. If this year is the Year of the Dog, the next year will be the Year of the Pig.

There is a Chinese saying, "There is an animal that hides in your heart." The Chinese believe the each zodiac animal exercises a profound influence over people born during its year. For example, if a person is born in the year of the Dragon, he/she is believed to have good luck in his/her life.

The following are stories associated with these twelve animal signs.

According to the first story, one day the Mouse was chosen to invite the animals to participate in a selection for the zodiac signs. Although the Cat was a good friend of the Mouse, the Mouse forgot to invite him. The Cat became angry and vowed then on to be the Mouse's natural enemy.

The second story recounts how the Mouse became the first of the twelve animal signs. Long ago, a god ordered all the animals to visit him on the New Year's Day. He said that those who arrived earlier would be on the list of the twelve animal signs. As the Ox heard of this, he said to himself: "Oh, it's a long journey to visit the god. I'd better start early." The Mouse heard what the Ox said. He quietly jumped onto the Ox's back without being noticed. The two set out on the eve of the Lunar New Year. Upon arrival of the god's place, the Ox was excited to know that he was the first to greet the god. Just before he was about to offer to the god his New Year greetings, the Mouse quickly jumped down over the Ox's head and kowtowed in front of the god. The god was so happy to receive the first greetings from the Mouse that he named him the first of the twelve animal signs.

The third story describes how the Twelve Earthly Branches are divided into two groups. One group belongs to the *yin* (阴) and the other to the *yang* (阳). Animals that belong to the *yin* would be placed in the *yin* group, and vice versa. But how were these twelve animals separated? Animals that have odd-number toes on each foot or paw fall into the *yang* and those who have even number on each foot or paw fall into the *yin*. The Tiger, the Dragon, the Monkey and the Dog each have five toes on each paw, and the Horse has one hoof. They all fall into the *yang* group. The cloven-hoofed Ox, the Goat and the Pig fall into the *yin* group because their hoofs are divided into two parts. The Mouse has both the *yin* and *yang* features because of his four toes on each fore leg and five on each hind leg. Therefore the Mouse represents *zi* (子), the first branch of the Twelve Earthly Branches since the *zi* branch covers a period from 11 o'clock in the evening (night or *yin*) to 1 o'clock (day or *yang*) early in the morning.

The Mouse's *yin* and *yang* features also give him the honor of being the first animal of the Chinese zodiac.

Notes: ①zodiac 黄道带 ②symbolize 象征 ③profound 深刻的 ④vice versa 反之亦然 ⑤odd number 单数 ⑥even number 偶数

汉字的产生与演变
Origin and Evolution of Chinese Characters

1 汉字是怎样演变的?

How have Chinese characters evolved?

Chinese characters have a history of at least four thousand years. Throughout Chinese history, there have been different theories concerning how or when characters were invented, but historians agree that before any writing system existed the ancient Chinese made records by tying knots with a rope. According to the most famous legend concerning the origins of Chinese characters, Cangjie(仓颉), an ancient legendary figure who worked as the Yellow Emperor's historiographer, often watched the footprints of birds and beasts as well as the appearance of stars. His careful observations inspired him to create the earliest written characters.

The earliest evidence of Chinese writing appears on oracle bones discovered mainly in Anyang (安阳), the late Shang capital. They appear as simple drawings of natural objects—trees, water, mountains, horses, and humans. These earliest pictographic characters are called the Oracle Bone Script (甲骨文), used during the Shang or Yin Dynasty (1600 BC – 1046 BC). Towards the end of the Shang Dynasty, people tended to engrave the Oracle Bone Script on the *ding* (鼎), a bronze cooking vessel; the *gong* (觥), a bronze wine container; the *gu* (觚), a bronze drinking vessel. One of the unearthed bronze vessels called *Mao Gong Ding* (毛公鼎) dates from the late period of the Western Zhou Dynasty (1046 BC – 771 BC). On its surface are 497 engraved characters. During the Zhou Dynasty (1046 BC – 256 BC), people tended to engrave scripts on bronze wares, and this writing style was called the Bronze Script (金文). The Large Seal Script (大篆) developed on the basis of the Bronze Script during the Zhou Dynasty. Legend has it that during the period of King Xuan of the Zhou Dynasty (周宣王) (827 BC – 781 BC), a historian named Zhou edited a text-book to help children learn characters. The book is named *The Book by Historian Zhou* (史籀篇), and its writing style is also called *Zhou* Script (籀文) or the Large Seal Script. The lines of the Oracle Bone Script seem thin, stiff and straight. Those of the Bronze Script seem thick, and characters are well rounded in form.

After the Warring States Period (475 BC – 221

BC), only seven states survived. The script used in the Qin State (秦国) fell into the category of the Large Seal Script. However, the scripts used in the other six states were different in their appearance. These scripts were called the Six-State Ancient Scripts(六国古文). During the Qin Dynasty(221 BC – 206 BC), Prime Minister Li Si(李斯) collected all the different systems of writing used in different parts of the country in an effort to unify the writing system. He simplified the ancient *zhuan*(篆) and created the Small Seal Script(小篆). These styled characters look more semiotic because they have fewer strokes and moved further away from earlier pictorial representations. *Lishu*(隶书), the Clerical Script, came into being during the period between the Warring States Period and the Qin Dynasty. At that time, government offices employed a large number of *liren*(隶人), low-grade clerks, to copy the huge flow of government documents. These clerks had to turn the curved and rounded strokes of the Seal Script into linear and square shapes to speed up the copying of documents. This script was thus called *lishu*, the Clerical Script. Initially, people used either the Small Seal Script or the Clerical Script. Gradually the clerical writing style became more widespread until it replaced the Seal Script in the Han Dynasty(206 BC – 220 AD).

The common use of the Clerical Script marks a

turning point in the development of written Chinese characters. According to etymologists, all the written scripts that are used before the birth of the Clerical Script should fall into the category of ancient style characters, which include the Oracle Bone Script, the Bronze Script, the Large Seal Script, and the Small Seal Script. The Clerical Script and other styled scripts born at a later date belong in the category of modern styled characters.

Notes: ①knot (绳等的)结 ②legendary 传说的 ③historiographer 历史学家 ④pictographic 绘画文字的 ⑤engrave 雕刻 ⑥simplify 简化 ⑦semiotic 符号学的 ⑧linear 直线的 ⑨etymologist 词源学者

2 你能告诉我一些今体汉字的情况吗?

Could you tell me something about the modern styled characters?

The modern styled characters mainly refer to the Clerical Script (隶书), the Cursive Script (草书), the Standard Script(楷书)and the Running Script(行书).

In the Han Dynasty (206 BC – 220 AD), people commonly would prepare a rough draft first and then write formally using the Clerical Script style. They usually executed strokes cursively in an attempt to speed up their draft writing. Thus the cursive script evolved from the Clerical Script, and people called this new style *caoshu*(草书), or "cursive script." There are various cursive forms. One of these forms is named "the Wild Cursive Script(狂草)," a script in which the writing appears to have been executed freely and rapidly so that parts of the characters are exaggerated.

The *zhengshu* script(the Square Script, 正书)from the Jin Dynasty(265 – 420) developed square in form, and non-cursive in style. By the Tang Dynasty (618 – 907), it started to be called *Kaishu*, the Standard Script. Modern calligraphy is generally written in the Standard Script because of its regularity and easy-to-learn strokes. There are eight different stroke patterns: the dot, the horizontal stroke, the vertical stroke, the falling to the left, the rising to the right, the falling to the right and rectangular hook right down.

Xingshu, the Running Script, is a semi-cursive script that developed out of the Han Dynasty. The characters of the Running Script are not abbreviated or connected, but strokes within each character often run together. The Cursive Script characters are hard to read and write, except among literati artists. The Running Script characters, however, remain comprehensible because the semi-cursive style develops naturally after writing daily for many years, as you write faster and faster. Before 1911, people would use a brush to write on a daily basis, and simply start with the Standard Script. By the teenage years, one would have developed a unique writing style. The Running Script would have been perfected at about 18 years of age.

Notes: ①standard 规范 ②execute 制作 ③stroke (写字, 绘画的)一笔 ④cursive 草书的 ⑤exaggerate 夸张 ⑥horizontal 横的 ⑦vertical 垂直的 ⑧rectangular 直角的 ⑨literati (literatus 的复数)文人 ⑩comprehensible 可理解的

3 汉字是怎样构成的?

What elements are used to define Chinese Characters?

Of all the major writing systems in the world, Chinese is the only one that has not developed a phonetic alphabet. Instead the Chinese writing system is a logographic script in the form of characters. Because there is a rich variety of dialects across the country, people who cannot orally communicate with each other can communicate through written language. A commonly heard expression in China is "*Qing xie xia lai* (please write it down, 请写下来)." There have been debates about whether

Chinese should abandon its characters and adopt Romanization as its writing system. However most Chinese people believe such arguments are fruitless as characters are the only way to distinguish words. Ten words may be pronounced in exactly the same way, and at the same time be represented by different characters.

Chinese characters are often thought of as hieroglyphics, pictures representing objects and/or concepts. This idea may be true of the earliest Chinese writing. However, pictographs were soon found inadequate to represent everything, especially abstract ideas. Ideograms were then introduced to represent abstract and symbolic concepts. After centuries of different refinements and style transformations, the characters with pictographic images and graphic quality have almost all disappeared.

Most modern Chinese characters are referred to as square characters, composed of two parts, a left part and a right part, or a top part and a bottom part. In either formation, one part is called the radical that usually appears on the left or the top. Radicals offer clues to the semantic classification of the words such as person, food, metal, plant, animal and language. If you know the radical of a character, but do not know the character itself, you can still get a general idea of its meaning. Apart from above-mentioned elements, there are also six principles used to define and clarify Chinese Characters based on the way they are formed. They are called the "Six Categories of Chinese Characters (六书)." The first four categories include "pictographs(象形)," "indicatives(指事)," "complex ideograms(会意)" and "semantic-phonetic characters(形声)," indicating the methods of forming the characters. The final two are "associative transformations (转注)" and "phonetic loan characters(假借)," which refer to the usage of characters.

Notes: ①phonetic 语音的 ②logographic 语标;略字 ③dialect 方言 ④hieroglyphic 象形文字的 ⑤inadequate 不适当的 ⑥refinement 优雅;高雅 ⑦transformation 变化; ⑧graphic 绘画的 ⑨radical 偏旁;部首 ⑩above-mentioned 上面提到的 ⑪ideogram 表意文字

4 学习汉字难吗?

Is it difficult to learn Chinese characters?

All educated Chinese can read Chinese characters, regardless of the dialect they may speak. However, the Chinese writing system is not nearly as easy to learn as other writing systems. Chinese characters are neither alphabetical nor phonetic. Each character represents a separate syllable, indicating both the meaning and the sound. Only after years and years of study can the proper amount of characters be memorized to achieve fluent literacy. There also exists a proper stroke order with regards to writing. Improper stroke order carries a stigma, and therefore Chinese teachers and parents keep a close eye on how children write, carefully correcting any strokes that fall out of sequence.

Why do foreign visitors learn Chinese characters? Chinese civilization has evolved for thousands of years around this remarkable and unique writing system. Moreover, traditional written Chinese and diversity of spoken forms are important factors in the development of Chinese society. Some foreigners study the language to communicate better while touring the country; others study for business reasons. Nevertheless, the study of Chinese characters is a rewarding road which gives access to some of China's most enduring cultural achievements.

Language learners often wonder how many characters are necessary for one to become literate. Estimates may range from 3,000 to 5,000. Statistics show that the majority of the 50,000 to 60,000 existing characters are not in common use.

Notes: ①regardless of 不顾 ②syllable 音节 ③memorize 记住 ④stigma 特征;小斑 ⑤keep a close eye on 仔细注意 ⑥sequence 连续 ⑦diversity 多样性 ⑧rewarding 有益的 ⑨enduring 耐久的 ⑩statistics 统计

5 拼音是什么时候出现的?

When was *pinyin* introduced?

Early Western missionaries in China devised a number of systems for writing Chinese phonetically in Roman letters. None of these systems was a true representation of the correct pronunciation of the language involved. By now one set, the Wade-Giles System, has come to be used fairly regularly by American and British scholars, but it gives misleading and undependable indications of the true Chinese sounds. The Wade-Giles system was designed around 1860 by Sir Thomes Wade, a British diplomat and professor of Chinese at Cambridge University, and was applied by Herbert A. Giles, another Cambridge scholar, in a basic Chinese-English dictionary. The system found its way into English-language reference book.

When the People's Republic of China was founded in 1949, a committee for reforming the Chinese written language was set up. Thousands of character forms underwent drastic simplifications to reduce the number of strokes and ease the difficult task of achieving literacy. In 1951, the committee began working on a new phonetic alphabet for the language. This new system was called *pinyin*, and in 1958, the *pinyin* system was introduced. In 1979, *pinyin* was put into formal use.

Although it is difficult for any system to render the sounds of Chinese in the Roman alphabet, *pinyin* in most cases comes closer than other forms. For instance, the Wade-Giles form is *Peking*, and the *pinyin* form is Beijing. The Chinese make only a few exceptions in their new Romanization of Chinese words like Sun Yatsen, China and Confucius. Anyhow, *pinyin* is to serve as a teaching aid in studying Chinese characters and in fostering the standard spoken language. It is also intended to provide a unified system of rendering Chinese names in Western languages, eliminating the various existing styles.

Notes: ①missionary 传教士 ②diplomat 外交官 ③simplification 简单化 ④literacy 读写能力 ⑤exception 例外 ⑥foster 培养 ⑦eliminate 排除

姓名的由来
Origin of Chinese Names

1 你能讲讲有关中国姓氏的来历吗?

Could you tell me something about the origin of Chinese surnames?

Prior to the Qin Dynasty, *xing* and *shi*(姓氏)functioned as surnames, and each indicated different meanings. The *xing*, the Chinese character(姓), is composed of a left part and a right part. On the left is the radical *nü*(female, 女), which offers clues to the semantic part and the right is called *sheng*(birth, 生). *Xing* means that "The female gives birth to a child." The female radical gives a clue to the origin of Chinese surnames, which can trace back to the time when China was a matriarchal society, and also symbolizes sincere respect to the mother. According to legend, there was a divine farmer named Shen Nong(神农)whose mother (女登)is the source of all the surnames *nü*. Examples of her descendents would be the Yellow Emperor(黄帝) whose surname is *ji*(姬) and Yu Shun(the Great Shun, 虞舜) whose surname is *yao*(姚).

The *shi* surnames began to be used since the Zhou Dynasty(1046 BC – 256 BC) in order to distinguish family's background and seniority among royal families and nobility. Most of the *shi* surnames came from noble rankings, states, official positions, fiefdoms, occupations and residential areas. After the Warring States Period (475 BC – 221 BC), both *xing* and *shi* surnames were merged and began to be shared by common people.

Notes: ①prior to 在之前 ②surname 姓 ③matriarchal 母系的 ④descendent 后裔 ⑤seniority 级别 ⑥fiefdom 封地 ⑦occupation 职业 ⑧residential 居住的

2 有些早期的姓氏是怎样出现的?

What are the origins of some early Chinese surnames?

As the population increased, the number of surnames also grew, many of them coming from the land on which people resided. Legend has it that Fu Xi(伏羲) resided in Dongfang(the east,东方), and his descendents would take their surname after *dongfang*. Another example is that during the Western Zhou Dynasty(1046

BC – 771 BC), the king of that time would invest the nobility with territories, and so each lord or prince would go there and set up his state accordingly. Afterwards the nobility's descendents would take their surnames after the names of the states owned by their ancestors. Additionally, the king or lord of each state divided his fiefdoms into rental lands and granted them to his state ministers. The descendents of these ministers would take their surnames from the names of the granted rental lands. For example, Zhan Qin(展禽), a minister from the State of Lu rented land by the name of *liu* (柳). Zhan Qin's descendents later adopted *Liu* as their surname. The lords and ministers of the State of Qi respectively resided in the four quarters inside the capital of the Qi, including Dongguo(the east quarter, 东郭), Nanguo(the south quarter, 南郭), Xiguo (the west quarter, 西郭) and Beiguo(the north quarter, 北郭). Afterwards these noble families' descendents took their surnames after the names of the quarters where their ancestors resided.

Some names of official positions of ancient times gradually became surnames. For example, *yue*(乐) can be traced back from the Zhou Dynasty(1046 BC – 256 BC) when the official position responsible for music was called *yuezheng*(乐正). The same goes with the surnames, *jia*(贾), which means "business." The official position responsible for business was called *jiazheng*(贾正)in the Zhou Dynasty. Some surnames have double-characters that are also associated with official positions such as *sima* (minister of military affairs, 司马), *sikong*(minister of architecture, 司空)and *situ*(minister of personnel management, 司徒). The descendents of these officials would take the titles as surnames as symbols of nobility. Prior to the Warring States Period (475 BC－221 BC), only aristocrats had surnames; common people began to have their own surnames later in history. Since the Han Dynasty (206 BC－25 AD), everyone has his/her own surname.

Notes: ①nobility 贵族 ②rental 出租 ③grant 授予 ④respectively 分别地 ⑤architecture 建筑 ⑥personnel management 人事管理

3 什么是《百家姓》和《千家姓》?

What are *The Hundred Family Surnames* and *The Thousand Family Surnames*?

Chinese surnames often confuse foreign visitors. A book printed during the Song Dynasty (960 – 1279) named *The Hundred Family Surnames*(《百家姓》) listed all of the known 468 Chinese surnames in use at the time. A similar book was printed during the Ming Dynasty(1368 - 1644) titled *The Thousand Family Surnames*(《千家姓》), which listed 1,968 surnames. At present, there are all together about 3,000 surnames.

Some double-character surnames have been transliterated from names used by ethnic groups in ancient China such as *chan yu*(单于), *yu wen*(宇文) and *hu yan*(呼延). There are even some surnames with three or more characters like *ai xin jue luo*(爱新觉罗).

Although there are thousands of Chinese family names, only 100 surnames can be considered common. Based on recent surveys, the three most popular are *li*(李), *wang*(王)and *zhao*(赵). To celebrate the 100 most common surnames in China, a special set of stamps were issued featuring a red Chinese knot, which symbolizes unity and luck.

Notes: ①transliterate 把……译成另一语系中相应的字母、音节或词 ②celebrate 颂扬 ③feature 以……为特色

4 请讲一讲"名"的事宜,好吗?

Please tell me something about Chinese given names.

Chinese given names(名字)are usually made up of

one or two characters. In ancient times, parents would give their child a name three months after birth. Traditional Chinese culture frowns upon naming a person after someone else. People have the same name most likely due to coincidence rather than intention. Frequently girls will be named after objects which reflect feminine characteristics, such as plants or flowers. Chinese personal names may also reflect periods of history. For example, many Chinese born during the Cultural Revolution have revolutionary-sounding names like *dongfeng* (the eastern wind, 东风).

Within families, adults rarely address each other by personal names. When addressing each other, they generally use a family title such as elder sister, second elder sister, third elder sister and so on. This traditional pattern symbolizes obedience and respect that the son should show to his parents; the wife to the husband; the younger to the elder, etc. In addition, there exists a large range of everyday formal titles people use with each other. Personal names are only used when addressing adult friends or children.

Nicknames are usually alterations of the given name sometimes based on a person's physical attributes or speaking style. Nicknames are rarely used in formal or semi-formal settings.

In ancient times, it was common for males to acquire a *zi* (style name, 字) at the age of 20. Rulers had posthumous names(谥号) and temple names(庙号).

Notes: ①frown upon 皱眉 ②coincidence 巧合 ③intention 意向 ④nickname 绰号 ⑤alteration 改变 ⑥attribute 属性 ⑦posthumous 死后的

5 在中国,常用的称谓有哪些?

What are some common titles and forms of address in China?

In China, the surname is followed by the given name, the exact opposite of Western custom. The Chinese sometimes reverse the order of their two names to conform to Western practice. Westerners may be confused upon finding out that in China family names are always placed first.

A woman in China does not take her husband's surname after her marriage but instead keeps that of her father. The Chinese address for a woman *nüshi*(女士) or "Ms" sounds rather formal for an unmarried woman. You may address any young woman who is not likely to be married as *xiaojie*(小姐), translated as "Miss." If you do not know whether a young woman is married, address her as *nüshi*.

Traditionally all Chinese receive a "milk name (乳名)" at birth, a "book name (学名)" upon entering school, and a "style (大名)" or "great name" upon marriage. Members of the family and very close friends normally use the "milk name." Teachers and school friends use the "book name." Both parents and relatives would also use a man's new "style name" after his marriage. In feudal days, scholars commonly assumed a "studio name (斋号)," which they used to sign their works.

Old people with no work-related title are commonly given the nickname *lao* (old or senior, 老); younger people with no identifiable name or job title may be addressed as *xiao* (young or junior, 小). To use an example, an old person of any age calls a younger person with whom he and she is familiar *Xiao* so-and-so; a younger person calls an old person Lao so-and-so. *Xiao* or *lao* may be used with persons of either gender.

Notes: ①reverse 使倒转 ②conform to 符合 ③assume 承担 ④identifiable 可认明的 ⑤gender 性别

6 "丈夫"这个称谓是怎样出现的?

What is the origin of *zhangfu*?

Presently in China the husband is called *zhangfu* (丈

夫), although this title has not always had that meaning. According to the *The Guliang Biography*(《穀梁传》), one of the 13 *Classics*, "At the age of 20, a man has to go through a ceremony, and it indicates that he has turned into a *zhangfu*(男子二十而冠,冠而列丈夫)." Here the *zhangfu* refers to an adult person. Then how did the *zhangfu* come to mean "husband?" In ancient times, some tribes had the custom of carrying away a man and marrying him by force. At that time, the man's height was the main criterion for a woman to pick her spouse. The basic height was one *zhang*(丈)that equals to 7 *chi*(尺), and one *chi* is about 0.33 meter. People thought that a man of one *zhang* tall would be able to resist being carried away by force. Gradually women began to refer to their spouses as *zhangfu*.

Notes: ①biography 传记 ②by force 靠力量 ③criterion 标准 ④spouse 配偶

7 "太太"这个称谓是怎样出现的?

What is the origin of *taitai*?

Overseas Chinese use the title *taitai*(太太)for wife, and the name is becoming popular in Mainland

China. However, during Emperor Liu Xin's rein in the Han Dynasty (6 BC – 2 BC) (汉哀帝刘欣), *taitai* meant a honorific title to the royal ladies of the older generation. Later in the Han Dynasty (206 BC – 220 AD), *taitai* became a popular title among aristocratic ladies, and the Han imperial family even used *huang-taitaihou* (皇太太后) to address the empress. During the Ming Dynasty (1368 – 1644), *taitai* was used to address women at age 30 and above whose spouses had obtained the high ranking status of artists or government officials (凡士大夫妻,年来三十即呼太太). During the Qing Dynasty (1616 – 1911), family male and female servants would likely use the title to address family hostesses. Gradually this *taitai* came to be used to address the wives of officials, business managers, school principals, and professors.

Notes: ①overseas 海外 ②honorific 尊敬的 ③ranking 等级高的 ④hostess 女主人 ⑤principal 校长

古代婚姻

Chinese Marriage in Ancient Times

1 怎么解释“婚姻”二字?

Could you explain the Chinese words *hunyin*?

Hunyin(婚姻) means “marriage.” It is composed of two characters, *hun*(婚) and *yin*(姻). The *hun* character has two parts: the left *nü* (female, 女) and the right *hun* (昏), which means “evening” or “dusk,” implying that the bride and groom meet in the evening. *Yin*(姻) is composed of the left nü(female, 女) and the right *yin* (rely on, by means of, 因). According to the etymological dictionary entitled *Shuo Wen Jie Zi* (Notes on Language and characters,《说文解字》), *Yin* (姻) means the husband's family, which the wife relies on.

Notes: ①imply 暗指 ②bride 新娘 ③groom 新郎 ④similar to 类似的

2 中国古代婚姻有什么礼节?

What were the rituals of Chinese marriage in ancient times?

Marriage as a custom became solidified in China during 402 BC to 221 BC According to the belief of the time, a marriage not only bound the husband and wife but also the two families involved. In ancient China, when parents looked for a prospective wife or husband for their son or daughter, they had to consider a number of factors. The most important factor was the other family's reputation and standing. The personal attributes of the prospective groom and bride came second. Below are six-rituals(六礼)of marriage that have been used for 2,000 years throughout the Chinese history.

(1) When an unmarried boy's family finds a prospective daughter-in-law, they will invite a "middle man" to approach the prospective daughter-in-law's family, present gifts, and propose the possible marriage between the two families. If the proposal is declined, the gift is rejected.

(2) If the girl's family accepts the proposal, the boy's family will write a letter to the girl's asking her date of birth.

(3) When her family replies, the boy's family will

pray to their ancestors to ask if the couple will be auspicious. If the prediction does not feel right, the marriage will be called off.

(4) If the couple appears auspicious, the boy's family will arrange the "middle man" to deliver the marriage documents and wedding gifts to the prospective daughter-in-law's home.

(5) Once the boy's family finalizes the wedding day, they will confirm the day with the girl's family by sending a formal letter and more gifts. If the girl's family refuses the gifts, another date must be found.

(6) On the wedding day, the groom departs with a troop of escorts and musicians who play cheerful music all the way to the bride's home. The bride's father meets the parade outside the home. He would take the groom to the ancestral temple where they will pray to their ancestors. At the same time, the wedding sedan chair is placed outside the home until the bride arrives. The groom bows his head low to invite the bride to take the chair, and then they both travel together for the wedding ceremony in the groom's home.

In ancient times, most families could not afford these expenses, and did not go through the above ritual process one by one. However, families had to share the information of what time the girl or boy was born. The information would include the hour, day, month and year. Upon the arrival of the information, the family would invite a fortuneteller to decide if the proposed marriage was auspicious.

Notes: ①solidify (使)变坚固 ②bind 捆,绑 ③prospective 未来的 ④reject 拒绝 ⑤auspicious 吉兆的 ⑥call off 取消 ⑦confirm 确定 ⑧escort 护送 ⑨fortuneteller 算命者

3 中国不同朝代的婚龄是一样的吗?

What was legal age to marry in ancient China?

Throughout the course of Chinese history, the prescribed age of marriage varied. During the Zhou Dynasty (1046 BC – 256 BC), a man should be married by the age of 30, and a woman by 20. At that time, people thought that a man's bones and muscles would be strong enough to withstand the burden of fatherhood at the age of 30; a woman would be full-grown and ready to be a mother when she reached the age of 20.

As the dynasties went by, the prescribed age for marriage gradually lowered. During the Spring and Autumn Period (770 BC – 476 BC), Qi Huangong(齐桓公), king of the Qi State, decreed a man should be married by the age of 30 and a woman by 15; towards the end of the Spring and Autumn Period, King Gou Jian of the Yue State(越王勾践)said that parents would be penalized if their son did not get married by 20 years of age and their daughter by 17. Princes or kings carried out the early marriage policy in their own states to promote population growth that later would provide more manpower to work in the fields or join the army.

During the Han Dynasty (206 BC – 220 AD), unmarried women of 15 years or older had to pay 5 times more taxes than required, thus forcing them to marry at an even earlier age.

In the Western Jin State (265 – 317)(西晋), local officials would select a groom for the woman who had not been married off by the age of 17. In the Northern Zhou State(557 – 581)(北周), a man was required to marry by 15 and a woman by 13.

In the early Tang Dynasty(618 – 907), the Tang rulers adopted a rehabilitative policy in order to relieve people out of the severe social conflicts. Part of the policy stated that a man should get married by the age of 20 and a woman by the age of 15. In the middle period of the Tang Dynasty, the latest age one could marry changed to 16 for a man and 13 for a woman. The local government would interfere if any man or woman failed to get married by the prescribed age. From the Song to the Qing dynasties(960 – 1911), the latest age for a man was about 16 years old and for a woman about 14.

Throughout ancient China, a large labor force was constantly in demand because of low economic productivity. After considerable pressure from the rulers of the earlier dynasties, the people later gradually accepted the early marriage policy.

Notes: ①prescribed 规定的 ②withstand 抵挡 ③full-grown 完全的；丰满的 ④penalize 处罚 ⑤conflict 冲突 ⑥interfere 冲突 ⑦productivity 生产力 ⑧considerable 相当大的

4 中国古代妇女是为何开始裹脚的？

Why did women begin to have their feet bound in ancient China?

The origins of foot-binding are unclear though legends exist that point to possible historical explanations. One of these legends recounts how foot-binding began in the court of the Southern Tang State(南唐)in Nanjing. The Tang prince ordered his concubine to bind her feet with silk to shape them like half moons and to whirl them around to give the appearance of dancing on clouds or over the top of golden lilies. This legend is probably not true because women with bound feet could hardly walk, let alone dance. However, this dancing concubine was renowned for her tiny feet and beautiful bow shoes (弓鞋).

Anyway, it was around the Tang Dynasty (618 – 907) that the practice became the standard for feminine beauty in the imperial court. The custom started with court dancers, and later all the women of the imperial court followed suit. In time foot-binding spread downward from the north to all parts of the country as the lower classes strove to imitate the style of the elite.

Notes: ①foot-binding 裹脚 ②concubine 妾 ③lily 百合花 ④feminine 女性的 ⑤elite 精英

5 以前妇女裹脚的情况是怎样的?

How did the women have their feet bound in ancient China?

Many women had their feet bound in ancient China. This tradition lasted for nearly one thousand years. Foot-binding was a sadistic attempt to stop the growth of women's feet and therefore people today are hard to understand the tradition. The reason for women binding their feet went deeper than fashion and reflected the role of women in ancient Chinese society.

Foot-binding consisted of wrapping the feet of a girl

at the age of 4 to 6 years. The process began early in life so that the arch did not have time to fully develop. The bandages, which were ten feet long and two inches wide, were wrapped around the smallest toes and pulled tightly to the heel. Every two days, the binding was removed and rebound. This part of the process went on for two years. After these two years, a girl's feet would be three to four inches long. To assure the feet stayed small, the ritual continued for at least ten more years. The aim was to produce a tiny foot, a "golden lotus(金莲)," which would be three inches long and was regarded as both lovely and alluring.

As time went on, the feet became so compressed that women usually hobbled about with difficulty, and had to lean on a wall or another person for support. Women with bound feet were physically prevented from moving about freely, and thus a young girl from a wealthy family would often receive a body servant at the time of her initial binding, to look after her personal needs and carry her into the garden when her feet were too painful to walk on.

How did this bizarre tradition continue for one thousand years? First, men in ancient China would not marry a woman who did not have bound feet. Every son's mother was always responsible for making sure the woman her son was to marry had bound feet. A family with a young girl had no choice but to submit to this tremendous social pressure and bind their daughter's feet; if not, their daughter would be ineligible for marriage.

Notes: ①sadistic 残酷成性的 ②arch 足背;足弓 ③bandage 绷带 ④alluring 诱惑的 ⑤compressed 压缩的 ⑥hobble 蹒跚 ⑦initial 最初的 ⑧bizarre 古怪的 ⑨ineligible 没资格的

6 妇女裹脚是如何终止的?

How was the custom of foot-binding discontinued?

In the mid-1600s, with the start of the Qing Dynasty, weak opposition against the foot-binding began to emerge. The Qing nobility, who were ethnically Manchu, attempted to prohibit this custom, but the foot-binding practice nevertheless continued. After over 500 years such a practice was so firmly rooted in Chinese culture that the Qing government could not prohibit it.

In 1911, the Qing Dynasty was overthrown, and foot-binding was officially made illegal. The social movement responsible for the ban used three strategies. First, a modern education campaign was organized to highlight that the rest of the world did not bind women's feet. Second, another education campaign explained the advantages of natural feet and the disadvantages of bound feet. Third, natural-foot societies were launched that had members pledged neither to bind their daughter's feet nor to allow their sons to marry women with bound feet. These three tactics effectively succeeded in bringing foot-binding to a quick end.

Foot-binding cannot be seen as a simple fashion statement as its roots spring from many parts of Chinese culture. Foot-binding started out as a definition of beauty and ended up crippling Chinese women for centuries. Unfortunately, it took much more than laws and protests to bring foot-binding to an end.

Notes: ①ethnically 种族上 ②prohibit 禁止 ③strategy 策略 ④highlight 使突出；强调 ⑤disadvantage 不利条件 ⑥tactics 战术 ⑦definition 定义 ⑧crippling 极有害的

7 “设男女之大防”是怎样出现的？

How did gender segregation begin?

In the beginning of recorded Chinese history there existed no strict gender segregation. Young men and women enjoyed each other's companionship freely. *Shi*

Jing (*The Classic of Poetry*,《诗经》) contains an early collection of poems and folk songs from ordinary people; here is an example of one:

Guan-guan go the ospreys,
On the islet in the river.
The modest, retiring, virtuous, young lady:
For our prince a good mate is she.
(关关雎鸠,在河之洲,窈窕淑女,君子好逑。)

During festivals of the Spring and Autumn (770 BC – 476 BC) or the Warring States Period (475 BC – 221 BC), men and women gathered together to personally select their spouses. Historical records are filled with examples. *The Zhou Rites*(《周礼·地官司徒·媒氏》) states, Mid-spring is a good season for men and women to meet together. It is also the time not to forbid men and women to be privately engaged for marriage(仲春之月,令会男女。于是时也,奔者不禁). *The Records of the Historian* (《史记·田敬仲完世家》) by Sima Qian (司马迁) of the Han Dynasty records, in 254 BC, Le Yi (乐毅), a general of the State of Yan led the army to attack the State of Qi. The King Min of the Qi (齐闵王) and his son Fa Zhang(法章) fled to Ju City(莒城) where the king was eventually assassinated. To protect himself, Fa Zhang changed his name and later started to work as a servant for Grand Astrologer Jiao (太史敫). Fa Zhang's handsome appearance attracted the attention of Jiao's daughter. Gradually, the two young people fell in love. After receiving the assistance from local people and officials of the State of Qi, Fa Zhang was chosen to be King Xiang of the State of Qi (齐襄王), with Jiao's daughter as the queen. Grand Astrologer Jiao was not happy about their marriage, complaining angrily, "My daughter chose her spouse and got married without a matchmaker to help. She is not my daughter." He swore never to see his daughter again. This story shows how sometimes even feudal ethical codes were unable to prevent young people like Fa Zhang and Jiao's daughter from getting married.

As late as the second century BC, courtship was still possible. The Han poet Sima Xiangru(司马相如) used his lute to court a widow whose name was Zhuo Wenjun(卓文君). He succeeded in persuading her to elope with him. Such occurrence would be impossible in a later period. After the Song Dynasty (960 - 1279), the gender segregation widened and became more rigid. What caused this change? The main reason came from the spread and acceptance of Confucian morals. For instance, Zhu Xi(朱熹) advocated strict gender separation, and also glorified widowhood. Because his philosophy dominated the intellectuals of the time, his bleak ideas were widely received, and thus the status of women began its decline in ancient China.

In 1949, the Chinese government passed "The Marriage Law" granting men and women equality and freedom to marry whomever they choose.

Notes: ①segregation 分离 ②osprey 鹭鸶羽毛 ③islet 小岛 ④virtuous 有美德的 ⑤assassinate 暗杀 ⑥persuade 说服 ⑦elope 私奔 ⑧advocate 提倡 ⑨widowhood 孀居

传统服饰
Ancient Chinese Clothes

1 汉代之前的中国传统服饰是什么样式？

What did ancient Chinese clothes look like before the Han Dynasty?

Ancient Chinese dress can be classified into two styles. The first style emphasizes the separation of the upper and lower garments (上衣下裳) which according to legend came into style during the days of the Yellow Emperor. Most upper garments have a Y shaped collar (交领), with the front side covered from left to right (右衽). The lower garment resembles a skirt with a ribbon around the waist.

The second style is called "the full clothing (深衣)" design, a kind of robe, which first appeared in the Zhou Dynasty (1046 BC – 771 BC). Similar to the contemporary dress in design, the clothing has upper and lower garments, but these two parts are sewn and united around the waist(衣裳连属制). As well, the rim of the cloth is embroidered with fabric. During the Han Dynasty(206 BC – 220 AD), women used this type of clothing as a ceremonial dress.

From the Xia to the Zhou dynasties(2070 BC – 256 BC), people usually wore the first style of clothing. In early Zhou Dynasty, however, laws strictly mandated different styles of clothing to reflect the different social classes. The full clothing started in the Zhou Dynasty, and by the Warring States Periods(475 BC – 221 BC), this style was quite popular. At the same time, the *hu* styled clothing(胡服)appeared. *Hu*(胡)refers to ancient nomadic people of the northwestern regions who wore short jackets and pants. During the Warring States Periods, King Wu Ling of the Zhao State(赵武灵王) ordered all subjects to wear the *hu* styled short jackets and pants, and to learn how to ride horses and shoot arrows, thus greatly promoting the fighting capacity of his army. Since then, the *hu* style of clothing became the norm across the country.

Notes: ①garment (一件)衣服 ②ribbon 缎带 ③contemporary 当代的 ④embroider 刺绣 ⑤mandate 命令 ⑥capacity 能力

2 自汉朝起古代中国传统服饰发生了什么变化?

What changes in ancient Chinese traditional clothes have happened since the Han Dynasty?

The full clothing still remained very popular during the Han Dynasty(206 BC – 220 AD). Pants worn by a person then had a split-seat covered by outer garments or full clothing. Even though the closed-seat pants were in use, the split-seat pants still existed for a long time.

From the Jin and Wei period to the Northern and Southern Dynasties(265 – 589), a large number of ethnic groups migrated to central China where the *hu* styled clothing had become the customary dress. At the same time, the Han styled clothing worn by common people had *hu*-style narrow sleeves, a close-fitting body, a round collar and slits up the sides of the garment; the Han ceremonial clothes still remained unchanged.

During the period of the Sui and Tang dynasties (581 – 907), typical male clothing consisted of the head bundle wrapped in cloth(袱头), the robe(袍衫), and the long boots. The robe had a round collar and narrow sleeves; the front pieces of the robe were covered from left to right.

The clothing in the Song Dynasty (960 – 1279) generally followed the same pattern of the Tang Dynasty with the exception of a more plain conservative look. The colors were not as bright as in previous dynasties due to the influence of Neo-Confucianism.

The clothing style of the Liao, Jin and Yuan dynasties (907 – 1368) generally followed the styles worn during the Han, Tang and Song dynasties, but also retained its own ethnic features. The cloth used mainly came in white, blue or reddish brown with cotton as the fabric of choice.

In the Ming Dynasty (1368 – 1644), the clothing style reflected influence from the Tang and Song dynasties. The clothes of the Qing Dynasty (1616 – 1911) exerted a great influence on present day traditional styles. There were three kinds of outfits for men: traditional Han styled clothes, the Manchu ethnic wear, and the Western suit. The Qing robe had narrow and tight sleeves, a round collar, and buttons on the right side. Towards the end of the Qing Dynasty, Chinese clothes underwent a great change due to Western influence, gradually evolving into modern day fashion.

Notes: ①split-seat pants 开裆裤 ②closed-seat pants 封裆裤 ③migrate 迁移 ④bundle 包裹 ⑤collar 衣领 ⑥conservative 保守的 ⑦exert an influence on 对……施加影响 ⑧undergo 经历

3 现在传统样式的衣服仍然受欢迎吗？

Are the traditional-style clothes still popular now?

Modern Chinese desire that clothes do not merely cover their bodies, but also express their personality, mood, and outlook. They scour shopping centers, boutiques, and wholesale markets hoping to keep up with the latest fashions. The Shanghai APEC meeting where various country leaders appeared at the closing ceremony wearing Chinese-style silk jackets gave impetus for a revival in traditional-style clothes. Subsequently traditional-style garments flooded stores, and appeared overnight in shopping malls, boutiques, and clothing wholesale markets. The design of traditional clothes has been revamped by younger designers who have given traditional clothes a more refined, elegant image. These young designers have a deep understanding of traditional Chinese esthetics, and skillfully mix classical and modern elements in their designs.

Notes: ①personality 人格 ②outlook 观点 ③scour 搜索 ④boutique 精品店 ⑤wholesale 批发 ⑥keep up with 跟上…… ⑦revival 复兴 ⑧subsequently 随后 ⑨revamp 修补 ⑩esthetics 美观性

4 有关裙子的出现有什么传说吗?

What are the legendary stories about the origin of the skirt?

According to legend, Xi Shi (西施) invented the skirt. The legend starts during the Warring States Period (475 BC – 221 BC) when the army from the State of Wu (吴国) destroyed the State of Yue (越国), King Gou Jian of the Yue (越王勾践) and his prime minister Fan Li (范蠡) were both captured and brought to the State of Wu. While being held captive, Gou Jian and Fan Li pretended to be subservient to the State of Wu in order to save revenge for later.

One day, the king of the Wu was ill, and the court medical doctors were unable to find out what illness he had. Gou Jian said to the king that he could cure the illness, and advised him: "You have caught a cold. The illness will be cured if you drink some warm wine."

The king followed Gou Jian's advice, drank the warm wine, and immediately felt much better. With the illness gone, the king trusted Gou Jian and Fan Li and decided to grant them the freedom to return to the State of Yue.

Upon arriving back home, Gou Jian and Fan Li began thinking of a plan to restore the State of Yue. They knew that the king of the Wu was fond of women, so they decided that the best scheme would be to present to him a beautiful lady from the State of Yue. This lady would then collaborate to help their future attack on the State of Wu.

One day, as they passed a river bend, Gou Jian and Fan Li found a woman washing clothes. Her name was Xi Shi, and she looked as beautiful as the goddess of the Yue.

Gou Jian and Fan Li took her to the royal palace. One day, Xi Shi said to Gou Jian, "Everyone says that I am beautiful, but I don't think so. Just look at my feet ... they are so big! It is too late to bind my feet, so I'll get a tailor to make a piece of clothing to cover them."

Of course, no tailors could make that kind of clothing because the skirt had not been invented yet, so Xi Shi did it herself. She spent three days and nights drawing a picture of an 18-folded long skirt and then gave this pattern to an extremely skilled tailor to have it made.

Afterwards, Fan Li sent Xi Shi to the Wu Kingdom. Her long skirt and beautiful looks seduced the king of the Wu. From then on the king idled away his time with Xi Shi from morning till night, neglecting his state affairs. Seeing that the king of the Wu had fallen into their trap, Gou Jian and Fan Li led a surprise attack on the State of Wu. The vulnerable Wu Kingdom could not resist the Yue army's strong attack and was thus destroyed.

In order to honor Xi Shi, Gou Jian had all the women in his state wear skirts. From then on, wearing long skirts became a custom that spread far and wide in China.

There is another myth about the origin of the skirt that comes from Chang'an(长安), capital of the Tang Dynasty(618 –907).

According to this legend, the Tang imperial court handpicked women to be the emperor's princesses or concubines based on facial appearance and well-rounded figure. A beautiful woman by the name of Wu Zetian (武则天) was selected because her figure and appearance satisfied the imperial court's standards.

Years later Wu Zetian was ordained to be the empress, but with the passing of time she had gained a lot of weight. She wore silk pants, but as she walked, her thighs rubbed against one another producing a *tss tss* sound. The empress felt embarrassed because people often looked around upon hearing the sound.

One day, Wu Zetian looked at her overweight legs and decided to use a piece of satin silk to cover her legs, hoping that might drive away her frustration.

Suddenly an idea came to her mind. She wrapped her legs up with satin silk, and looked at herself in front of a mirror. Walking back and forth, a smile appeared on her face. She then had tailors make a piece of clothing according to this pattern. After the tailors finished, Wu Zetian had a court maid put on this new piece of clothing. As the maid walked around, Wu came up with ways to further improve on its look, and ended up liking the final design so much that she wore it inside and outside the court. Gradually more and more women copied her new clothing design.

When people asked Wu Zetian to name this kind of clothing, she thought it over and then said, "Let's call it '*qun*(skirt, 裙).'" *Qun* is composed of two parts: the radical *yi*(clothing, 衣) appears on the left, and *jun* (monarch, 君) on the right. These two parts suggest that the skirt might have been invented by the empress.

Notes: ①prime minister 宰相 ②subservient 卑屈的 ③revenge 报仇 ④collaborate 协作 ⑤a folded long skirt 折叠长裙 ⑥seduce 引诱 ⑦vulnerable 脆弱的 ⑧handpick 仔细挑选 ⑨well-rounded 丰满的 ⑩thigh 大腿 ⑪frustration 挫折

5 旗袍是怎样出现的?

Could you tell me the origin of *qipao*?

Between the late Kang Xi and the Yong Zheng periods

(1662 – 1736) of the Qing Dynasty, men mainly wore gowns and Mandarin jacket outfits. The Manchurian women usually wore a gown called qipao while Han women had separate jacket and skirt.

From the middle of the Qing period, the clothing designs of both Manchurian and Han cultures influenced each other; palace robes were cut short and made into jackets and Manchurian styled clothing prevailed among *Han* high officials and noble lords.

Since the Qing Dynasty, woman clothing was more diversified in design; it included undershirts, skirts, overcoats, scarves, and belts. By 1840 as Western culture entered China and gradually influenced the local culture, clothing styles also changed, particularly in Shanghai and other cities along the coastal areas. The clothing designs and styles varied because there was no professional clothing research center to uniform the designing system. For example, *qipao* underwent constant changes in accordance with individual designers. *Qipao* was a one-piece dress originally worn by the Manchurian women during the Qing Dynasty. Designers further updated *qipao* by absorbing some elements from the Western clothing style. The dress was easy and comfortable to wear, fitting the female Chinese figure well. The neck was high, and collar closed; its sleeves were short or full in length, depending on season and taste. The outfit was buttoned on the right side and had slits running up along the sides. From the 1920s to 1940s, *qipao* was in fashion, becoming the Chinese women's standard clothing. From school girls to feminists, Chinese women from all levels of society wore *qipao*. *Qipao* trend even became popular in foreign countries.

Notes: ①mandarin (满清的)官吏的 ②diversified 多样化的 ③overcoat 大衣 ④professional 职业性的 ⑤outfit 配备

6 你对古代帝王服装知道多少?

How much do you know about the emperors' clothing in ancient China?

According to the records of *The Classic of Rites*, monarchs of the Zhou Dynasty(1046 BC – 256 BC) had ceremonial clothing to perform sacrifices to Heaven. In addition, kings had special clothing available for their court services, field hunting and military activities. The ceremonial clothing consisted of the crown hat(冕冠), *xuanfu*(玄服) and *xunfu*(纁服). *Xuanfu* is a black material clothing, and *xunfu* a red outer garment hanging from the waist. During sacrificial ceremonies, the Zhou monarchs wore large black lambskin coats in order to show respect to Heaven.

During the Qin Dynasty(221 BC – 206 BC), officials of the 3rd rank or above wore silk robes and the full clothing(深衣). Emperor Qin wore an unlined garment made of light silk fabric when Jing Ke(荆轲)tried to assassinate him.

In the Western Han Dynasty(206 BC – 25 AD), emperors wore robes, but the colors of their robes varied according to seasons. In spring, emperors wore blue or green robes; in summer, they wore bright red ones; in autumn, they wore white ones; in winter, they wore black ones. In the Han Dynasty, a highly valued robe had its large sleeves and narrow sleeve cuffs.

In the Tang Dynasty(618 – 907), an emperor wore a large fur coat, bright red lower garments and shoes when he performed sacrifices to Heaven and Earth. His ceremonial hat had no silk hanging strings. He wore a dark blue coat and *xunfu*, a red outer garment hanging from the waist, when he received congratulation from his court officials upon his marriage or returned from his expedition. Since the Zhenguan Period (贞观年间), emperors usually wore informal clothing except on the New Year's Day, in the Winter Solstice or during the sacrificial ceremony.

In the Song Dynasty(960 – 1279), when an emperor performed a sacrificial ceremony in the Winter Solstice, he wore a large fur coat that appeared blue in color but red inside, and its collar was made of a dark lambskin. On the New Year's Day when he had an audience with his court officials, he wore his crown hat with 12 silk hanging strings, and blue clothing drawn with the moon, stars, the mountain, the dragon, flowers, fire, and other images.

In 1370, the Song court tentatively mandated different styles of clothing for imperial families such as the emperor's crown hat, ceremonial clothing, and informal daily dresses and formal clothing for the queen and maids of honor of different ranks.

During the Qing Dynasty (1616 – 1911), clothing worn by emperors for a sacrificial ceremony was called *yanfu*(兖服) which was embroidered with four golden dragons, each having five claws; the sun was embroidered on the left shoulder, the moon on the right shoulder and a seal-styled character "longevity" on the front and colorful clouds on the back. The Qing emperor usually had two kinds of court dresses. One was for winter and the other for summer. In the design, the upper and lower garments were sewn and united around the waist. Although the clothing appeared bright yellow, the Qing emperor had to wear blue clothing when he performed a sacrificial ceremony in the Imperial Vault of Heaven(皇穹宇) and the Hall of Prayer for Good Harvest (祈年殿); he wore red ones when he worshipped the morning sun.

Notes: ①monarch 帝王 ②lambskin 羔羊皮 ③unlined (衣服)没有衬里的 ④sleeve cuff 袖口 ⑤have an audience with 接见 ⑥tentatively 暂时的 ⑦vault 拱顶 ⑧ worship 崇拜

7 古代官员穿的是统一颜色的袍服吗?

Did ancient officials wear robes in the same color?

When you watch a Chinese opera, you will be amazed by long gowns or robes worn by actors playing officials of ancient China. These robes' different colors and embroidery signified official ranks in feudal times. Starting from the Tang Dynasty(618 – 907), robes had different colors: a government official of the third rank or above wore a purple robe with a goldfish pocket; an official of the fourth or fifth rank wore a bright red robe with a silverfish pocket; and an official of the sixth rank or below wore a green robe without a fish pocket. When some officials were promoted to higher posts, their ranks stayed the same, but the robe's color would change to indicate the promotion. For example, when someone was promoted to be prime minister, he would wear a purple robe with a goldfish pocket even though his rank was below the third.

The Qing (1616 – 1911) officials abolished the

robe color system, and instead required all robes to be blue. Deep red robes were used only on special occasions and festivities. In the late Qing period, the clothing became more diversified as Qing officials wore robes embroidered with python and garment outfits with bird or animal patterns. For example, the nine-python and five-claw robes were offered to the 1st to 3rd ranked officials, the eight-python and five-claw robes to the 4th to 6th ranked officials, and the five-python and four-claw robes to the 7th to 9th ranked officials.

A square pattern in shape of a bird or beast was embroidered right in the center of a garment outfit. Bird patterns specified civil official ranks. The red crowned crane was given to the 1st ranked officials, the golden pheasant to the 2nd ranked officials, the peacock to the 3rd ranked officials, the white wild goose to the 4th ranked officials, the silver pheasant to the 5th ranked officials, and the egret to the 6th ranked officials. The oriole pattern went to official staff that had no ranks at all.

Beast patterns specified military official ranks. For example: the Chinese unicorn was given to the 1st ranked officers, the lion to the 2nd ranked officers, the leopard to the 3rd ranked officers, the tiger to the 4th ranked officers, the bear to the 5th ranked officers, and the young tiger to the 6th and 7th ranked officers. There was one exception: those who served in the departments of law or justice had the pattern of a supernatural sheep called "*xiezhi*(獬豸)." It is said that this sheep is able to distinguish right from wrong.

Notes: ①embroidery 刺绣 ②signify 表示 ③abolish 废除 ④python 蟒蛇 ⑤pheasant 雉 ⑥oriole 金莺 ⑦unicorn 独角兽 ⑧leopard 豹

8 你可以告诉我中山装是怎么出现的吗?

Could you tell me the origin of the Sun Yat-sen Suit?

The Sun Yatsen Suit(中山装)or Chinese tunic suit is a simplified outfit introduced by Dr. Sun Yatsen. Dr. Sun found Western style suits uncomfortable, and traditional Chinese-style robes and garments unsuitable for the Chinese people's new spirit after the overthrow of the Qing Dynasty. Therefore in 1923, while working as leader of China's Revolutionary Government based in Guangzhou, Dr. Sun introduced a business suit based on a popular style worn by the overseas Chinese in Southeast Asia at the time. In line with Dr. Sun's suggestions, tailors added a fold-down collar and four visible pockets to the suit. In order to have the option to carry more things, the pants also had two hidden big pockets, one on the left and the other on the right, with a small pocket in the front of the pants called the "wrist watch bag" and another pocket with a flap on the back right side. The Sun Yatsen suit came in grey, blue or black, and was considered convenient as well as economical. Since the 1920s this style became very popular throughout China.

Notes: ①uncomfortable 不舒服的 ②unsuitable 不合适的 ③fold-down 折叠的 ④hidden 隐藏的 ⑤convenient 方便的 ⑥economical 节俭的

饮食
Chinese Food

1 请你略谈一下中餐，好吗？

Could you give me a briefing on Chinese food?

Chinese cooking has developed through the centuries, and also makes traveling in China a real joy. Eating out is more than just food; it can be considered a social occasion, a time when families get together, and major leisure activity among friends and businessmen.

Many tourists wonder whether it is possible to eat a nutritionally balanced diet while traveling in China. Quality, availability of ingredients and cooking styles vary by region, and tourists will always find something to suit their tastes.

Chinese livestock are primarily raised by individual families to supplement their income. In the last few years, the Chinese have developed several large livestock farms, and farmers have been encouraged to raise larger herds of animals, but family-raised animals still predominate. Pork, chicken, and fish are readily available in street markets.

In the U. S. A. chickens mature faster. They are usually ready to sell in seven to eight weeks compared to twelve to eighteen weeks required for Chinese chickens. Chinese chickens are better suited for being cut into thin small strips. Are you tempted to buy a live chicken in the free market? Freshly killed chicken definitely tastes best.

Fish generally cook very fast and are usually prepared in eight different ways—poached, steamed, braised, stewed, baked, broiled, grilled, and fried. The best method will depend on the fish you are cooking. Remember that fish vary considerably in their fat content, so fatter fish taste better if they are baked or broiled while some of the leaner fishes may be poached or steamed.

There are many restaurants in China that are small family-run businesses. Some restaurants have buffet kitchens, where customers go to the back of the restaurant to select their vegetables and meats such as chicken, duck, and fish. Customers may even have a chance to observe how the chef cooks food.

Most restaurants provide a packet of napkins, chopsticks, and even sunflower seeds, while tea is normally free. Most waiters will ask you what kinds of alcohol you want as Chinese often have meals with rice wine or beer. Overseas visitors can find out at least one restaurant he/she likes best. Because English menus are still hard to come by, a phrase-book will be very helpful to bring.

There are regional differences in Chinese cooking that offer a diverse range of dishes. Most comprehensive and popular of these regional styles originated in the North, South, East, and West. Basically the four gastronomic areas include Shangdong, Guangdong, Sichuan and Yangzhou. Each regional recipe has at least one hundred attractive dishes. In addition, there are more than one hundred minor schools of Chinese cuisine.

Cantonese cooking is probably the most famous of all Chinese cooking styles. Cantonese food has its origins in Guangzhou and Hong Kong and tends to be lighter and less spicy than other cuisine. Most restaurants abroad tend to be Cantonese, but as you will soon discover, the Chinese food served abroad is very different from that enjoyed in China.

Sichuan cuisine is the spiciest of all because it uses *huajiao*(literally flower pepper, 花椒)to add subtlety to the blast of the red chili. Popular dishes include Pork with Peanuts, and "Strange Tasting" Chicken (怪味鸡).

Shandong cooking belongs to the Northern cooking style, and includes the menus of the emperors of the Yuan, Ming, and Qing dynasties, as well as many seafood dishes. Beijing-food falls under the category of Shandong cooking. A famous and delicious dish is Peking Duck; its tender duck meat is eaten in wrapped pancakes with shallots and plum sauce, and the bones are boiled up into soup.

The Yangzhou menu has a great variety of dishes from the provincial kitchens of Jiangsu and Zhejiang provinces. Yangzhou cuisine tends to be heavier than the Cantonese variety and usually takes slightly longer to prepare so that vegetables and meats can properly absorb the rich sauces.

The key to ordering Chinese dishes is to get a variety and balance of textures, tastes, smells and colors. Most Chinese will order at least one cold dish, a main dish, a watery soup, and finish off with a bowl of rice. Pork and chicken are the main meats throughout China, but you will also find beef and lamb, especially in *hui* Muslim restaurants.

In addition, some great tasting snacks are worth trying out, as they are cheap and quick to make. The best places to track them down are night markets and old town backstreets.

Notes: ①nutritionally 滋养地 ②availability 可得性 ③ingredient （烹调的）原料 ④livestock （总称）家畜 ⑤supplement 补充 ⑥predominate 占主导（或支配）地位 ⑦strip 条；带 ⑧braise 以文火炖煮 ⑨stewed 炖的 ⑩poached 用文火煮的 ⑪buffet 小吃店 ⑫napkin 餐巾 ⑬gastronomic 美食法的 ⑭subtlety 微妙之处 ⑮pancake 薄煎饼 ⑯shallot 葱 ⑰plum sauce 李子酱 ⑱texture （织物的）组织；结构 ⑲backstreet 后街

2 你可以再谈谈中餐吗？

Could you give me some more information about Chinese food?

Chinese food consists of plants and animals that have existed in China since remote times, but ingredients are not the same everywhere, and so Chinese food assumes a local character simply by virtue of the ingredients in use.

In the Chinese culture, the whole process of food preparation is impressive. A balanced meal must have an appropriate amount of ingredients of both *fan*（饭） and *cai*（菜）. *Fan* is grains and other starch foods, and *cai* are vegetable and meat dishes. In a narrow sense, *fan* means "cooked rice," which makes up half of a typical Chinese meal. *Fan* also includes steamed wheat or corn-flour bread and noodles. Traditionally Chinese chefs use multiple ingredients and mixed flavors. Vegetable and meat ingredients are usually cut up. Pork, for example, may be diced, sliced, shredded, or ground. Combined with various vegetable ingredients and seasonings, the cut pork is usually cooked into individual *cai* dishes with vastly differing flavors, shapes, colors, and aromas.

Because Chinese chefs are very adaptable, they can prepare dishes even in a foreign country without many familiar ingredients. This tradition of adaptability comes out of a historic knowledge of wild plant resources. The Chinese peasants apparently knew every edible plant in their environment, most of which do not ordinarily belong on the dinner table but may be easily adapted for consumption. The knowledge of these wild plants has been carefully handed down. Another feature of the adaptability is the great variety of preserved foods like grains, meat, fruit, eggs and vegetables. These foods are preserved by smoking, salting, or drying. In ancient China, preserved foods were invaluable during famine period.

Throughout history, some restaurants won high praise from their customers and became famous because of good service, delicious food, and reasonable price. The names of these restaurants have been handed down from one generation to another. Among the famous names are the Quanjude restaurants(全聚德)in Beijng, the Songhelou Restaurant(松鹤楼)in Suzhou, and the Goubuli Restaurant(狗不理)in Tianjin.

In the Qin and Han dynasties(221 BC - 220 AD), dishes were named after their major ingredients and cooking methods but at present fancy and beautiful names are bestowed on many dishes to make them more noticeable to customers. For example, *stir-fried clam, water chestnut and mushroom*(天下第一鲜)in Jiangsu's menu, *fish ball soup with eel, shrimp and pork*(七星鱼丸汤)in Fujian's menu, and *stewed beef with innards in a hot sauce*(夫妻肺片)and stewed chicken wings in red wine (贵妃鸡翅) in Sichuan menu. Beautiful dish names create an exciting atmosphere when customers are eating their food.

Notes: ①by virtue of 凭借 ②multiple 多样的 ③aroma 香味 ④adaptability 适应性 ⑤invaluable 无价的 ⑥bestow 把……赠与/给予 ⑦noticeable 显著的 ⑧innards 内脏

3 历史上烹调发展的概况是什么?

How has Chinese cooking evolved throughout history?

Chinese cooking is an art which grew out of a highly developed civilization, and has roots which go further back in history than Western cuisine. Chinese cuisine has evolved through the centuries. When man first learned how to cook, he simply baked a food over hot stones or roasted food over fire, some food wrapped with mud and straw. When ceramics were invented, man could also prepare food using utensils and pottery. During these remote ancient times, there were five kinds of grains: millet, broomcorn millet , wheat , hempseed and bean (稷、黍、麦、麻、菽). Vegetables used at the time were mainly bamboo, mustard, melon, taro, sunflower seeds, garlic, onions, and ginger.

In ancient times, most common people mainly ate millet or other cereal food and had very few meat or vegetable dishes. Princes, nobles and senior officials had a greater variety of cooked dishes to enjoy. *Book of Rites · Neize*(《礼记 · 内则》) lists 20 different dishes made with fish and other meat. According to this book, during a funeral ceremony, people kept a vegetarian diet, but after the ceremony fruits and meats were available.

Before the Han Dynasty(206 BC – 25 AD), only animal fat was used. During the Zhou Dynasty, kings ate lamb and piglet meat cooked in butter in the spring, dried chicken and fish cooked in dog fat in the summer, veal and fawn cooked in lard in the autumn, and fresh fish and wild geese cooked in sheep fat in the winter. In the Han Dynasty, cooking oil was pressed out from plant seeds. People learned to fry ingredients and then further crackle-fry or stir-fry them over a blazing fire. By the late Warring States Period, an essay on culinary theory appeared that detailed how to control the fire temperature, and use seasonings. The book also detailed that the right temperature with the correct cooking time and seasonings would bring out certain flavors.

During the Wei, the Jin, and the Northern and Southern dynasties (220 – 589), China witnessed a massive migration as people of various ethnic origins came and lived together in the same communities where they exchanged food and cooking styles. People from Xinjiang and Central Asia offered roasted and quick boiled sliced meat. From Fujian, Guangdong, and the southeast coastal areas of the country came distinctive seafood cooking. A book entitled *Qi Min Yao Shu*(《齐民要术》) by Jia Sixie (贾思勰) from the Northern Wei Dynasty describes a number of cooking techniques and includes many recipes. Between the Tang and Song dynasties, varied cuisine flourished. These focused not only on the smell and taste of food, but also on color and design.

During the Ming and Qing dynasties (1368 – 1911), the development of sea transportation brought delicacies like shark's fin, sea cucumber, and swallow's nests to the banquet table. *Menus of the Su Garden*(《随园食单》) by Yuan Mei(袁枚) from the Qing Dynasty describes the preparation of many delicacies and sumptuous foods and analyzes various theories of cooking. The Manchu-Han banquet(满汉全席) of the Qing Dynasty displayed the exquisiteness of Chinese cuisine which included extravagant minor and main courses, desserts, and other services.

Foreign cuisine has been readily adopted even since early history. Wheat, sheep, and goats were introduced from western Asia in prehistoric times, and many fruits and vegetables came from central Asia during the Han and Tang dynasties that include alfalfa, grapes, walnuts, broad beans, carrots, onions, pepper and cucumbers. Since the Ming Dynasty, new food staples from the Americas like maize, potato, sweet potato, peanut, tomato have become integral ingredients of Chinese food.

Notes: ①utensil 器皿 ②millet 小米 ③broomcorn 高粱 ④hempseed 大麻籽 ⑤funeral 葬礼 ⑥piglet 小猪(尤指乳猪) ⑦culinary 烹调的 ⑧seasoning 调味品 ⑨migration 迁移 ⑩delicacy 精美 ⑪exquisite 精美的 ⑫extravagant 奢侈的 ⑬prehistoric 史前的 ⑭alfalfa 紫苜蓿 ⑮integral 不可缺少的

4 你对清代皇帝进膳的情况知道多少?

How much do you know about imperial meals prepared for the emperors of the Qing Dynasty?

In the early years of the Qing Dynasty (1616 – 1911), court feasts were not customized for specific events. Upon approval by emperors, anyone could attend court feasts. Attendants might be queens, princesses, emperor's sons, princes, prefecture governors, and civil and military officials.

During the Kangxi Period (1662 – 1722) of the Qing, the imperial palace set up a special department to manage the emperor's meals and beverages and to take care of affairs related to court feasts. In addition, this department was responsible for the preparation of important feasts that occurred on the New Year's Eve, the New Year's Day, the Dragon Boat Festival, the Mid-Autumn Festival, and wedding ceremonies. These days have been listed as official feast holidays in the book called *The Common Etiquette of the Great Qing* (《大清通礼》). This book also deals with the etiquettes of beverages during these feasts.

The *jinshan* (进膳) or *chuanshan* (传膳) meals refer to the food eaten by the Qing emperors at ordinary times. *Jinshan* means "having meals;" *chuanshan* "passing on dishes." On a desk was a number of big and small bowls that contained a variety of dishes and soup, which were all covered until the emperor started to eat. The emperor usually had two meals a day. In winter, his first meal was at six or seven o'clock in the morning and his second meal at half past one in the afternoon. In addition, he had snacks and cakes at about six o'clock in the evening. Before the preparation of each meal, cooking staff had to submit a list of food, soup, and dishes to be approved by the office minister of the internal affairs.

In the court palace, the imperial kitchen prepared the emperor's meals; the imperial tea house supplied varied tea, and made milk tea with tea, cream and salt; the imperial bakery produced pastries and cakes.

The Qing emperor's family feasts fell on New Year's Eve and New Year's Day. When Emperor Qian Long (乾隆) came to the throne (1736 – 1795), he held his initial feast on New Year's Eve in the second year of his rein. As the feast started at two o'clock in the afternoon, court servants were engaged in the feast preparation. The emperor's golden dragon banquet table was placed in the centre of the Qianqinggong (Palace of Heavenly Purity, 乾清宫); on the left was the queen's golden dragon banquet table. The other smaller banquet tables were placed along the east and west sides in the palace. These tables were offered to highest-ranking imperial concubines. Additionally, some other desks were set up and offered to other important attendants. At three o'clock, as musicians in the place galleries played music, the emperor would arrive, and sit at his table, and the feast would start. To begin, warm dishes were provided. The queen would then be offered a pair of boxes which contained mixed soup and food. Each concubine also had a soup-food box afterwards. Milk tea followed the soup-food box which was first presented to the emperor, and then to the queen, and finally to the concubines. Fruits were the final course which again, would be presented first to the emperor, and then to the queen, and finally the concubines. When the feast was over, the emperor was the first to leave. All attendants would kneel down to show respect as the emperor left the feast.

Notes: ①customize 定制 ②etiquette 礼仪 ③beverage 饮料 ④submit 提交 ⑤internal 内部的 ⑥bakery 面包房 ⑦additionally 另外

5 阴阳特点与中餐有什么关系？

How is *yin* and *yang* featured in Chinese food?

Chinese food has long been prepared and consumed with more than just nutrition in mind. Traditional Chinese doctors have been using diet to cure diseases for more than two thousand years. As early as the Shang and Zhou dynasties (1600 BC – 256 BC), the people of the Han ethnic group drank and ate in accordance with the ancient principle of *yin* and *yang*, which holds that everything in the universe is positive or negative and that there must be a harmonious balance between these opposing forces if we are to stay in accord with the cosmos. *Book of Rites · Jiaotesheng* (《礼记 · 郊特牲》) says that in the Zhou Dynasty, drinking is *yin*, and eating is *yang*. Moreover, the foods also have *yin* and *yang* characters. Cereal food is usually classified as *yin*; meat cooked over fire as *yang*. Within this belief, every food category—meat, fowl, vegetable, fruit, nut, liquid, etc. —has its own specific *yin* or *yang* character. *Yin* foods are thin, bland, cooling, and low in calories; *yang* foods are rich, spicy, warming, and high in calories. Boiling foods makes them *yin*; deep frying makes them *yang*.

The Chinese believe that the five tastes of food—spicy, bitter, sweet, sour, and salty—are intimately linked with the five primary elements of the Chinese cosmology—metal, wood, water, earth, and fire. Spicy foods clean the lungs; bitter foods relieve gastroenteritis; sour foods refresh and strengthen the liver; salty foods strengthen the kidneys and bones; sweet foods invigorate the spleen. Some foods had specific effects on the body. Ginseng helps regulate the functions of the glands; seaweed reduces inflammation; lotus root has a significant sedative effect that greatly benefits insomniacs. Pickled plums have long been famous for refreshing the stomach and bowels. Red beans relieve fatigue and stimulate both the heart and urinary system. Garlic stimulates the internal organs and keeps the body warm.

Notes: ①harmonious 调和的 ②in accord with 与……一致 ③cereal food 谷类食品 ④calorie 大卡(表示食物营养价值的单位) ⑤intimately 亲密地 ⑥cosmology 宇宙学 ⑦gastroenteritis 肠胃炎 ⑧invigorate 刺激 ⑨spleen 脾脏 ⑩inflammation 炎症;发炎 ⑪sedative 使镇静的 ⑫insomniacs 患失眠症的人 ⑬stimulate 刺激

6 你对中餐中的豆类食品知道多少？

How much do you know about soy bean foods in China?

Soy bean first appeared in written Chinese annals some 3,000 years ago. At that time its food use had already been highly developed and has continued development up until today. The place soy bean foods hold in Chinese society could easily be compared to that of dairy foods in Europe and America. Following are brief descriptions of categories of soy bean foods that are general considerations for shopping.

Bean curd, or tofu (豆腐) is the largest and the most important of the soy bean categories. Generally, Bean curd is made by grinding soybeans, filtering the resulting soymilk, adding a coagulant and pressing out the excess water. Northerners traditionally prefer a harder Bean curd while southerners prefer a softer, more watery product. A large portion of the bean curd made in China is further processed.

One of the most common processed products is the pressed bean curd (豆腐干). This is often smoked or stewed in flavorful sauces and sold on the streets.

Another common processed product is fermented bean curd (豆腐乳). This is made by taking very hard, small bean curd cubes, inoculating them with bacteria or mold and allowing them to ferment. These are sold in the markets in bottles or earthenware jars.

Bean curd junket (豆腐脑) is a favorite of street vendors in the south. It is extremely soft, looking very much like vanilla pudding. You will see the vendors scooping it out of large pots into bowls, adding sauces according to the customer's specifications.

Bean Paste, or soybean milk (豆浆) is called *miso* in Japan. Bean paste is made by combining steamed soybeans with a starch—usually wheat or rice.

Fermented Soy beans (豆豉) is steamed, cooled soy beans. The beans are fermented for three weeks and then mixed with salt, alcohol and water. This mixture is sealed in an earthenware vessel and stored for six months. The final product is fried or braised with meat dishes for a wonderful flavor.

Notes: ①soy bean 大豆 ②dairy food 奶制食品 ③grind 磨碎 ④coagulant 混凝剂 ⑤ferment 发酵 ⑥inoculate 灌输 ⑦bacteria 细菌 ⑧mold 霉;霉菌 ⑨earthenware jar 陶器罐子 ⑩vanilla pudding 香子兰布丁 ⑪specification 规格;明细单

传统酒文化
Chinese Alcohol Culture

1 中国人在喝酒时有哪些礼节?

How do Chinese behave when drinking?

In ancient China there existed a formal drinking etiquette to follow. When guests attended a feast, the host and guests would kneel down face to face to show respect to each other. As they began to drink, the host would pour a bit of alcohol on the ground in appreciation of the kindness of the earth that provided them with grains and food. When drinking, the host and guests would first savor the alcohol before swallowing it to convey their appreciation. Younger guests at the feast had to wait for the elders to finish drinking before they themselves could start to enjoy the wine.

Nowadays at the beginning of a friendly meal or dinner party, a host or hostess will often raise his or her glass and say, "Drink and enjoy yourself!" Generally after two or three dishes have been served, guests will respond to the toasts. Other individuals on the host's side normally take the lead in toasting guests seated closest to them. These toasts may involve only two people or everyone at the table.

When there are more than one table, the host, after his opening remarks, will often go to each additional table to toast each individual. At official banquets, the chief guest is expected to follow the same custom.

In Chinese etiquette, the host is permitted to merely sip his or her drink—or not drink at all—in order to stay sober and properly manage the banquet. Hosts may also choose to join their guests in drinking if they are still able to take care of the banquet's duties. Guests may respond to the host by calling for a *ganbei* (干杯) toast. Women, particularly if they are not important guests of the party, are generally excused from the *ganbei* ritual. Of course if the host or some other party member proposes a "sip" toast, anyone at the party can still go "bottoms up." As for toast, it is especially polite to follow suit, usually between courses. Drinking in China expresses interest or pleasure during the banquet, but also demonstrates prowess, particularly among males.

Traditionally in Chinese culture there has been a strong tie between alcoholic drinking and establishing new personal, political or business relationships. A common saying goes, "If you respect each other, drink up your wine; if you respect them less, just sip(感情深,一口闷;感情浅,舔一舔)." As the host drinks first, sometimes he will turn his cup upside down to show there is no wine in his cup. After this, the guests will also finish the wine in their cups. The more the guests drink, the happier the host, so refusing to drink is regarded as impolite unless you have a good reason such as high blood pressure, an upset stomach. In this case, joining the toast with water or soft drink is acceptable. Another popular way of limiting the amount you drink is not to fill your cup or glass to the top.

Notes: ①alcohol 含酒精饮料;酒 ②appreciation 欣赏 ③toast 祝酒 ④bottoms up 干杯 ⑤prowess 非凡的能力 ⑥stomach 胃

2 在饮酒时,人们做什么游戏?

What drinking games do people play?

Chinese people sometimes play drinking games with friends. The goal of the game is not to get drunk; drunkenness is the penalty for the loser.

Common drinking games include *the Rock-Paper-*

Scissors. According to this game, the rock beats the scissors; the scissors cut the paper; the paper wraps up the rock. Two players throw out the signs of either object, and if both players show the same sign, they continue the game until one player loses and has to drink.

The Finger Guessing Game is also well known. Two players give a sign for a number using their right hands while shouting out a number from zero to ten. The numbers from each player's hands are added together. If the sum matches either player's announced number, he/she wins. The player who loses has to drink.

The Food Chain is yet another two-player game. Each player begins by banging chopsticks on the table. The two players then touch chopsticks and call out one of the following: stick, tiger, rooster, and worm. According to the game's rules, the stick beats the tiger, the tiger eats the rooster, the rooster eats the worm, and the worm eats through the stick. If the two players say the same item, they keep chanting the items until someone loses and has to drink.

Fajiu (罚酒), literally meaning "drinking as a punishment," occurs when someone arrives late to a feast or banquet. The latecomer usually takes three cups of liquor as a lighthearted penalty.

Notes： ①drunkenness 酗酒 ②penalty 惩罚 ③chant 反复单调地唱 ④lighthearted 随便的

3 酒对中国文化有影响吗?

Have alcoholic beverages exerted any influence on Chinese culture?

Alcohol drinking is a common cultural heritage enjoyed by almost all people of the world. Alcohol has existed in China since antiquity. During these ancient times people would pour out alcohol in honor of their forefathers and then toast their relatives and friends. Chinese men of letters of that time might write poems or monographs after tasting liquors or wines. Alcoholic beverages were also important in banquets or feasts held by ancient emperors or kings.

Alcohol always accompanies delicious dishes either when people first meet or when old friends have a reunion. China produces various types of wine like yellow wine, fruit wine, and distilled liquors[in English wine and liquor are not the same thing. Wine is from grapes, but vodka or *baijiu*(白酒) would be considered liquor]. The most famous Chinese liquor is Maotai (茅台)which comes from the wheat and sorghum of Maotai, Guizhou Province. Wuliangye(五粮液) and Erguotou

(二锅头) are also popular Chinese brands of alcohol.

In the Zhou Dynasty (1046 BC – 256 BC), alcoholic beverages were classified into two types: rice wine and *li* (醴) wine. Some scholars think that *li* wine was similar to beer due to its low alcoholic content. Many stories tell the origins of varied alcoholic drinks from ancient China. One story attributes alcohol's origin to Yi Di (仪狄), the daughter of Emperor Yu (禹). She presented to Yu (禹) a tasty drink made from fermenting rice wrapped in mulberry leaves.

One legend points to Du Kang (杜康) of the Zhou Dynasty (1046 BC – 256 BC) as the inventor of alcohol. One day when he was herding sheep, he mindlessly dropped a bamboo tube in the pasture. Over time the forgotten tube was filled with millet. When Du Kang found the tube again 14 days later, the millet inside had turned into fragrant liquid. This new discovery made him happy, and he began brewing the drink. Today some Chinese still use his name synonymously with alcohol.

There are many ancient stories that tell of wise scholars' drinking experiences. These stories recount their pleasure before and after alcohol drinking, and even describe how these scholars produced their masterpieces while intoxicated.

Tao Yuanming (陶渊明), a prominent poet of the

Wei and Jin Dynasties(220 – 420), often drank alone. He brewed his own alcohol, and meticulously described the rapture he had for drinking; many believe his poems are imbued with alcohol.

The Tang(618 – 907) writer Li Bai(李白)wrote many poems that reflected his fondness for alcohol. One night he was drifting on a lotus pond while totally drunk. He leaned over to embrace the reflection of the moon and fell overboard into the pond. In one of his poems, he wrote, "Happiness is to be savored to the full. The golden cup must not face the moon untouched(人生得意须尽欢，莫使金樽空对月)."

Du Fu(杜甫)was another well-known poet of the Tang Dynasty. He came to Chengdu in 759, where he lived peacefully and composed over two hundred poems. One of his poems said, "So far from town, the food is very plain. And all we have to drink is this home brew. If you like, I'll call across the fence to my old neighbor; to help us finish off the last few drops(盘飧市远无兼味,樽酒家贫只旧醅。肯与邻翁相对饮,隔篱呼取尽余杯)!"

Su Shi(苏轼)was a poet of the Northern Song Dynasty(960 – 1279). He composed many *ci*-poems, one of which asks "How often can you come back to drink with us merrily and linger tipsy(使君能得几回来？便使樽前醉倒更徘徊)?"

People drink alcoholic beverages during traditional Chinese festivals. The Eve of the Lunar New Year is an important occasion for family members to gather together. On this occasion, people eat rich food and drink to their family members and the New Year's coming. In rural, China farmers celebrate an abundant crop harvest and pray for happiness. Once they finalize a lucky date, each family starts to prepare a big dinner. All the family members sip alcohol and enjoy themselves to their hearts' content.

Notes: ①cultural heritage 文化遗产 ②antiquity(尤指中世纪前的)古代 ③men of letters 文人 ④monograph 专题著作 ⑤mulberry 桑树 ⑥inventor 发明者 ⑦mindlessly 不费心思地 ⑧synonymously 同义词性质的 ⑨intoxicated 喝醉的 ⑩meticulously 细致的 ⑪fondness 喜爱 ⑫overboard(自船上)落水 ⑬to one's heart's content 尽情地

4 你能讲讲中国历史上禁酒的情况吗？

Has there been any prohibition against drinking alcohol in Chinese history?

The Book of Shang(《尚书》) and *The Classic of Poetry*(《诗经》) contain the earliest moral judgments concerning alcoholic drinking. They say that alcoholic drinkers should maintain social morality and not indulge to excess. Confucianism has no objection to drinking, but does emphasize moderation as well.

Alcohol should be consumed slowly to enhance its pleasure. Chinese people are unlikely to exhibit reckless behavior in public settings in order to avoid embarrassment and the loss of face. When drinking, people's face may turn red. All these factors work as powerful forces against drunkenness and restrict the use of alcohol.

Yu the Great was the first Chinese ruler to prohibit the consumption of alcohol. During the Han Dynasty (206 BC – 220 AD) various laws were passed with the aim of controlling consumption. For example, in 206 BC in order to curtail drinking at banquets, a fine of four ounces of silver was imposed if three or more people were found drinking together. In 147 BC alcohol production was totally prohibited, but by 98 BC a revision in the law specified that only government officials could manufacture and sell alcohol, thus establishing a government monopoly. Throughout the courses of Chinese history, prohibition against alcoholic consumption was common. Some were for political reasons, and some for the control of grains. For the most part, what determined whether the government lifted a ban or not was the quality of the grain harvest that year.

Notes: ①morality 品行 ②indulge 放任 ③moderation 适度 ④reckless 不顾后果的 ⑤consumption 消耗 ⑥monopoly 垄断

5 中国有哪些名酒?

What famous liquors are there in China?

There are many famous liquors, wines or beers on sale in China. Below are some alcoholic beverages, which are well-known across the country.

茅台酒 Maotai

Maotai Liquor has long been regarded as the number one liquor in China. Maotai was first distilled in the town of Maotai near the Chishui River(赤水)in Guizhou Province. At the Panama World Fair of 1915, it won a gold medal for its excellent quality and unique flavor.

泸州老窖特曲 Luzhou Laojiao Tequ

Tequ(特曲)is the most prestigious liquor produced in Luzhou area, Sichuan Province, followed by Touqu (头曲)and Erqu(二曲). Laojiao Tequ has a strong fragrance and tastes mellow and a bit sweet.

五粮液 Wuliangye

This liquor is produced in Yibin(宜宾), Sichuan Province. Wu liang(五粮) means "five food grains." In 1988, the distillery received both the quality certificate for its products from the national government and the Quality Control Prize from the National Ministry of Commerce; and in 1991, the liquor was put on the list of Top Ten Chinese Liquors.

古蔺郎酒 Gulin Langjiu

This liquor is produced in Gulin County, Sichuan Province and has the same strong fragrance and taste of Maotai. In 1984, at the annual National Wine Appraisal Conference, Gulin Langjiu won a gold medal and was put on the list of the Top Ten Chinese Liquors.

汾酒 Fenjiu

This liquor won a gold medal at the Panama International Exhibition in 1916. The high-quality of the liquor is due in great part to the natural water of wells located at the Apricot Blossom Village(杏花村) in Shanxi Province. Fenjiu looks clear and tastes soft and sweet.

竹叶青 Zhuyeqing

This liquor is Fenjiu brewed with a dozen or more

of selected Chinese herbal medicine. One of the ingredients is bamboo leaves which give the liquor a greenish color and its name.

高粱酒 Gaoliangjiu

Gaoliang is the Chinese name for sorghum. Besides sorghum, the brewing process also uses barley and wheat. In the Ming Dynasty (1368 – 1644), the liquor was originated in the place east of Tianjin.

五加皮酒 Wujiapijiu

This liquor is a variety of Gaoliangjiu with a unique selection of Chinese herbal medicine added to the brewing process. Alcohol content is around 54%.

绍兴黄酒 Shaoxing Yellow Wine

This wine takes its name from its color. It is made in Shaoxing City (绍兴), Zhejiang Province and is also called Shaoxing Rice Wine and noted not only for its yellow color, but also for its mellow fragrance and good taste.

青岛啤酒 Qingdao Beer

This beer is regarded as the number one beer in China. It is brewed with pure spring water from Laoshan (崂山), a mountain area in Qingdao, Shangdong

Province. Qingdao Beer has a pleasant aroma and a well-balanced taste.

Notes: ①unique 独特的 ②prestigious 有声望的 ③mellow(酒)芳醇的 ④certificate 证明书 ⑤appraisal 评价 ⑥apricot 杏 ⑦greenish 带绿色的 ⑧sorghum 高粱 ⑨well-balanced 匀称的

品茶
Chinese Tea Culture

1 请你简要谈谈茶，好吗？

Could you give me a briefing on Chinese Tea?

China has produced tea for five to six thousand years, and tea drinking has been a part of Chinese daily life for at least 1,500 years. In the 6th century tea was introduced to Japan. It is said that tea was introduced into Indonesia in the seventeenth century. Later the Dutch arrived and brought it back to Europe.

The word for tea in many countries comes from the Chinese character "*cha*." The Russians say "*cha'I*", which sounds like "*chaye*" (tea leaves) as it is pronounced in northern China, and the English word "tea" sounds similar to the pronunciation of "*te*" or "*tah*" from South China. The Japanese character for tea is written exactly the same as it is in Chinese, though the pronunciation is slightly different.

Tea processing falls into three categories. Green

tea is heated soon after picking and is not subjected to further processing. Black tea, known as "red tea"(红茶)in China, is dried and then exposed to the air before it is heated. Semi-fermented tea like Wulong tea has an oxidation time somewhat between that of green and black tea. Green tea and black tea differ noticeably in appearance, taste, and chemical composition. Some ethnic nationalities drink compressed tea, known also as "brick tea" (砖茶) due to its shape. Jasmine tea (茉莉花茶) falls into the category of semi-fermented tea; jasmine buds are put into the tea in an attempt to produce a delicate aroma.

It usually takes five years for a tea-plant to grow before its leaves may be picked. After 30 years, however the plant's trunk has to be cut off to let new stems grow out of the same root and thus continue to produce tea.

When do people start picking tea? Each local tea production area has its own tea-picking period depending on local climate. Along the shores of the West Lake in Hangzhou(杭州), from the end of March to October tea-pickers pick the Longjing tea from the same tree every 7 to 10 days.

The picked leaves are dried by heating in a large and deep iron cooking pot, which used to be done by hand. At present, many tea producers use electricity-heated pot to dry tea leaves. The temperature in the pot is about 25℃ or 74 ℉. There are other machines used for grinding or rolling tea leaves into a certain shape.

Notes: ①semi-fermented 半发酵的 ②noticeably 显著地 ③compressed 压缩的 ④delicate 精美的 ⑤electricity-heated pot 电热锅

2 饮茶有什么好处吗？

What are the benefits of tea drinking?

From its very beginning, tea has been considered a medicine and could even relieve poison. In *The Eating Classics*(《食经》), Hua Tuo(华佗) said that continuously drinking bitter tea helps a man to think.

Both green tea and black tea contain an alkaloid (5%, mainly caffeine), a drug that has a mild stimulating effect. The quantity of caffeine provided by a cup of tea depends on its strength; the stronger the "brew", the greater the quantity of caffeine. A medium-strength cup of tea will provide about one third as much caffeine as a cup of percolated coffee, and about two thirds as much as a cup of instant coffee. Caffeine intakes that result from drinking four or five cups of tea each day are not associated with any harmful effect to health in adults. In addition, the tea leaf contains a number of chemicals like tannic acid, a substance known for its anti-inflammatory and germicidal properties.

Drinking tea may help protect against heart disease because its antioxidants help protect blood cholesterol from being oxidized. Oxidized cholesterol is strongly associated with increased risk of heart disease. Studies comparing people who drank either tea or water showed that, shortly afterwards, the tea drinkers had lower levels of oxidized cholesterol in their blood than those who drank plain water. The same chemicals that prevent blood cholesterol also reduce the likelihood that blood will clot in the arteries of the heart.

Green tea, black tea, and black tea with milk all have similar health-promoting effects. Population studies suggest that as little as one cup of tea per day has healthy benefits.

Aromatics in tea may help digest meat or fat, but one point worth noting is that drinking tea with a meal will interfere with iron intake from foods of plant origin. Unless you have a problem with too much iron in the blood, your iron intake will be better if you drink tea between meals rather than with a meal.

Notes: ①alkaloid 生物碱 ②caffeine 咖啡因 ③percolate 过滤 ④anti-inflammatory 消炎的 ⑤germicidal 杀菌的 ⑥antioxidant 抗氧化剂 ⑦oxidize 使氧化 ⑧cholesterol 胆固醇的 ⑨artery 动脉 ⑩aromatic 芳香剂

3 请你谈谈饮茶的礼节,好吗?

Could you tell me something about Chinese tea etiquette?

Tea is the most popular beverage in China, and it plays an important role in Chinese daily life. Traditionally Chinese drink tea before or after a meal, but really anytime is ok.

People usually host guests with tea at home or work. At a special tea party, serving a cup of tea is more than a matter of mere politeness—it is a show of respect to the guests. Before brewing tea for guests, the host should wash his hands and clean all tea cups. A ceramic tea set is preferred. The host should ask guests what kind of tea they prefer: green tea, black tea or jasmine tea. Each cup is 70% full with hot boiled water, and the tea water tastes neither too strong nor too light. Generally the host places the teacups on the saucer before he/she presents them to guests. As the host uses his two hands to present the teacups to guests, they should rise to their feet and take over them also with both hands. At the same time, guests should express their appreciation by saying "thank you."

In Southern China, traditional family-type teahouses with casual atmospheres abound in towns and market villages. Tea servers offer hot boiled water and tea snacks, and provide a comfortable setting with bamboo armchairs, low tables, and sooty kettles. Local people who go to the teahouses are not really thirsty, but usually go there just to sip tea and chat. Elderly persons may pass their whole day there, drinking tea, chatting, playing cards, or dozing off in their armchairs.

As for the tea ceremony, different areas may have different ways to display their unique ceremony. Unlike the Japanese tea ceremony, the Chinese tea ceremony emphasizes the tea rather than the ceremony. During a Chinese tea ceremony, participants are most concerned with what the tea tastes like, smells like, and how one kind of tea tastes compared to another kind of tea.

The tea ceremony does not mean that each server will perform the ritual in the same way, nor is there a relationship to religion. This style of tea-drinking uses small cups to match the small, unglazed clay teapots; each cup is just large enough to hold about two small servings of tea. This particular use of tiny cups is practiced in Fujian and other areas in southern coastal China. In Shanghai and Beijing, large cups are used.

The tea used in tea ceremonies is particularly refined. They aren't the teas you would have with food. The server passes the dry and unbroken tea leaves around for everyone to see and smell. Then he displays a tiny teapot made from red sand clay. After heating water to boiling, the teapot is first rinsed with hot water. The server uses pointed chopsticks to put the tea into the teapot and pours hot boiled water into it. The server rinses the tea leaves by filling the pot half full with the water and draining the water out immediately, leaving only the soaked tea leaves.

The server then fills the pot to the top with more hot water. As he does this, he holds the pot over a large bowl allowing the bubbly water to run into the bowl. The first infusion should be steeped for only 30 seconds before he pours the tea into the tiny cups. Instead of pouring one cup at a time, the server moves the teapot around in a continual motion over the cups so they are all filled together.

As the server empties the pot, he passes out the tiny cups, telling drinkers to smell the tea first. When they drink the tea, the tea tastes much different than it smells. It has a bitter, green-twig taste, very satisfying.

The server refills the teapot with hot water. He refills the cups as the drinkers hand back them for the next round. Each pot of tea serves three to four rounds and up to five or six, depending on the tea and the server with the goal that each round tastes the same as the first.

Notes: ①brew tea 泡茶 ②doze off 打瞌睡 ③unglazed 没有上釉的 ④continual 连续的 ⑤server 侍者

4 你对古代茶的发展了解多少?

How did tea develop in ancient China?

Historians are unsure when exactly tea drinking started. Lu Yu(陆羽)of the Tang Dynasty(618 – 907) published *The Classic of Tea*(《茶经》), the first book about tea in China. In this book, he explains "Shen Nong(神农)made tea as a drinking beverage(茶之为饮,发乎神农氏)." Shen Nong was a divine farmer in Chinese mythology who taught people agriculture and medicinal practice. According to *General History of Huayang*(《华阳国志·巴志》)by Chang Qu(常璩)of the Jin Dynasty(265 – 420), "When King Wu(1046 BC – 1041 BC) of the Zhou Dynasty sent his army to attack Zhou(纣), the last king of the Yin Dynasty, the troops from the states of the Shu and Ba assisted King

Wu. Tea and sweet fermented rice wine were all tributes (周武王伐纣，实得巴蜀之师……茶蜜……皆纳贡之)."

Much literature of the Han Dynasty (206 BC – 220 AD) show that tea was mainly for high class people. According to one of the stories, "When the queen saw the emperor coming, she had her servants prepare tea for him. The servants told the queen that the emperor probably did not like that kind of tea."

During the period between the Jin Dynasty and the Northern and Southern Dynasties (265 – 589), cultured members of the society advocated drinking tea in place of alcoholic drinks in an attempt to avoid wastefulness and misbehavior after drinking. Buddhism began to flourish during the period of the Northern and Southern Dynasties. At that time, Buddhists drank tea to help themselves stay awake for meditation. Tea bushes grew around monasteries on mountains and in valleys.

During the Tang Dynasty (618 – 907) tea became more mainstream. At the same time, the government started to impose tea tax on tea products. *The Classic of Tea* by Lu Yu carefully illustrates the tea plantation, tealeaves processing, and the tea drinking habits. During the same period, tea drinking spread to Japan and Korea.

In 907, the Tang Dynasty fell, and China split into

a number of independent states. The tea production in the south of present day Jiangsu and Zhejiang provinces developed so quickly that they gradually became the center of tea art and culture. People in the Song Dynasty came to drink tea even more stylishly than in Tang times. During the Song Dynasty, teahouses in some cities sprang up where common people could go and drink tea.

Tea industry in the Tang and Song dynasties (618 – 1279) focused on tea processing, especially in tribute tea to the court government. The technology was more advanced than previous dynasties. During the period between the Song and Yuan dynasties, the tribute tea was still *tuanbing* tea (团饼茶), a kind of tea compressed in the shape of a round cake. However, more and more common people drank another kind of tea called "*san* tea (散茶)," which means "the loose tea," "the whole piece tea" or "uncompressed tea." This tea did not go through the complex process like *tuanbing* tea, and thus remained natural with whole and even leaves.

During the Ming and Qing dynasties (1368 – 1911), green tea was the most common; Wulong and black tea were also popular. People came to drink tea even more tastefully and cared about the places where they drank, preferring natural environment on the quiet mountains, in forests, by a small stream or under quiet pine trees.

During the same period, especially in the Qing Dynasty, tea houses developed very fast like the bamboo shoots appearing after a spring rain. Some towns of just a few thousand residents had over one hundred tea houses.

Notes: ①mythology 神话 ②tribute 贡物 ③advocate 提倡 ④wastefulness 浪费 ⑤misbehavior 品行不端 ⑥stylishly 时髦地

5 如何选茶叶,怎样沏绿茶?

How to select tea and how to brew green tea?

Tea customers can buy green tea, black tea or jasmine tea. The following are some simple ways that may help tea drinkers select tea: the shape of the leaf, the color of the liquid, the aroma, the taste, and the appearance of the infused leaf.

Tea leaves should always be kept dry. Customers can use their fingers to press tea leaves to test the dryness, but be careful as the slightest pressure easily breaks dry tea leaves into small pieces. Aroma is the most important factor. Good tea always smells good. The color of the tea liquid and the shape of tea leaves vary with different types of tea. Generally, the tea liquid should remain clear and free of impurity, and the shape of good tea leaves in the liquid should be whole and even.

There are dozens of green tea to choose from in most supermarkets and tea shops. The length of brewing time as well as the temperature of the water can affect the flavor and sweetness of green tea. Water should be below boiling temperature when added to most green tea. One way to adjust the water to the right temperature is to heat the water to the boil, immediately remove it from the heat and allow it to cool for one to three minutes. Higher temperatures should be used only for lower-quality tea in order to more easily extract the most flavor and substance.

Ideally, tea should be made in a teapot with a sensible amount of tea in order to allow enough room for the leaves to "blossom," or open, and move through the water. Good choices for teapots are glass, which makes it easy to monitor the strength of the tea. Although china or porcelain cups are most commonly used, clear glass mugs can enhance appreciation of the delicate color of most green tea. Never boil the water in an aluminum pot, and never steep the tea in teapots or cups made of plastic or aluminum as they have a bad effect on the taste.

Notes: ①infuse 泡(茶等) ②liquid 液体 ③impurity 不纯;不洁 ④extract 提取 ⑤mug(有柄)大杯子 ⑥plastic 塑料的 ⑦aluminum 铝

6 你对中国的茶具了解多少?

What can you tell me about Chinese teapots?

Traditional tea-drinking utensils consist of teapots, teacups, tea bowls, and trays. A good teapot is a sculptural artwork, giving satisfaction in its appearance. Teapot customers usually stand in front of varied teapots in a store, idly comparing the shapes. A customer should choose a pot which meets his/her needs: some pots are primarily aesthetic, and others, more practical.

Before the Ming Dynasty (1368 – 1644), original Chinese pottery resembling a teapot was called a "medical pot", used to hold wine or herbal medicine. In the Ming Dynasty, people used the medical pot to brew tea with hot water. Only gradually did the term teapot come into use.

During the same period, white tea ware became

popular. By the middle of the Ming Dynasty, teapots made of porcelain and purple clay were in fashion. Jingdezhen (景德镇) in Jiangxi Province and Yixing (宜兴) in Jiangsu Province are two key places where teapots are produced.

Notes: ①utensil 器皿 ②aesthetic 审美的 ③practical 讲究实际的 ④in fashion 流行

7 中国有哪些名茶?

What well-known teas are there in China?

There are many famous teas in China. Below are some teas well-known across the country.

西湖龙井 Longjing

Longjing means "Dragon Well" and is a green tea that grows along the shores of the West Lake in Hangzhou, Zhejiang Province. Each bud grows two leaves that appear flat and narrow.

洞庭碧螺春 Dongting Biluochun

This tea grows in the western and eastern Dongting areas, Jiangsu Province. Its tiny and slightly curled leave is covered with white fluffy substance. Its liquid appears bright yellow.

黄山毛峰　Huangshan Maofeng

Maofeng grows in Mt. Huangshan, Anhui Province. Tea leaves, which are picked on March 28 and 29, are regarded as of the best quality. Each tea bud may grow one leaf or two leaves. One of its other names is *Guo Jia Li Pin Cha* (the National Gift Tea).

六安瓜片　Lu'an Guapian

This tea grows in Lu'an County in Anhui Province. Since the Tang Dynasty(618 – 907), it has been regarded as a high-quality green tea. Usually its long and narrow leave is two centimeters in length.

君山青针　Junshan Qingzhen

This tea grows in Junshan, Hunan Province. It is a green tea made of unopened buds. As it is brewed, its leaves in the liquid stand upright, presenting the appearance of a forest of stalagmites.

信阳毛尖　Xinyang Maojian

This tea grows in Xinyang, Henan Province. The best Maojian tea usually comes from tea bushes growing on high mountain areas in Xinyang. When infused, its leaves quickly lay down on the bottom of a cup, and its liquid appears light yellow.

祁门红茶　Qimen Black Tea

This tea leaves mainly grow in several areas, including Qimen, Anhui Province. After the tea leaves are brewed, the liquid appears red, and it tastes heavily fragrant. At the Panama World Fair of 1915, Qimen black tea won a gold metal.

都匀毛尖　Duyun Maojian

This tea is a highly valued green tea that grows in Duyun County, Guizhou Province. The tea consists of selected buds as well as tender leaves that are finely twisted through a careful process.

武夷乌龙　Wuyi Wulong

This tea grows on Wuyi Mountain, Fujian Province. Usually tea workers roll the leaves with their hands and bake them over a charcoal-fire. When it is brewed, its liquid produces a smooth aroma with a deliciously sweet and roasted taste.

安溪铁观音　Anxi Tieguanyin

This tea grows in Anxi, Fujian Province. Its leaves are thick and dark green in color, and the edge of leaves slightly folds like Guanyin Bodhisattva's folded palms. Tieguanyin has several varieties. Its leaves picked in spring are called the Spring Tea, the best tea of this kind. The other varieties include the Autumn Tea and Summer Tea.

Notes: ①bud 芽 ②fluffy 绒毛(状)的 ③centimeter 厘米 ④stalagmite 石笋 ⑤charcoal 木炭

风俗习惯
Traditional Customs

1 什么是麒麟?

What is Chinese unicorn?

In ancient China, the unicorn, phoenix, tortoise, and dragon were regarded as "the Four Spiritual Animals(四灵)" that symbolized auspicious signs. The unicorn, phoenix, and dragon are all mythical animals in Chinese legends.

The Chinese unicorn has the body of a deer, the tail of an ox, and the hooves of a horse. His body is covered with scales, and a single horn stands out on his head. The unicorn personifies all that is good, pure, and peaceful. Legendary stories say that the unicorn always desires to do good for others. In the ancient dynasties, emperors all regarded the unicorn as the symbol of times of peace and prosperity. Stone or bronze unicorns are found in the Imperial Palace, the Summer Palace, and other imperial residences and gardens.

Common people also love the Chinese unicorn. During the Spring Festival, people along the southern side of the Yangtze River have a custom of carrying a paper-made unicorn while visiting each family. They give a performance in front of each entrance door to extend good wishes. In addition, some legends say that the unicorn even has the power to bless women with children. Couples often use the unicorn to pray to have children as soon as possible after marriage.

Notes: ①tortoise 乌龟 ②spiritual 超自然的 ③unicorn 独角兽 ④personify 使拟人化 ⑤legendary 传奇的 ⑥prosperity 繁荣 ⑦bless 祝福

2 什么是凤凰?

What is phoenix?

The phoenix has a beautiful crest on its head, and her body is covered with colored feathers. She appears noble like the queen of birds. In Chinese legends, the phoenix symbolizes auspiciousness and peace. Emperors in the ancient dynasties regarded the phoenix and dragon as symbols of power and dignity. The phoenix later became an auspicious animal among common people whose presence is supposed to bring good luck. Especially on traditional Chinese weddings, the phoenix image serves as a happy ornament on a brides wedding gown and coronet. In traditional designs, the phoenix appears with other mythical animals like the dragon and unicorn, further illustrating the symbol of auspiciousness. "Prosperity brought by the dragon and the phoenix (龙凤呈祥)" is one popular saying.

Notes: ①crest (鸟的)冠; 冠毛 ②auspiciousness 吉祥 ③dignity 尊严 ④ornament 装饰 ⑤illustrate 说明

3 什么是龙?

What is dragon?

People in China are all familiar with the image of the dragon, but few know the story behind the mythical animal. The dragon has the head of an ox, the horn of a deer, the eyes of a shrimp, the claws of a hawk, the body of a snake, and the tail of a lion. Scales and shell cover the whole body. The dragon can walk on land, swim in water, and fly among the clouds. Because the dragon symbolizes infinite supernatural power, ancient emperors regarded him as the symbols of power and dignity while common people respect him as the incarnation of virtue and strength. The image of the dragon can be seen carved or drawn on roof ridges of imperial palaces, temples, and on the utensils used by imperial families. During some traditional festivals, common people show their reverence to this mythical animal by hanging pictures of the dragon, displaying a variety of dragon lanterns, performing the dragon dance, or rowing dragon boats.

Notes: ①shrimp 虾 ②infinite 无限的；无边的 ③incarnation 化身 ④utensil 器皿 ⑤reverence 崇敬；敬畏

4 什么是龟？ What is tortoise?

Tortoises may be found in the ocean, rivers and zoos. Tortoises usually have much longer life-span compared with other animals, so people regard him as the symbol of longevity and good health. In addition, the tortoise is thought to have the power to see the future. In ancient times, prior to an important event, a soothsayer would burn tortoise-shells and predict an event according to the lines that appear on the burnt tortoise-shell. Huge stone or bronze tortoises were placed in ancient imperial palaces, residences, and mausoleums, which shows the early dynasties' desire to continue forever.

Notes: ①life-span 寿命 ②soothsayer 算命者 ③predict 预言 ④mausoleum 陵墓

5 "紫气东来"有什么含义?

What does "the purple cloud coming from the east" mean?

"The purple cloud comes from the east" means that something auspicious is approaching. Because of its bright sign, Chinese people like to write it on paper and paste it on top of a door of a house or an apartment. The written sign functions as the horizontal wall inscription, joining in a couplet to welcome the traditional Spring Festival.

According to one legend, Lao Zi(老子) worked as an archivist in the Imperial Library of the Zhou court. As the Zhou Dynasty (1046 BC – 256 BC) declined, dukes of the Zhou Dynasty frequently declared war in order to gain power and position. Lao Zi anticipated that greater chaos caused by war would take place in near future. He rcsigned from his post, and upon a purple buffalo traveled west.

One early morning, a guard in charge of the western-most gate saw a huge purple cloud approaching from the east. He walked out of the gate to see more clearly. He soon saw an old man with long snow-white bread arrive leisurely on a purple buffalo. He looked like an immortal. As he passed through the gate, the guard said to him, "Since you are about to leave the world behind, can you write a book for my sake?"

Lao Zi did so. Lao Zi complied and wrote a book in two parts: the Way (道) and Virtue (德). The whole book has some 5,000 characters and is called *Dao De Jing* (《道德经》). After he finished his writing, he continued to travel on the buffalo and disappeared.

In the early Western Han Dynasty (206 BC – 25 AD), the ruling class believed in Huang Di and Lao Zi's way to seek a peaceful life and hoped that this belief would dominate the whole country. At the beginning, Daoists worshiped both Huang Di and Lao Zi, but later emphasis shifted only to Lao Zi who was generally seen as the founder of Daoism.

Liu Xiang (刘向) of the Han Dynasty wrote a book called *The Biography of Immortals* (《列仙传》). He said in this biography, "Lao Zi traveled to the west. Yi Xi, a gate guard, saw that a purple cloud drifted over the gate. Then Lao Zi passed by, riding on a purple buffalo (老子西游,关令尹喜望见有紫气浮关,而老子

乘青牛而过也)."

Notes: ①approach 靠近 ②horizontal 水平的；横的 ③inscription 碑文 ④duke 君主 ⑤anticipate 预期 ⑥for one's sake 为了……缘故

6 为什么人们常常倒贴"福"？

Why is the Chinese character "happiness" often pasted upside down on a door or a wall?

During the Spring Festival, each household pastes a big or small Chinese character "*fu*(福)" on its entrance door or on walls inside houses as part of the Spring Festival celebration.

The character's present meaning is happiness and in the past referred more to good fortune. Throughout the course of Chinese history, people have kept the custom of pasting the character during the Spring Festival, yearning for good fortune and a bright future.

How did this custom start? Legend has it that when Jiang Ziya(姜子牙) granted titles to deities, his wife came and asked him to offer her a title. Jiang said to her, "You are a spendthrift. All thc families suffer from misfortune and become poor after you visit them, so I am going to offer you the title of Poverty Deity." Upon hearing this, his wife asked, "Where am I going to stay as the Poverty Deity?" Jiang answered, "You are welcome to stay anywhere except places where fortune exists." Jiang's words spread far and wide among the common people, and they quickly pasted the Chinese character "good fortune(福)" in the hope that the Poverty Deity might not enter their houses. This practice was passed on from generation to generation until it became a custom during the festival celebration.

Sometimes the *fu* character is pasted upside-down. Why? The word "reverse or upside down" is "*dao*(倒)"in Chinese. This "*dao*(倒)"and another "*dao*(arrive, 到)"are pronounced exactly the same although the former one has a radical on the left, and the latter has none. People use the same pronunciation simply to demonstrate that "the happiness or good fortune has arrived."

There is a folktale that explains the origin of why the character is put upside-down. One time during the Spring Festival, ZhuYuanzhang(朱元璋), the first emperor of the Ming Dynasty(1368 - 1644) arrived in a small town. He took off his emperor's dress, decided to put on common clothes, and then left the guesthouse. As he toured the town, he saw a group of people staring at a drawing of a bare-footed woman who carried a huge watermelon in her arms. The caricature made fun of bigfeet women. At that time, many women had bound-feet as the style was considered lovely and alluring. Incidentally the empress happened to have big feet, so this drawing irritated the emperor. He returned to the guest-house and ordered his palace men to find out who was involved in the mischief. His men then pasted the character "*fu*" on the doors of houses to indicate the families that were not involved. Next morning the palace men would arrest the people whose doors did not have any character.

Upon hearing this plan, the kind-hearted empress immediately ordered all the people in the town to paste the "*fu*" character on the doors of their houses, emphasizing that this task had to be done before daybreak. One illiterate local man pasted the character upside-down by accident. The next morning the emperor and empress went out into the street and found that each household had the character on their doors. The overturned character caught their eyes, and the emperor stopped to view it for a moment. He became angry again and ordered his palace men to arrest the man and his whole family and to put them in jail.

The empress quickly came to the illiterate man's defense and said, "This family pasted the character upside-down on purpose because they were told that you would pass by their house today. The overturned character actually means ‘arrival of the fortune.’” The empress' explanation convinced the emperor to set the man and his family free. From then on people began to follow this custom.

Notes: ①household 户 ②spendthrift 挥霍无度的 ③misfortune 不幸；厄运 ④reverse 颠倒，翻转 ⑤bare-footed 赤脚的 ⑥caricature 漫画 ⑦incidentally 偶然地 ⑧irritate 激怒 ⑨illiterate 文盲 ⑩overturn 翻倒 ⑪convince 使确信

7 红、黄颜色有什么特点？

What are the implications of red and yellow colors?

In China the color red refers to auspiciousness. The walls of monasteries and royal buildings are painted red. In addition, people usually paste red couplets during Spring festival or joyous occasions; the bride and groom are traditionally dressed in red during the wedding ceremony; red-painted eggs are offered to a woman who has given birth to a child; the money given to children at New Year is wrapped in red paper(压岁钱).

In remote ancient times, however, Chinese used yellow to represent auspicious signs. In addition, black or white were also colors associated with good fortune.

During the Han Dynasty (206 BC – 220 AD) Liu Bang (刘邦), the first emperor of the Han Dynasty, proclaimed himself the son of the Red Emperor (赤帝之子). Since then, the color red came to be an auspicious color and enjoyed the growing esteem among people across the country. People continued to use the color red for festivals or joyous occasions even after the Han Dynasty.

Since ancient times, yellow has been considered an imperial color. When you visit the Imperial Palace, the Summer Palace, and Beihai Park, you will find that the tiles on the top of the royal buildings are usually yellow. The Five Elements (五行) assign earth the color yellow in the central position. During the Tang Dynasty (618 – 907), laws were passed that only allowed the imperial family to use yellow. In the Song Dynasty, the yellow glazed tiles were used for imperial building, and this custom continued throughout the following dynasties. In addition, many things used by emperors appear yellow in color like imperial robes, imperial edicts, and interior ornaments in the emperor's rooms.

Notes: ①joyous 充满快乐的 ②given birth to 生(孩子) ③assign 分配 ④edict 法令

8 祝寿送寿桃的由来是什么?

Why do people often give longevity peaches to express birthday good wishes?

When someone holds a birthday celebration, his/her relatives and friends may give peaches to express good wishes. We call these peaches "longevity peach (寿桃)." When did this tradition start? According to legend, the practice started with Sun Bin(孙膑).

During Spring and Autumn Period and Warring States Period (770 BC – 256 BC), Sun Bin left his hometown and traveled a thousand-*li*(里) to visit a famous scholar named Gui Guzi (鬼谷子). Sun Bin decided to study the art of war from this respected scholar, and thus began his lessons upon arrival. Twelve years passed and Sun Bin still had no desire to go back home.

On the fifth day of the fifth lunar month Sun Bin remembered that it was his mother's birthday. He thought that his mother might be expecting him to return home as soon as possible since he had not been home for 12 years, and his mother was 80 years old. He did not even know if his mother was still in good health.

On the same day all the family members gathered to celebrate Sun Bins mother's birthday at Sun's home. The aged mother felt so sad and wept because everyone was at home except Sun Bin. The whole family tried hard to console the old woman, but their attempt did not lessen her grief.

At that moment Sun Bin walked into the room. Sun Bin met his mother and felt extremely sad as he saw his mother had withered so much with age and grief. He quickly took a peach out of his pocket and gently presented it to her, saying, "I asked my teacher to let me come home today, and so my teacher offered this peach, asking me to present it as a best wish for your happy birthday."

Sun Bin's mother ate the peach, which soon made her look much healthier and younger. Since then, many families follow Sun Bin's example by presenting peaches to their parents, relatives, and even friends on their birthdays.

Notes: ①express a good wish 表达美好的愿望 ②upon arrival 当到达时 ③as soon as possible 尽快 ④console 安慰 ⑤wither 枯萎

9 民间四大传说讲的是什么?

What are the four great legends about?

The Buffaloboy and the Weaving Girl (牛郎织

女), Tale of the White Snake(白蛇传), Meng Jiangnü (孟姜女), and Liang Shanbo and Zhu Yingtai(梁山伯和祝英台) are four great legends known by all Chinese.

The Buffaloboy and the Weaving Girl

In ancient China, people believed that deities resided in Heaven, Earth, and Hell, and that the Heavenly royal parents had seven beautiful daughters; the youngest was the prettiest and brightest of them all.

Once upon a time, there was a boy who was clever, diligent, and honest. He lived with his wicked big brother because his parents had died. The big brother drove him out of his home, giving him nothing but a buffalo. This animal was loyal to the boy, and the two became good friends. Eventually the boy became known as the Buffaloboy.

Meanwhile, the youngest of the seven celestial princesses had grown tired of her life in the Celestial Palace, and longed for a common life like the ones she saw so often down beneath her. To pursue her happiness, she descended onto earth and landed in front of the Buffaloboy.

They married and had a lovely son and a lovely daughter. While the Buffaloboy worked in the fields with his buffalo, the Heavenly princess wove at home to help support the family. Villagers all admired her excellent weaving skill and eventually gave her the nickname the Weaving Girl.

The family enjoyed a moderate but happy life until the celestial royal family traced the seventh princess to the village. A day in Heaven amounted to years on Earth, so the years she had spent with the Buffaloboy were but a few days in Heaven.

The Celestial Empress was so angry that she ordered her daughter to go back to Heaven or otherwise see her husband and children be killed. The Weaving Girl was a good wife and mother, and so decided to return to her celestial home, sadly leaving behind the Buffaloboy and her two children.

The Buffaloboy was at a loss at discovering that his beautiful wife had disappeared when suddenly the buffalo began to speak. The buffalo said that he would be dead very soon and asked the Buffaloboy to use his hide as a vehicle to catch up with his wife. The Buffaloboy did so and soared into the sky, carrying his young son and daughter in a basket on each side of a shoulder pole. When the empress saw the Buffaloboy approaching, she took out her hairpin and drew a line across the sky in front of the Buffaloboy that instantly became a torrential river called the Silvery River (known as "Milky Way" in Western culture). She thought that the couple would never have a chance to get together again.

All the magpies in the world, deeply touched by the devotion of the young couple, flocked to their rescue. Each year, on the seventh day of the seventh month on the Chinese lunar calendar, the birds would manage to gather enough force in number to form a bridge so that the family would have a brief reunion.

Tale of the White Snake

Long ago on Mt. Emei(峨眉山)there lived two snakes; one was white and the other green. They had been engaged in ascetic practices for a thousand years, and had gained the ability and desire to become beautiful ladies and thus transformed themselves into Bai Suzhen(白素贞)and Xiao Qing(小青). They appeared at the West Lake(西湖)and began enjoying the scenery around them. Rain started to pour down as they reached a bridge, and the two ladies took temporary refuge under a willow tree.

Soon an affable young man named Xu Xian(许仙) passed by who was carrying an umbrella. When he saw the two beautiful ladies sheltering under the tree, Xu Xian lent them his umbrella and helped them take a boat home.

Bai immediately fell in love with him, and told him to come to their house the next day so that they could return to him the umbrella. She learned that he was an orphan, living with his elder sister, and working in a herbal medicine shop.

Bai proposed that they be married. Xu was delighted. Under the direction of Xiao Qing, they worshipped Heaven and Earth and joined in marriage. They opened their own herbal medicinal shop, and Bai proved to be excellent at compounding drugs or herbs. Soon more and more local people came to their shop for drugs.

At the Golden Mountain Monastery(金山寺) nearby, there dwelt a monk named Fa Hai (法海). He recognized Bai as a snake demon(蛇妖), and he thought that this snake was of great potential danger to humans so he warned Xu Xian.

Xu refused to believe that his wife was a snake demon so the monk told him to get her drunk at the day of the Dragon Boat Festival (端午节), and she would revert to her true form. Xu followed his advice, and after Bai became quite ill after drinking, she retired to bed. Soon on the bed appeared an enormous white snake. Xu saw what had happened. He was so frightened that he fell down on the ground dead.

When Bai recovered, she was horrified to discover her husband dead, and she appealed to her sister Xiao Qing to help find the herbs to bring him back to life. Bai even made a special trip to steal the magic medicine and finally succeeded in saving Xu. However, Xu was still worried a bit about Bai's true form.

The monk was disgruntled and so kidnapped Xu and took him into protective custody at the monastery. Bai was upset and at the same time her sister Xiaoqing urged her to give up her inappropriate marriage to Xu. Finally Xu managed to escape from the monastery and rejoined Bai who confessed everything to him. Xu swore his love for her anyway, regardless of her true form. Their son was born shortly afterward.

But the monk remained determined, and managed to capture Bai and imprison her under the Pagoda of the Thunder Peak(雷峰塔). She was saved once again by her sister Xiao Qing, who journeyed to Mount Emei for further practice of martial arts, and then returned for the final defeat of the monk.

Liang Shanbo and Zhu Yingtai

The story of Liang Shanbo and Zhu Yingtai, also known as "Butterfly Lovers," is deeply rooted in Chinese folk tradition, and has always been close to the hearts of the ordinary people. It tells a tragic love between Liang Shanbo and Zhu Yingtai.

Zhu Yingtai was a young girl who decided to go to school. Prior to attending school, Zhu disguised herself as a boy. In school, she met a humble but intelligent young man named Liang Shanbo. They two quickly became good friends as they were of similar minds and temperament.

Every day they studied together as delightful companions. Their studies covered poetry, music, and philosophy. As days passed, Zhu fell in love with Liang because of the growing friendship and true affection. During their stay in school, however, Liang never suspected the true feelings of his companion.

One day, Zhu received a letter from her parents asking her to return home, and so when she left school, Liang came to see her off. As they walked together along the way, Zhu subtly tried to convey her feelings. Unfortunately Liang failed in catching what she said, so finally Zhu told him a lie, saying that she had a twin sister at home, and she promised to introduce her to Liang. So before they departed, Liang said that he would go and visit Zhu at her home as soon as possible, and at the same time he would confirm the wedding date with her twin sister.

When Zhu arrived home, she found out that her parents had agreed to a marriage proposal from the Ma family, a very wealthy and powerful family in the province. Zhu was distressed. She vehemently disagreed with her parents' arrangement since they had not asked for her opinion, and therefore wished that her parents would break off the engagement. However, her parents had accepted wedding gifts, and they had to force their daughter to accept. Traditionally a bad name would be given to a family if they broke off an engagement after they had accepted the gifts.

In the meantime, Liang came to Zhu's home as scheduled. Upon his arrival, he was surprised to see that Zhu was a girl. His surprises then quickly melted into happiness and joy. They were very happy when they met again. Many beautiful memories that occurred in the past three years still remained fresh in their minds. Liang took this opportunity to propose a possible marriage with her. Under this circumstance, Zhu told him of her arranged marriage engagement with a son from the Ma family. The possible marriage between Zhu and Liang vanished into thin air. Lament appeared on their faces, and their eyes were filled with tears when Liang and Zhu departed.

Liang came back home. He was heart-broken and became sick. Soon he died. Upon hearing this news, Zhu was desperately sad. Liang's death completely took away from her any hope of happiness although she had agreed to marry into the Ma family.

As the wedding sedan chair and escorts passed by Liang's grave, Zhu asked to stop because she wanted to mourn Liang at his grave. The whole team stopped. Zhu got off the chair and walked to the grave where she tearfully offered her prayers to the memory of Liang. As she knelt down, a mysterious storm appeared and a flash of lightning broke out. The grave opened. Without hesitation, Zhu jumped into the opened grave which immediately closed afterwards. The windstorm stopped and lightning disappeared. There was no sign of the bride except for two butterflies that flew above the grave.

This story spread far and wide so that people began to refer to Liang Shanbo and Zhu Yingtai as the Butterfly Lovers, symbolizing the reunion of their spirits in Heaven.

Meng Jiangnü

This story occurred during the Qin Dynasty (221 BC – 206 BC) when Emperor Qin unified the country. The construction of the Great Wall was under way which required the physical labor of thousands upon thousands of people. Local soldiers across the country rounded up as many men as possible to send them to the construction sites where they had to do hard physical labor around the clock. The work was exhausting and led to many deaths.

A scholar named Fan Qiliang (范杞良) in Suzhou hid himself wherever possible in order to escape being caught by local soldiers.

One day he arrived at a village where he saw a garden. He quietly walked into the garden and stayed there through the night. The garden happened to belong to Meng Jiangnü's family; Meng was a beautiful and clever girl.

The next morning Meng strolled into the garden. She came across Fan as she enjoyed viewing flowers. Soon after that her parents came, and Fan told his story. Meng and her parents decided to hide Fan in their home. Meng's parents liked the young scholar and thus arranged Fan to marry their daughter.

They got married but three days after the wedding ceremony, local soldiers broke into Meng's house and took Fan away to the construction site at the Great Wall. Meng wept day and night, and prayed earnestly, wishing her husband to come back. She waited half a year without a sign of him.

Late autumn came. The shrilly wind blew, and the weather was getting colder day by day. Meng sewed some winter clothes for her husband to wear. Meng left the village and started her thousand-*li* journey to the construction site where her husband worked.

Meng experienced much hardship and trouble along the way, but finally arrived at the foot of the Great Wall. Workers there immediately recounted how her husband had died and was buried inside the newly built wall.

The heart-breaking news overwhelmed Meng, and

she fell unconscious on the ground. Upon regaining consciousness, she started crying so bitterly that the sky, the earth, the sun, and the moon darkened. For a long time, she cried, and suddenly a thunderous noise broke out and shook the earth. One section of the Great Wall collapsed unearthing heaps of bones.

Meng bit her fingers and let blood drop on the bones. She prayed quietly, saying if her blood oozed into the bones, those bones were her husband's; if not, these bones were of others. At last, Meng found her husband's bones and corpse. She cried again while holding up in her arms the pile of bones of her dead husband.

At that moment, Emperor Qin passed by. Fascinated by her beauty, the emperor invited her to be his concubine. Meng pretended to accept his offer. She required the emperor to do three things for her before they held their wedding ceremony. One of the three things was to invite Buddhist monks to chant Buddhism scriptures for her husband while he was buried; the second was to hold a memorial ceremony for her husband that the emperor and all officials had to participate in; the third was that after the funeral services, Meng would take a three-day sightseeing tour.

The emperor agreed to her three requests. After the requests were fulfilled, Meng severely scolded the emperor, and then threw herself into the sea.

Notes: ①cowboy 牧牛人 ②wicked 有恶意的 ③celestial 天国的 ④grow tired of 变得厌倦 ⑤eventually 最终地 ⑥vehicle 运载工具 ⑦to catch up with 赶上 ⑧soar 往上飞舞 ⑨hairpin 发夹 ⑩torrential 汹涌的 ⑪ascetic 苦行者 ⑫temporary 暂时的 ⑬affable 和蔼的 ⑭under the direction of 在……指导下 ⑮compound 使混合 ⑯ ⑰recognize 认出 ⑱potential 潜在的 ⑲revert to 回复 ⑳horrified 可怕的 ㉑disgruntle 使不高兴 ㉒custody 监禁 ㉓confess 承认 ㉔imprison 监禁 ㉕temperament 性格 ㉖affection 爱慕感情 ㉗subtly 微妙地 ㉘vehemently 激烈地 ㉙break off 中断 ㉚lament 悲伤 ㉛a flash of 闪烁，闪光 ㉜exhaust 筋疲力尽 ㉝heart-breaking 令人心碎的 ㉞overwhelm 战胜 ㉟regaining consciousness 恢复意识 ㊱thunderous 像打雷的 ㊲ooze 渗出 ㊳a pile of 一大堆 ㊴fascinate 使着迷 ㊵sightseeing 观光

10 什么是“八仙”？

Who are the Eight Immortals?

The Eight Immortals (八仙) are Chinese deities. Their portraits are seen everywhere — on porcelain vases, teapots, teacups, fans, scrolls and embroidery. Each immortal's power can be transferred to a tool of power (法器) that can give life or destroy evil. Not only are they worshipped by Daoists but also are popular subjects in general Chinese culture.

Traditionally, "eight" is a lucky number. People often add this number to names in order to give good luck, and therefore the "Eight Immortals" are associated with good fortune. In the Ming Dynasty (1368 – 1644), Wu Yuantai (吴元泰) wrote a book called *The Origin of the Eight Immortals and their Trips to the East* (《八仙出处东游记》). Hereafter, the legend of the Eight Immortals gradually spread across the country, and the above-mentioned images became popular among Chinese people. Below are some descriptions of each immortal.

Li Tieguai or Iron-crutch Li (铁拐李) is the most ancient of the Eight Immortals. He is depicted as a lame beggar, carrying a crutch. His spirit frequently leaves his body to wander on the Earth and Heaven.

Han Xiangzi (韩湘子) is a happy immortal. He is depicted holding a lotus flower, and sometimes with a *sheng* (a flute, 笙) to accompany him. His lotus flower improves mental or physical health of people and animals.

Lan Caihe (蓝采和) is the least known of the Eight Immortals. Lan Caihe's age and gender are unknown. Lan is depicted often as a girl or a boy, but sometimes as a woman or a man, she/he carries a flower basket. His/her behavior is out of norm and deemed strange by most people.

Lü Dongbin(吕洞宾) is the most widely known of the Eight Immortals and hence considered by some to be the de facto leader. Dressed as a scholar, he often holds a sword that dispels evil. The kindness of Lü Dongbin is demonstrated in the Chinese proverb "dog bites Lü Dongbin(狗咬吕洞宾)," which means an inability to recognize goodness and repaying kindness with vice.

Cao Guojiu(曹国舅) was said to be the uncle of the Emperor of the Song Dynasty. He is shown in the official's court dress with a jade tablet which can purify the environment.

He Xiangu(何仙姑) was born with six golden hairs on her head, and she spent her life as a hermit in the mountains. In a dream, she was instructed how to achieve immortality by the other Immortals.

Zhong Liquan(钟离权) is one of the most ancient of the Eight Immortals and the leader of the group. In Daoism, he is known as Original Master Truly-*yang*(正阳祖师). His fan can revive the dead.

Zhang Guolao(张果老) is the last of the Eight Immortals. Known as Master Comprehension-of-Profundity (通玄先生), he claims to be several hundred years old.

Notes: ①transfer 转移 ②above-mentioned 上述的 ③description 描述 ④de facto 实际上 ⑤dispel 驱逐 ⑥hermit 隐士 ⑦comprehension 理解 ⑧profundity 渊博

11 灶神的由来是什么?

What is the origin of the Kitchen god?

There once was a fat mighty lord who loved to eat. His palace was full of all kinds of delicious food, and sometimes he went out to find new food.

One day he came to the house of a simple peasant woman. The mighty lord begged to taste her food so she gave him some sugar cakes(糖饼), and soon he ate them all. He was still hungry and wanted more cakes, and he even threatened the woman to take her back to his palace to continue to make cakes for him.

The woman became angry and slapped the mighty lord across the face. Her sharp blow was so strong that the mighty lord fell back and became embedded into the wall. He was completely stuck and could do nothing but watch other people eat food.

When the Jade Emperor(玉皇大帝)heard this story, he appointed the mighty lord to be the Kitchen god (灶神). Since then, his altar has been set up somewhere near every family's kitchen stove. As the Kitchen god, his responsibility is to report to Heaven what the family has done the whole year. For this reason, each family carefully minds their conduct and behavior because they are afraid that a bad report would be given to the Jade Emperor.

In order to make the Kitchen god happy, each family renews the Kitchen god's picture each year. On the 23rd day of the 12th lunar month, people usually offer the god some melon-shaped candies called "candy melons (糖瓜)." This candy tastes sweet. The kitchen god's mouth will be so full with sugar that when he makes his report, everything will sound good. Others believe that the candy is so sticky that it will keep his mouth shut when he gives his report.

Notes: ①mighty 强大的 ②slap 掴；拍击 ③responsibility 责任 ④candy 糖果 ⑤be full with 充满……的

传统节日 Traditional Festivals

1 “年”是怎么来的?

What is the origin of *nian*?

The Chinese character *nian*(年) or *xin nian*(New Year, 新年) means “harvest.” The Spring Festival always falls sometime before or after *li chun*(the beginning of Spring, 立春). There is a folktale that tells the origin of *nian*.

A long time ago there lived a frightful demon named *nian* (年) who had a large horn, a huge mouth, and sharp teeth, and he did evil things wherever he went. The heavenly gods always locked him up in a prison somewhere in a remote mountain, and he was permitted to leave the prison only once each year.

When the demon left prison, he would come down to the villages and look for food, sometimes even eating local people. During this time, villagers would hide inside their houses and place some of their livestock outside, hoping to satisfy the demon's appetite.

Later, local people discovered that the demon was afraid of red color, flames, and loud noises. So in the evenings, when he was released, people would light up their houses, set off firecrackers, and beat gong and drums. The next day everybody would rejoice and congratulate each other on avoiding the disaster.

Notes: ①folktale 民间故事 ②demon 妖魔 ③livestock 家畜 ④appetite 胃口 ⑤firecracker 爆竹

2 人们在春节前和春节期间主要做些什么？

What do people mainly do before and during the Spring Festival?

The Spring Festival, also known as the Lunar New Year, is the most important traditional national festival in China. Preparations for the New Year Festival start during the last few days of the old lunar year. Some traditional families make *laba*（腊八）porridge, a porridge made of glutinous rice, millet, berries, lotus seeds, beans, and gingko. They also offer sacrifices to the Kitchen god. Most families will also purchase necessities for the New Year. Their shopping items include not only oil, rice, flour, chicken, duck, fish and meat, but also fruit, candies, and nuts. In addition, new clothes and shoes for the children, gifts for the elderly, friends and relatives, are all on their purchasing list.

At home, family members clean their homes, cut their hair, and take baths. In addition, they paste *Chunlian*(春联), spring couplets in red color on entrance gates or doors. All of these poems contain auspicious words to send off the old year and usher in the new one. In some traditional families, people burn joss sticks or incense to their ancestors.

On the Eve of the Spring Festival, people stay up late or even all night and pray for peace in the coming year. That night every house or apartment is brightly lit in the hope that anything that might bring people bad fortune will disappear under the dazzling light. At the same time, a large family dinner is served, which includes southern-styled round-shaped rice dumplings and *jiaozi*(饺子), or northern-styled steamed dumplings. People set off firecrackers as the New Year approaches, and greet each other with good wishes for the happy New Year.

On the New Year's Day, it is a folk custom not to cut your hair or do any housework associated with clothing or utensil washing for fear that the good luck will be washed away. The same goes to the use of knives, scissors, or nail clippers. Sharpened blades might cut off the thread that links good fortune and families in the coming year. During the New Year celebration, people do their best not to say words concerning sickness and death.

Everyday from New Year's Eve to the fifteenth day of the first month, there are various New Year activities. Many people hold up a bamboo-framed dragon and parade it through the streets. The lion dance is a traditional activity which brings joy and happiness. Percussionists beat drums and gongs as the accompaniment to the dances. Wedding ceremonies are also popular in cities and villages throughout the land at this time.

Notes: ①porridge 粥 ②joss stick(中国祭祀用的)香 ③dazzling 耀眼的 ④percussionist 打击乐器演奏者 ⑤accompaniment 伴奏

3 关于门神的由来有什么传说?

What are the legends about the origins of the Door god images?

In rural areas, some families still paste images of the Door god on their doors or on the walls inside their rooms. There are many interesting folktales about the Door gods.

One source says that these images derived from Qin Shubao(秦叔宝) and Yuchi Gong(尉迟恭), military generals who had helped found the Tang Empire(618 – 907). Emperor Tai Zong of the Tang Dynasty fell sick and heard ghosts howling in his dreams. The next morning, he told his dream to Qin Shubao and Yuchi Gong who buckled on their armor; the former grabbed a mace, and the latter an iron staff. They stood on guard in the night outside the door of the emperor's chamber. Henceforth the emperor dreamed no more of ghosts. However, the emperor felt it was improper for his two generals to stand guard night after night. He told a painter to draw the images of the two on a piece of paper that he hung on the palace entrance as "Door gods." As the story spread far and wide, many ordinary people followed suit, pasting the same pictures of Door gods on their doors for the purpose of driving away evil spirits.

The second source says that a long time ago there grew an orchard of magical peach trees on the top of Mt. Dushuo(度朔山). On the top of each peach tree dwelt a giant rooster that crowed at dawn to wake up the roosters in other villages. Some of the peach branches formed archways where thousands of demons passed back and forth.

One day some demons began gnawing at these trees, and their behavior disturbed the order of the world. So the Jade Emperor assigned two generals, Shen Tu(神荼) and Yu Lei(郁垒), to go to the mountain to drive away the demons. When they arrived at the mountain, the two generals stood guard and threw the demons to feed the tigers on the mountain. When the Yellow Emperor learned of this, he had painters paint images of the two generals on peach-wood tablets and place on the doors of houses to keep demons away. Since then, it became a custom to paste pictures of the two ferocious generals on the doors of their houses on New Year's Day to keep demons away.

The third source says that a long time ago, there was a beautiful island called Shuodu (朔度) where a people of great virtue lived, and they pursued a simple, happy and peaceful life. To the northeast of the Shuodu Island was an ugly island called the City of the Ten Thousand Demons(万鬼城). This awful place was the home of vicious demons(恶鬼). One day, the demons attacked Shuodu Island and took all the people to the demon city as slaves. These Shuodu people suffered, and many of them died from starvation or beatings. While the Shuodu people suffered, two huge creatures appeared from the sea, and one was named Shentu(神荼)and the other Yulei(郁垒). Both of them carried thick peach-wood sticks. They used the sticks to break the wall and kill the demon king. The other vicious demons gave up the fight and begged for mercy. The huge creatures promised to protect the Shuodu people from further attack by the demons. Since then, the Shuodu people started to place their images on the doors of their houses in an attempt to keep demons away.

Notes: ①howling 咆哮的;哭哭啼啼的 ②buckle 扣住;扣紧 ③grab 抓住 ④mace 权杖 ⑤ferocious 凶猛的

4 为什么人们要在春节时放爆竹?

Why do people set off firecrackers during the Spring Festival?

Originally people set off firecrackers to keep away evil spirits and demons, and to seek happiness. Legend has it that there was a humanlike beast that was extremely savage and hid itself in remote mountains. Toward the end of every year, it would come out to kill people and animals. However, when the New Year was approaching, people set off firecrackers to scare away the beast because the beast was afraid of light and loud noise.

There is another saying about the origin of burning

firecrackers. Once there were small but terrible monsters, called Shanxiao(山魈), who lived in the forests. They lived on raw shrimps and crabs from the mountain streams. They used to come out of the forests and steal salt from places where human beings lived. However, they were afraid of fire and loud noises. So when they entered villages, people would burn fire in their courtyards. They would also throw bamboo in the fire that would make a loud popping sound after being heated; this sound would also scare away the monsters.

Setting off firecrackers is a tradition started in the remote past with burning bamboo stems. As you know, bamboo stems have joints and are hollow inside. When they are burnt, the air inside expands after being heated, and the stems themselves bust open and crack. Later on, people placed gunpowder into bamboo stems and invented firecrackers. Later, paper rolls replaced bamboo stems. In the end of the Qing Dynasty (1616 – 1911), there were already special workshops in China, making all kinds of firecrackers. In a book entitled *Dijing Suishi Jisheng* (*Wonderful New Year Days in the Imperial Capital*, 《帝京岁时记胜》), the author vividly described how people in Beijing during the Qing Dynasty set off firecrackers on the first day of a year. "The noise of firecrackers like roaring waves and thunderclaps was heard in and outside the palace; it went on without stopping for the whole night(闻爆竹声如击浪轰雷,遍于朝野,彻夜无停)." Firecrackers indeed liven up the New Year holiday as they are a thrilling sight that brings great joy to adults and children alike.

Notes: ①savage 野性的;凶猛的 ②hollow 空的 ③liven up 使活跃 ④thrilling 令人激动

5 你对元宵节知道多少?

How much do you know about the Lantern Festival?

The Lantern Festival falls on the 15th day of the 1st lunar month, and has many fun activities. The highlight is to watch colorful lanterns in varied shapes which include electric wall lamps and electric-powered lanterns of life-size animals. In addition, groups of lanterns recount episodes from classic novels. The brightness of the moonlight and the lantern light enhances each other.

This festival dates back to the Warring States Period(475 BC – 220 BC), when people watched lanterns under the moonlight. At first, they did this on this day to offer sacrifices to the Sun God, who was known as the Lord of the East. Lantern Festival became official in the Han Dynasty. According to ancient Chinese history, after the death of Liu Ying (Han Emperor Hui, 汉惠帝刘盈), Queen Lü (吕后) usurped the power of the state and set up her own dynasty. Zhou Bo (周勃), Chen Ping (陈平), and other top court officials wanted to continue Liu's dynasty. Therefore after the death of Queen Lü, they jointly started a campaign to get rid of Queen Lü's administration and made Liu Heng (刘恒) the emperor of the Han Dynasty. The campaign was successful, and the Han Empire was restored. Because Queen Lü's dynasty ended on the fifteenth day of the first month, Emperor Wen (汉文帝) named the fifteenth day of the first month *yuan xiao jie* (元宵节). In ancient times, the word *xiao* means "evening," and *yuan* "the first month of a year."

Why is *yuan xiao jie* translated to the lantern festival in English? Maybe it is due to a variety of lanterns on show. This custom at first was related to the night curfew in ancient China. Common people had been forbidden to go outdoors or get together at night. Later, the imperial rulers relaxed the night curfew during this festival because the rulers also wanted to have fun themselves.

By the Southern and Northern Dynasties (420 – 589), oil lanterns, lacquer lanterns, some burning incense, and burning candles were on display in the festival. The lights beamed together, reflecting in the water.

The exhibition of lanterns was part of the festival.

In the Tang Dynasty (618 – 907), the Lantern festival was a three-day national holiday and all government offices were closed on the fourteenth, fifteenth and sixteenth. Curfew was lifted for three nights for city residents to go out and have as much fun as they liked. Emperors would watch lanterns from an imperial tower on the night of the festival. The imperial household, the Daoist and Buddhist temples, and the households of the nobility and the rich would all put up colorful lanterns.

In the Song Dynasty (960 – 1279), the lantern exhibition was prolonged from three to five nights. There were lanterns made of colored glass, or even of white jade. Human figures, landscapes, flowers, and birds were all drawn on the lanterns. There were also lantern pagodas, lantern hills, lantern balls and lantern arches.

By the Ming Dynasty (1368 – 1644) under Zhu Yuanzhang (朱元璋), the lantern exhibition was extended to ten nights. In the Ming and Qing dynasties theatrical performances were staged alongside the exhibition.

Lantern-making is a distinct craft of unknown origin, but some believe that it has existed for around two thousand years. Lantern-making combines craft skills in metal and wood working, paper-cutting, drawing, oil painting, weaving, and embroidery. Different areas in the country have developed their own distinctive styles.

Notes: ①highlight 最突出(或最精彩)的部分 ②electric-powered 电动的 ③episode 片断 ④usurp 篡夺 ⑤get rid of 除去 ⑥curfew 宵禁 ⑦nobility 贵族(阶层) ⑧distinctive 有特色的

6 端午节是怎样产生的?

What is the origin of the Dragon Boat Festival?

Duan wu jie (the Dragon Boat Festival) is one of the three main folk festivities in China. The other two are the Spring Festival and the Mid Autumn Festival. The Duan Wu Festival used to be the day that a tribe of the ancient Wu and Yue (now Jiangsu and Zhejiang) would offer sacrifices to its totem—the dragon. These people would cut their hair short and tattooed their bodies with dragons. They considered themselves descendents of the dragon. With the decline of the totem culture, the old practice typical of a totem society gave way to the building of dragon boats. However, as days went by, the festival has lost its original significance and is now used to honor a great Chinese poet named Qu

Yuan of the Warring States Period (475 BC – 221 BC).

Qu Yuan was a patriotic poet from the State of Chu during the Warring States Period. There Qu Yuan proposed a series of progressive reforms, including domestic political reforms and a new legal system. However, the forces of corruption, represented by Jin Shang (靳尚), opposed Qu Yuan and led the king to distrust him. So Qu Yuan left the capital and lived as a drifter. With patriotic fervor, he produced many odes to express his concern for the fate of his state and people. In 278 BC, when the Qin troops stormed the capital, and the downfall of Chu became imminent, Qu Yuan drowned himself in the Miluo River (汨罗江) near the present-day Changsha (长沙). He chose not to live and see his state be destroyed. When the news of his death came, the local people rushed to the scene and rowed boats along the river in an attempt to find his remains, but they were never recovered. The people of the Chu mourned his death, and every year afterwards they threw bamboo tubes filled with rice into the river as a sacrifice to him. This is supposed to be the origin of the custom of rowing dragon boats and eating *zong zi* (粽子) during the Dragon Boat Festival.

Zong zi is glutinous rice wrapped up in reed leaves. Originally it was made as an offer to the dragon as a sacrifice. According to a legend, during the Eastern Han Dynasty (25 – 220) there lived in Changsha a man named Ou Hui (欧回), who one day met another man named the Minister in Charge of the Affairs of Three Aristocratic Families (闾大夫). This man told Ou Hui, "It is very good of you to offer me gifts of rice, but most of them are stolen and devoured by the river dragon. In the future, please wrap them up in chinaberry leaves and tie them up with color threads. The leaves and threads will scare away the dragon, and he will never touch them again."

Notes: ①totem 图腾 ②tattoo 文身花纹 ③corruption 腐败 ④drifter 流浪汉 ⑤imminent 即将来临 ⑥devour 吞没 ⑦chinaberry 楝树果

7 什么是清明节？

What is the Clear and Bright Festival?

The Qing Ming Festival (the Clear and Bright Festival, 清明节) has been one of the most popular festivals in China for thousands of years, and continues to this day. On this day, people go and pay respects to the deceased at their tombs. As a custom people sweep and clean the tombs and mourn the dead. This festival gives the living an opportunity to honor their deceased ancestors.

The festival takes place in early spring, when all life begins to renew and the fields are green with life, and is a good time for outings in the countryside to enjoy the beauty of the land. In ancient times, *Qing Ming* was the day for all urban inhabitants to have an outing on the city outskirts. This outing was called *taqing* (treading on greens, 踏青). During the *taqing* time, people would make garlands out of willow tree twigs and wear them on the head. Women would plait the twigs into fine rings and pin them on the hair as a sign of their desire to stay youthful forever.

Poets throughout the ages have expressed the activities and sentiments on that day. Here is one by the Tang Dynasty(618 – 907) poet Du Mu(杜牧):

It continues to rain in the Qing Ming season,

Which makes a traveler on the road very sad indeed.

When he asks where to find an inn,

A cow-boy points to a place in the distance

— the Apricot Blossom Village.

(清明时节雨纷纷,路上行人欲断魂。借问酒家何处有? 牧童遥指杏花村。)

It is worth mentioning *Riverside Scene at Qingming*

Festival (《清明上河图》), the most exceptional scroll painting of the Northern Song Dynasty (960 – 1127). The painting vividly portrays life in Bianliang(汴梁), the capital city of the Northern Song Dynasty, during the Qing Ming Festival and begins with a few people paying respects to their dead kinsmen at the tombs, then follows with scenes along the banks of the Bianhe River lined with willow trees common of the spring-time in the Qing Ming Festival. As the river course gradually widens, the picture shows more people towing boats, and others loading and unloading goods. Onlookers crowd a nearby bridge; restaurants and tea houses are by the river; the road is full of carts and people carrying things on shoulder-poles.

Notes: ①deceased 已故的 ②mourn 哀悼 ③outing 郊游 ④inhabitant 居民 ⑤outskirt 郊区 ⑥garland 花冠 ⑦sentiment 情感 ⑧apricot 杏 ⑨exceptional 特别的 ⑩kinsman 亲属 ⑪shoulder-pole 扁担

8 什么是中秋节?

What is the Midautumn Festival?

Every year the Midautumn Festival (中秋节) falls

on the 15th day of the eighth lunar month. According to the ancient calendar system, the eighth lunar month is in the middle of the autumn season and the fifteenth day of the eighth month falls in the middle of that month. On that night, the moon is supposed to be brighter and fuller than any other month. In China, a full moon is symbolic of family reunion, so the day is also known as "The Day of Reunion."

This day is a grand occasion because there exist many myths and legends about the moon. The most popular one is about Chang E(嫦娥), the girl who swallowed a magical potion, and suddenly found she could fly. She flew to the Moon Palace and decided to stay there for a while. In the Moon Palace, she met an old man, who called himself Wu Gang (吴刚) who had been sent there to cut down a laurel tree as a punishment for the mistakes he had made while studying to be an immortal. But the opening on the tree closed immediately after he withdrew his axe and so he had to keep on cutting and cutting.

During the Midautumn Festival, when night falls, the moon shines overhead, and a gentle breeze blows with the smell of cassia blossoms in the air. In some places, people go and see the beautiful sight of cassia blossoms at the festival; in other places, they have a family reunion dinner, drink sweetened wine, and eat lotus roots and water chestnuts.

Moon cakes(月饼) are the most popular food during the festival. These cakes appear round in shape. People began making moon cakes during the Tang Dynasty(618 – 907), and the food became a very popular pastry in the Song Dynasty(960 – 1279) when they were available everywhere as an offering to the moon. Big cakes then were over one foot in diameter, with carvings of the moon palace and the moon rabbit on them. Some people ate them after a sacrificial ceremony while others kept them until the New Year Eve. In the Ming Dynasty (1368 – 1644) people exchanged moon cakes as a way to express the happiness at their family reunion. In the Qing Dynasty(1616 – 1911), moon cakes were stuffed with walnut paste, similar to the ones we now have. The ways of making moon cakes vary from place to place, and so their flavors are also not the same. The stuffing includes cocoanut paste, lotus seed paste, assorted fruit seeds and nuts, egg yolk, chicken, ham, cassia, and date paste.

Notes: ①symbolic 象征的 ②swallow 燕子 ③laurel 月桂 ④pastry 糕饼 ⑤assorted 什锦的 ⑥yolk 蛋黄

古代科举
Imperial Examination System in Ancient China

1 什么是科举考试?
What is the Imperial Examination System?

One of the great innovations of ancient China was to recruit officials through open examinations. This idea even influenced the West in their formation of civil servant systems in modern times.

In the Shang Dynasty(1600 BC – 1046 BC), aristocrats took on main positions in the court and served as officials in government departments. The enfeoffment system was also implemented at this time. During the Western Zhou Dynasty, rulers attached great importance to the blood relationship based on patriarch principles and set up the social estate system accordingly. During the Warring States Period, the feudal landlord class adopted the system of granting titles of nobility according to meritorious services performed in battle fields. In addition, aristocrats extensively accepted small and middle landlords or scholars as their family tutors(门客) in favor to the consolidation and development of the feudal regime.

In the Han Dynasty(206 BC - 200 AD), ministers, high-ranking officials, and local authorities recommended to the imperial court talented and virtuous people. The court would offer them government posts or promote them from lower positions to higher ones. In addition, emperors would directly employ some people to be officials, working in the court; local authorities would also employ persons and appoint them to work in local government departments.

Since the Sui Dynasty(581 - 618), the system of imperial examinations was gradually established. Unlike former recruitment, the imperial examination system allowed the participation of people from all social stratums, regardless of family background or recommendations. All men, virtuous and healthy, could take the exam.

During the Tang Dynasty(618 - 907), appointments to government positions, however, went mainly to aristocrats rather than to people who passed the civil service examination. Only ten percent of government officials were selected from the imperial examinations.

There were two kinds of examinations during the Tang Dynasty. One kind involved Confucian studies and the Five Classics; the other Daoism. Exam questions had many sections: interviews, writing from memory, answering questions, composition writing, and poetry. Other subjects included history, law, calligraphy, and mathematics.

In the Song Dynasty (960 – 1279), the examination was based entirely on the Confucian Classics. Over fifty percent of government officials were recruited from the civil service examination. The candidates had to memorize the Five Classics, interpret passages, master their literary style, and use Confucian philosophy to interpret the Classics and construct political advice. The Daoist examination was totally discarded.

By the end of the Song Dynasty, the imperial examination became insupportable. Since the contents of imperial examinations were narrow, and since written examinations alone did not show the candidates' practical experience, the system of imperial examinations gradually lost its worth and hindered the development of society. This system was abandoned for a time in the Yuan Dynasty and the Heavenly Kingdom of Taiping(太平天国), and was completely abandoned after the fall of the Qing Dynasty.

Notes: ①recruit 征募(新兵) ②enfeoffment 赐以封地 ③patriarch 家长；族长 ④meritorious 有功劳的 ⑤consolidation 巩固 ⑥virtuous 有美德的 ⑦regardless of 不关心的 ⑧recommendation 推荐 ⑨discard 丢掉 ⑩insupportable 不能忍受的 ⑪hinder 妨碍 ⑫abandon 抛弃

2 你对科举考试还了解多少？

How much more do you know about the Imperial Examination System?

Imperial examinations were done openly. In order to ensure objectivity in evaluation, candidates were identified by number rather than by name, and exam papers were rewritten by a third person prior to being evaluated. This endeavor was to cover the candidates' handwriting. Candidates were confined during examinations. As for examiners, they were usually asked to live together in a place where any contacts were cut off from the outside world, and their family members were not allowed to sit for the exam. Candidates had to go through provincial and metropolitan examinations first. These two examinations would eliminate most of the candidates. Only the lucky few could take part in the final examination. The emperor himself presided over this examination that took place in the imperial palace. When the examination was over, the court announced the list of successful candidates. Winners would be granted with titles and escorted in a parade by palace guards of honor. At that time, people would go out into the streets to join the celebration of winners.

During the Qing Dynasty (1616 - 1911), the degree types were classified as follows:

Shengyuan (生员), quasi-bachelor's degree, administered at the local level each year.

Juren (举人) quasi-master's degree, administered at the provincial level every three years.

Jinshi (进士), quasi-doctoral degree, administered in the capital every three years.

The degree types are labeled as "quasi-" degrees not to denigrate their content, but to point out that while they may roughly correspond to Western conceptions of bachelor, master and doctoral degrees, they had different contents, different methods of instruction, and very different social functions.

Notes: ①objectivity 客观性 ②confine 限制 ③metropolitan 大都市 ④quasi 类似 ⑤administer 管理 ⑥denigrate 诋毁 ⑦conception 概念

3 科举制度的优点和缺点是什么?

What were the advantages and disadvantages of the Imperial Examination System?

Like all other systems, the examination system had its advantages and disadvantages. On the positive side, the exam had broadened the government base by drawing officials from all levels of society. Theoretically at least, it was entirely possible for a man of the humblest origin, by passing the specified examinations, to rise in power, wealth, and prestige. More than anything else, the examination system accounted for a large degree of social mobility.

Second, the civil service examination system was adopted for the purpose to find the right man for the right task; nothing could be more objective than a test impartially administered. Many great statesmen in China were products of this system.

Third, the examination system brought to mind the importance of education and learning and thus indirectly raised the cultural level of the country as a whole. In ancient China, the most respected had always been the scholars while landlords, merchants, or industrialists in other countries might be the men of greater prestige.

However, only a small fraction (about 5 percent)

of examinees passed and received titles. Those who failed to pass did not lose wealth or local social standing; they served, without the benefit of state appointments, as teachers, patrons of the arts, and managers of local projects, such as irrigation works, schools, or charitable foundations.

Well, those who criticized this system could point out that the examination was a test of literary learning which should not be used as the sole criterion to judge a man's true ability. A good administrator was more often a man of the world than a man learned in Confucian classics or skillful in writing poetry. Moreover, while the examination system might have increased social mobility, it did not end social stratification. A peasant's son might pass the examination and thus be accepted as one of the social elite, but this did not help the rest of the peasants who were still regarded as lower class.

Furthermore, except for the wealthy few, who could afford to spend years of study just to prepare for the examinations? The so-called democratic look of the examination system was perhaps more appearance than reality. Critics of this system were anxious to point out that the over-emphasis on literary learning at the expense of other intellectual pursuits had done great damage to other areas of learning of equal importance. This accounted for, at least in part, China's lagging behind some other countries in the field of science and technology, despite its achievements in the humanities. Society did not attach much importance to the study of natural science and offered no reward for its development. People generally looked down upon manual work, and there was no intellectual tradition outside the study of humanities.

Notes: ① theoretically 理论上地 ② humble 谦逊的 ③mobility 机动性 ④merchant 商人 ⑤industrialist 工业家 ⑥charitable 慈善的 ⑦criterion 标准 ⑧stratification 阶层的形成 ⑨elite 精英 ⑩over-emphasis 过分的强调 ⑪humanities 人文学科

4 你对唐朝以后的学校了解多少?

How much do you know about the ancient schools after the Tang Dynasty?

During the Tang Dynasty(618 – 907), the country entered a prosperous period. There were twenty types of central schools in the Tang Dynasty that included Great Schools(太学), *Si Men* Schools(四门学), Book Schools(书学), and Mathematics Schools(算学). In addition, there were many more types of local schools across the country. However, the Tang Dynasty attached great importance to the imperial examination rather than schools themselves. So schools tended to have students study the same material designated to examinations.

Zhao Kuangyin(赵匡胤), the founder of the Song Dynasty(960 – 1127), followed scholar-first politics. Imperial examinations during the Song Dynasty were virtually identical to those of the Tang Dynasty. Both official and private schools co-existed, with the official schools being divided into central and local schools. Local official schools included the Great School and Law Schools(律学). The most common private schools included the Enlightenment Schools (蒙学) and *Dong* Schools(冬学). A new type of school emerged in the Song Dynasty. It was called the Academy of Classical Learning (书院). Students in this school studied classical texts on their own, and teachers used their own teaching materials to teach students individually.

Schools in the Yuan Dynasty(1206 – 1368) consisted of national schools, local schools, academies of classical learning and "*She schools*" (社学). There were also a few special schools in the Yuan Dynasty, including Mongolian Characters Schools.

Schools in the Ming Dynasty were similar to those of the Song and the Yuan dynasties. School regulations were very strict, and those who broke them were severely punished. There were three levels of imperial examinations in the Ming Dynasty that included the township exam(乡试), the national exam(会试)and the palace exam(殿试).

In the Qing Dynasty (1616 - 1911), official schools were the same as those of the Ming Dynasty. Some special schools were set up for those who had imperial lineage. Math Schools, astronomy Schools, and medicine Schools were also included. Private academies of classical learning turned into official schools and large organizations. Some of these schools focused on preparation for the imperial examinations, and some others on academic research programs related to classical literature and history. In the Qing Dynasty, foreign missionaries came to China. They brought to the Chinese people mathematics, astronomy, the Western calendar, geography, and firearms. These missionaries also translated *The Four Books*, *The Five Classics*, and many other classical texts into Latin and other languages for the purpose of introducing them to the Western World.

Notes: ①designate 指定 ②be identical to 完全相似的 ③enlightenment 启发 ④academy 高等学校 ⑤be similar to 类似于

5 什么是“四书五经”?

What are “The Four Books and the Five Classics”?

Confucius is the most famous sage of China. Through his followers, Confucius founded the principle basis of the Chinese tradition of ethics that has deeply influenced Chinese society and culture.

The Han rulers founded a unified dynasty. They felt the need of a philosophy that could guide and strengthen their rule. Seventy years after the founding of the Han Dynasty, Emperor Wudi (汉武帝) called on scholars to present suggestions for effective government. Dong Zhongshu (董仲舒) suggested that Confucianism be made the official orthodox philosophy, and that all other schools of thought be discredited. From then on, in the civil service examination system of ancient China, it was compulsory for candidates to study Confucianism for imperial government positions.

“Si Shu Wu Jing” means “The Four Books and the Five Classics(‘四书五经’).” The Four Books are as follows.

The Great Learning (《大学》) is one section of *The Classic of Rites*(《礼记》). The subject is self-cultivation as the key to the good society, giving a fundamental introduction to Confucianism.

The Doctrine of the Mean (《中庸》) is the name of another section in *The Classic of Rites*. This book looks at moderation in man's conduct which enables him to live in harmony with the universe.

The Analects of Confucius(《论语》) is a collection of sayings of Confucius and incidents in his life, compiled by his disciples.

The Book of Mencius (《孟子》) consists of the sayings of Mencius, Confucius' great successor who was born about 100 years after Confucius' death and lived from 372 to ? 289 BC. This book was probably written by Mencius' disciples.

The Five Classics consist of:

The Classic of Poetry (*The Book of Odes* or *Songs*, 《诗经》), a collection of ceremonial and folk verse, probably of the early Zhou period. These poems are actually songs based on musical types and have had a profound influence on the later development of poetry.

The Classic of History or Documents (《书经》) is short sections of material of varying date and authenticity ascribed to early sovereigns and officials.

The Book of Changes (《易经》) is a book used for divination built on the oracle bones. Represented by the *bagua* diagram (八卦) of whole and broken lines, it combines, in one interrelated whole, all of human life and fate and the physical elements of the world in symbolic form.

The Classic of Rites (《礼记》) is a compilation of articles that explain ancient social forms and ceremonies. Confucian scholars, from the middle Zhou Dynasty down to the first part of the Han Dynasty, wrote these when they imparted *The Rites*.

The Spring and Autumn Annals (《春秋》) are chronicles of Confucius' state of Lu covering the years from 722 to 479 BC, with appended commentaries.

Notes: ①Confucianism 儒教 ②orthodox 正统的 ③discredit 使丢脸 ④self-cultivation 自我修养 ⑤moderation 适度；节制 ⑥in harmony with 和谐 ⑦compile 编辑 ⑧disciple 弟子 ⑨authenticity 真实性 ⑩ascribe 把……归属(于) ⑪chronicle 编年史 ⑫append 附加

6 古代社会有哪四个等级？

What were the four classes in the ancient Chinese society?

In ancient China the Chinese spoke of their society as composed of four classes: the scholars, the farmers, the artisans and the merchants. The scholars were given the highest status because they performed what Chinese regarded as the most important function: the transmission of an ancient heritage and the personification of Chinese virtues. The farmers' standing was second only to the scholars because they were primary producers, feeding and clothing the nation. The artisans processed what the farmers had produced, and their function was not regarded as an essential as that of the farmers. At the bottom of the social scale were the merchants whom the Chinese regarded as exploiters, making profits from what others had produced or processed.

Some 2,300 years ago, Mencius advanced a classification of the Chinese people. He believed that in an ideal society there were two kinds of people: the educated who ruled and the uneducated who were ruled. Though Mencius was only speculating on what an ideal society should be, the Chinese applied his theory until modern times.

Notes: ①be composed of 由……组成 ②artisan 工匠；技工 ③transmission 输送 ④personification 人格化 ⑤exploiter 剥削者 ⑥make profit 获利

不同朝代的文化发展
Cultural Development in Ancient China

1 新石器时代文化发展的概况是什么？

Could you tell me about the culture in the Neolithic times?

During the Neolithic age man lived a comparatively settled life in villages. Houses were usually semi-subterranean, round, and rectangular. Central pillars supported a roof made of clay and thatch. The walls were of pounded earth, and inside were amenities such as ovens, cupboard, and benches all made of clay. The population worked in agriculture, hunting, and fishing. Stone tools and weapons like arrowheads, harpoons, and needles were of both chipped and polished varieties; some were even made of bone.

Different types of pottery distinguished early cultures. The Yangshao Neolithic culture(仰韶文化)had reddish pottery of varying shapes and black designs. For example, one bowl from Banpo Village (半坡) has a highly stylized fish design with a prominent snout, eyes and an open mouth, all of which exhibit the vitality and rhythm typical of Chinese art.

The Longshan culture (龙山文化), which overlaps and succeeds the Yangshao Neolithic culture, developed ceramics that are thin, hard, black and burnished, and the profiles are more angular than those of the Yangshao.

At Erlitou (二里头) in central Henan Province, the discoveries include remains of a bronze foundry as well as the foundations of two large houses. These discoveries show that Erlitou culture developed out of the Longshan, but their relationship remains subject to dispute. Some scholars say that the Erlitou culture belongs to the early Shang period, but others identify it with the Xia (夏朝).

Notes: ①comparatively 对比地 ②semi-subterranean 半地下的 ③rectangular 矩形的 ④pillar 支柱 ⑤amenities (常用复) 便利设施 ⑥arrowhead 箭头 ⑦harpoon 鱼叉 ⑧Neolithic 新石器时代 ⑨reddish 淡红的 ⑩stylized 程序化的 ⑪prominent 突出的 ⑫snout 鼻子 ⑬rhythm 节奏 ⑭burnish 磨光 ⑮profile 外形 ⑯angular 有角的 ⑰foundry 铸造厂 ⑱identify with 视……与……为同一事物

2 夏、商、周文化发展的概况是什么?

Could you tell me about the culture in the Xia, Shang and Zhou dynasties?

At one time the Shang Dynasty (1600 BC – 1046 BC) was considered a legend. Among the cultural heroes admired by the Chinese, Yu is particularly interesting because of his innovations related to flood control and irrigation. The oracle bones, the bronze-ware, and the tombs of the Shang reveal a civilization of splendor.

The story of the oracle bones of the Shang is very fascinating. The bones were considered magical because they had characters inscribed upon them, dating from about 1,300 BC, and some of the signs found on the Yangshao pottery represent the earliest known form of the Chinese language. Some 5,000 characters have been distinguished, and of these 1,500 have been deciphered.

In the Shang Dynasty, the kings were buried in coffins placed in immense pits along with numerous treasures. Among the most valuable of these objects were bronze vessels such as fine bronze fittings for chariots and harness. These artifacts were considered sacrifices to ancestors and gods, and at the same time were used to gain royal favor. The bronze-ware was solid yet decorous and usually derived from earlier pottery shapes. These bronze objects were usually owned by the wealthy. Bronze workmanship attained an extremely high standard rarely surpassed anywhere else in history.

During three centuries of the Zhou Dynasty (1046 BC – 256 BC), society and culture continued along the lines established by the Shang. Magnificent bronze vessels were still cast, but the inscriptions on bronze became longer and more detailed, and some vessels were made in large sets. Writing became more prevalent and records were kept in much greater quantity. By the end of the Zhou Dynasty, there were works on history, music, rituals, archery, and other topics. Most of these records were kept on bamboo or wood which consisted of slats bound by a cord.

The Zhou Dynasty is by far the longest in Chinese history of which the second half (known as the Eastern Zhou Dynasty) is divided into two sections: the Spring and Autumn Period and the Warring States Period. A great technical advance of that time was smelting and casting iron. Iron was used to cut the edges of wooden spades and to make other tools such as hoes, knives, and sickles.

The Eastern Zhou Dynasty (770 BC – 256 BC) also saw the rise of major ideologies. Confucius and Mencius founded the Confucian School (儒家), and Shang Yang

(商鞅) and Han Fei(韩非) founded the Legalist School (法家). A new style of poems and songs appeared in the south called *chu ci* (Ballads of Chu,《楚辞》), whose representative work was *Li Sao*(《离骚》) by the poet Qu Yuan(屈原).

Notes: ①innovation 创新 ②fascinating 极美的极好的 ③decipher 解释 ④chariot 战车 ⑤decorous 端庄得体的 ⑥workmanship 工艺品 ⑦surpass 优于 ⑧archery 箭术 ⑨cast 浇铸

3 秦、汉文化发展的概况是什么？

Could you tell me about the culture in the Qin and Han dynasties?

In 221 BC, the first emperor of the Qin Dynasty ended the chaos of the Warring States Period by promoting feudal landownership, developing means of communication, and unifying the written language, monetary currency, and weight and measurement systems. To protect against the threat of the nomadic tribes in the north, sectional walls already built by three of the former kingdoms were strengthened, joined and extended to form a single wall along the northern frontier, thus building the Great Wall(长城). The Great Wall we see today is 1,400 miles long and was mainly built in the Ming period.

After the Qin Dynasty, the Han emperors restored Confucianism by appointing specialists in *The Five Classics* and making filial piety one of the criteria for appointing officials. Although Confucianism enjoyed new favor and imperial support, Daoism was also a potent factor. Daoism had influenced Emperor Wu Di and impressed the father of the noted historian Sima Qian(司马迁). Daoism is a religion native to China which took shape during the reign of Emperor Shun Di(顺帝年间, 125 – 144) of the Eastern Han Dynasty. Daoist doctrine is rooted in age-old witchcraft, recipes for immortality, and the concepts of Huang Di (the Yellow Emperor) and Lao Zi. The philosophy greatly influenced economic, cultural, and political thinking of feudal China for more than 1,700 years.

Sima Qian lived during the reign of Emperor Wu Di. He continued the work of his father by completing *Records of the Historian*(《史记》). This record covers a period of some 3,000 years, from the legendary age of the Yellow Emperor to the Han Emperor and is the first comprehensive history in the form of biographical records in China. Sima Qian's work set a standard for all subsequent Chinese historical writing. This work was followed by *The Book of the Earlier Han Dynasty* (《汉

史》) by the *Ban* family: Ban Biao(班彪), Ban Gu(班固) and Ban Zhao(班昭). This book records the historical period from the first year of Gaozu(高祖), the first emperor of the Han Dynasty until the fourth year of Dihuang of the Xin Dynasty(王莽地皇).

In other Han literature, the most distinctive type is the *fu*(赋), which has sometimes been classified as poetry, sometimes as rhythmic prose since the *fu*'s meter and length of line are irregular. The themes revolve around the court, palace, capital, landscapes, hunting, and court amusement.

Technological inventions also advanced at this time. Zhang Heng(张衡) invented a seismograph and various astronomical instruments powered by water; the physician Zhang Zhongjing(张仲景) wrote *Shang Han Lun*(*A Treatise on Fevers*,《伤寒论》); Cai Lun (蔡伦) of the Eastern Han used bark, bast-fiber, and pieces of cloth as material to make better paper.

Notes: ①chaos 混乱;杂乱的一团 ②monetary 金融的;财政的 ③measurement 测量 ④filial piety 子女的虔敬 ⑤potent 强有力的;有权势的 ⑥witchcraft 巫术 ⑦recipe 烹饪法 ⑧immortality 不朽 ⑨legendary 传奇的 ⑩comprehensive 综合的 ⑪biographical 传记的 ⑫subsequent 随后的 ⑬irregular 不规则的 ⑭amusement 娱乐 ⑮fever 发烧

4 六代文化发展的概况是什么？

Could you tell me about the culture during the Six Dynasties?

The Northern Wei is perhaps best known for its legacy of Buddhist art, particularly the sculpture found in the Yungang Grottoes(云冈石窟), West of Datong(大同)and the Longmen Grottoes (龙门石窟) near Luoyang. Such works of art are but one of the visual signs that mark the beginning of the complex process by which Buddhism was assimilated into Chinese culture. At about the 2nd century, Mahayana Buddhism entered Central China but did not have a wide appeal until about the time of the Northern Wei. Buddhism spread further during the subsequent period. One of the several social factors that made wide acceptance possible at this time was the fusing of Buddhism and Daoism together which allowed the former to fit Chinese culture and thought.

Tao Yuanming (陶渊明) is regarded as one of China's greatest poets. After a short career in government, he retired to live the life of a country gentleman. In his verse there are many references to wine, the simple country life, books, and nature. His poems convey a serene harmony with nature. Other fine poets also wrote during this period, but there was at the same time a tendency for poets to indulge in increasingly artificial styles and to show off their virtuosity by using an exotic vocabulary.

During the later Han Dynasty(206 BC – 220 AD), the development of cursive script turned writing into a personal art which suited well the educated class who had practiced calligraphy since childhood. Calligraphy came to be especially valued as a means for self-expression and a creative outlet. During the Jin Dynasty, there were some great calligraphists, including Wang Xizhi (王羲之) and Wang Xianzhi(王献之) whose art served as a model for generations. During the period of the North Wei, stone tablets were engraved with the Standard Script, a type of style based on the Clerical Script. People named the engraved calligraphic works of this period the Wei Tablets(魏碑), which have been regarded as the model of calligraphy.

In painting, the main subject continued to be the human figure. One famous painter was Gu Kaizhi(顾恺之) who was well known for capturing with his brush the essential character of his subjects. A hand-scroll with the poem "*Admonitions of the Instructress to the Court Ladies*(《女史箴图》)" is still extant. The heightened interest in painting led to the development of art criticism and stimulated the classic formulations of the six rules(六法) or principle of paintings by Xie He(谢赫)

of the Qi State.

Notes: ①legacy 遗产 ②sculpture 雕刻 ③complex 错综复杂的 ④assimilate 吸收 ⑤convey 表达 ⑥indulge 放任 ⑦show off 炫耀 ⑧virtuosity 艺术鉴别力 ⑨exotic 奇特的 ⑩clerical 文书的 ⑪hand-scroll 手卷轴 ⑫admonition 训诫 ⑬extant 现存的 ⑭stimulate 刺激

5 隋、唐文化发展的概况是什么?

Could you tell me about the culture during the Sui and Tang dynasties?

The Tang Dynasty (618 – 907) was a period of great economic prosperity and cultural growth in Chinese Feudal society. The Tang culture opened up to cultural influences from India and the distant west; it was also the cultural model for other Eastern Asian countries. There were a considerable number of foreigners who lived in Chang'an(长安), some of whom came from as far away as India, Iran, Syria, and Arabia. Some were students, and other foreigners were merchants.

Chinese Buddhism continued to develop as Buddhist monasteries flourished and fulfilled important social roles. The most outstanding monks had sufficient insight to develop their own doctrine and teaching styles. Eight Buddhist sects appeared between 581 and 755. The Tiantai, Huayan, Pure Land and Zen schools (天台宗、华严宗、净土宗、禅宗) were the four major sects that had considerable influence in ancient China.

Large scale Tang sculpture in wood and bronze has not survived. However, there are many stone statues, including sculptures in the Yungang and Longmen Grottoes. The Buddha drawn in caves at the time is depicted as a majestic personage radiating goodness and compassion. Stone Sculptures in Dazu(大足)started in the first year of Jingfu (景福)of the Tang Dynasty, and completed by the end of the Southern Song Dynasty. Dazu's sculptors developed vividness and grace both in form and content. The caves are filled with delicately carved statues that prominently show full and stately appearance. The figures are draped in their simple and flowing garments.

The Tang literature is most famous for its poetry, which reached a new height in romanticism and realism, known as the golden age of Chinese classical poetry. Two important forms of poetry came to maturity at this time: "regulated poetry (a eight-line verse form with either 5 or 7 characters per line,排律)" and "cut-short poetry (a four-line version of the regulated form,绝句)." Scholars in China commonly regard Li Bai and Du Fu as the greatest poets in the history of Classic literature. Li Bai used the conventional verse forms, which frequently contain a strong element of fantasy and super-nature. His poetry sounds lyrical and innovative. Like the works of Shakespeare in English tradition, Du Fu's poetry came to be so deeply bound up with the literary value that generation after generation of poets and critics rediscovered themselves and their interests in some aspect of the poet's work. In the 790's, Han Yu(韩愈) and Bai Juyi(白居易) began to write in their own distinctive styles. Unlike Du Fu, Bai wrote in simple and easy language. Like Du Fu, he had a strong social conscience.

Notes: ①considerable 相当多的 ②flourish 繁茂 ③sufficient 足够的 ④insight 洞察力 ⑤survive 幸存 ⑥majestic 雄伟的 ⑦personage 人物 ⑧radiate 散发出 ⑨compassion 怜悯;同情 ⑩sculptor 雕刻师 ⑪prominently 显著地 ⑫romanticism 浪漫主义 ⑬maturity 成熟 ⑭conventional 传统的 ⑮fantasy 空想;幻想 ⑯lyrical 抒情诗般的 ⑰innovative 创新的 ⑱critic 批评家 ⑲conscience 良心;道义心

6 宋朝文化发展的概况是什么?

Could you tell me about the culture in the Song Dynasty?

The fall of the Tang Dynasty was followed by more than fifty years of disorder before the country was finally reunited under the Song(960 – 1279). The gap between dynasties did not lesson the interest of what scholars had in cultural pursuit. *Ci*-poems(宋词) of the Song dynasty are a type of poetry that emerged during the Tang Dynasty and reached its full development under the Song dynasty as a major achievement of Song literature. *Ci*-poems again became very popular during the Qing Dynasty. *Ci*-lines are in unequal length and set to music. Most of the poems do not even have their own titles, but are named after an original melody. Composers and writers use this melody to write a new poem. The original melody is a tune pattern. In the Song Dynasty, this type of poetry may be divided into two groups. One is known for its *wan yue* (delicate restraint, 婉约), and the other for its *hao fang*(heroic abandon and vigor, 豪放). The vigorous *ci*-poem type is represented in the works of Su Shi(苏轼) of the Northern Song and Xin Qiji(辛弃疾) of the Southern Song. Under the influence of the great writer Su Shi, the *ci*-poem began to free itself from its musical background and became primarily a literary art form.

Beginning in the Tang Dynasty, landscape painting came to the fore and reached its peak during the Five Dynasties and the early Song, in the hands of Li Cheng (李成) and Fan Kuan(范宽) who continued their tradition into the 11th century. One of Fan's paintings is

Travellers Along a Mountain Stream(《溪山行旅图》). His paintings' impressive scope, strength, and dark tones have replaced the rich colors, the clarity of line, and the decorative charm of earlier landscape paintings. The most famous example of landscape painting in this period is the Northern Song painter Zhang Zeduan(张择端)'s *Riverside Scene at Qingming Festival* (《清明上河图》). The Song painters produced classic works of art strikingly different from the paintings of the earlier times. The minds of the great Song artists were affected by philosophical influences from both Daoism and Buddhism. More subtle expression appeared in the same dynasty, and painters emphasized the spiritual qualities of the painting and the ability of the artist to reveal the inner harmony between man and nature.

Ceramics also developed unique qualities during this time. The color glazed ceramics of the Song are among the most highly valued by collectors. Song wares include stoneware and porcelain. Vessels are covered with a clay coating that has been carved away to produce a design; others are covered with enamel or decorated with a painting. Colors run from white through gray to black as well as various hues. Some of Song ceramics were made especially for the imperial household and represented the artistic refinement of the age.

In the second half of the eleventh century, Confucianism reemerged out of the works of Zhou Dunyi (周敦颐) and Chengyi (程颐), but by no means was the same as in the days of Confucius and Mencius. The challenge of Indian Buddhist metaphysics and Daoist thought required that some attention be given to a philosophic frame-work, which would serve to explain the world and human nature. There was a considerable debate between the various schools of thought, but in the end the comprehensive views of Zhu Xi (朱熹) prevailed, and he became the leader of a new orthodoxy, known in the West as Neo-Confucianism.

According to Zhu Xi's ideas, everything in the world is constituted by the interaction of two factors, the *li*(理), or form of the object, and its *qi*(气), or matter. (The meaning of the second term is literally "breath.") The *li* of all things is summed up in the Great Ultimate (太极). *Li* is the origin of everything and governs nature and human society. As to man, the *li* of human nature is common to all and is basically good, but men vary in their exemplification of good or evil according to their *qi* or physical endowment.

There had been a long-continued debate between the realist Confucian school descended from Xunzi(荀子), who said that human nature was evil, and the idealists depending on Mencius, who maintained that it was good. Zhu Xi supported Mencius' view but said that the education Mencius recommended must be backed up by self-cultivation(修身). Zhu Xi understood it in a particular sense. For him it meant something much deeper than the English word implies in the nature of personal commitment. He says that the goal should be reached by the extension of knowledge through "the investigation of things(格物)" and "attentiveness of mind(精思)." Zhu Xi says that the investigation of things means that we should seek for what is above shapes by what is within shapes.

In 1313, a century after Zhu Xi's death, by a decree of the Yuan Dynasty, Zhu Xi's commentaries on *The Four Books* were made the official standard for the civil service examinations. The ethical teachings by Zhu became accepted state philosophy from the Ming to the Qing Dynasty.

Notes: ①pursuit 追求 ②unequal 不相等的 ③original 原先的 ④melody 美妙的音调 ⑤delicate 精美的 ⑥restraint 抑制;克制 ⑦primarily 主要地 ⑧strikingly 显著地 ⑨refinement 高雅 ⑩by no means 绝没有 ⑪metaphysics 形而上学 ⑫constitute 形成 ⑬interaction 相互作用 ⑭ultimate 极限;顶点 ⑮exemplification 例证 ⑯endowment 捐助 ⑰commitment 承诺 ⑱clarity 明晰

7 元朝文化发展的概况是什么？

Could you tell me about the culture in the Yuan Dynasty?

In 1279, the Yuan Dynasty (1206 – 1368) conquered the Southern Song and reunited China. The outstanding achievement of the Yuan Dynasty in literature is Yuan drama(元剧), which appeared around the end of the Jin and the beginning of the Yuan. Yuan drama consists basically of a single and complete story in four acts or song sequences. Protagonists, either male or female, sing its song or arias. Apart from the arias, there are also dialogues, stage action and dance performed to music accompaniment. The Yuan drama touched on all levels of the Yuan Dynasty. Guan Hanqing(关汉卿) and Wang Shifu(王实甫) were the most famous *beizaju* (北杂剧) creators. 530 Yuan operas have survived, including masterpieces such as *Snow in Midsummer* (《窦娥冤》), *The Western Chamber* (《西厢记》) and *The Orphan of Zhao* (《赵氏孤儿》). Music played an important part in the theater. The songs or song sequences in each act were in a single mode. The lute and zither were the standard instruments of the northern Yuan drama.

Yuan free-song(元曲) was a new form of rhymed

verse, which developed out of popular northern ballads and folk songs. The tunes are derived from several different ethnic groups and do not correspond to Song lyric tunes. Most free-songs are quite short, and these are known as "minor songs (小令);" those consisting of two or more stanzas are called "free-song sets(套曲)."

The Yuan Dynasty is known for its outstanding ink-wash paintings. Amateur artists found a vehicle for self-expression and cultivation with brush and ink. Zhao Mengfu(赵孟頫) was a major painter and one of China's truly great calligraphers. His *Autumn Color on the Que and Hua Mountains* (《鹊华秋色图》) greatly appealed to the Yuan literati. In Zhao's painting, the use of space for calligraphy does not disturb his painting. In a sense, the painting is calligraphy, too; in another sense, the calligraphy is painting. Calligraphy in the Yuan was prized as one of sublime characters which gave way to a variety in painting and writing styles.

Notes: ①basically 基本上 ②protagonist 主角 ③aria 抒情调 ④masterpiece 名作 ⑤ballad 民歌 ⑥correspond(+ to/with) 符合;一致 ⑦stanza 诗的一节 ⑧appeal(+ to) 有吸引力

8 明、清文化发展的概况是什么?

Could you tell me about the culture in the Ming and Qing dynasties?

Feudalism began to decline in the Ming and Qing dynasties(1368 – 1911) while handcraft industries developed and the beginnings of a capitalist economy emerged. The spread of democratic and nationalist ideas gave the progressive literature its anti-feudal flavor. The traditional episodic novel thus developed as a literary form during the Ming and Qing dynasties, with a broad thematic range, including historical romances, chivalric tales, ghost stories, social satires and love stories. *The Romance of the Three Kingdoms* (《三国演义》) is thought to have been compiled by Luo Guanzhong(罗贯中) between the end of the Yuan Dynasty and the beginning of the Ming Dynasty. The book is based on existing written and oral accounts of the last years of the Eastern Han Dynasty and the Three Kingdoms Period of Wei (魏), Shu (蜀) and Wu (吴). *The Outlaws of the Marsh*(《水浒传》) recounts the stories of 108 men and women who during the Northern Song Dynasty gathered at Liangshan Mountain (梁山) in present Shandong Province under the leadership of Song Jiang (宋江). Most of the chapters can be thought of as independent biographies, and they have been told and retold by Chinese people for generations. *The Journey to the West* (《西游记》) is based on the actual pilgrimage of a Chinese monk, Xuan Zang, who traveled to India in the 7th century for Buddhist scriptures. This novel has had a profound influence on Chinese literature due to its romantic style, imaginative content and humorous expressions. *The Dream of the Red Chamber* (《红楼梦》) contains 120 chapters in all and is a masterpiece of world literature. Most scholars believe that the first 80 chapters were written by Cao Xueqin (曹雪芹); the final 40 chapters were added by Gao E (高鹗) along the lines of the original author's intention. The novel focuses on the tragic love stories of Jia Baoyu (贾宝玉) and his beautiful cousins, Lin Daiyu (林黛玉) and Xue Baochai (薛宝钗). The story also depicts the gradual decline of the aristocratic Jia family and represents the peak of the development in the traditional Chinese realistic novel.

During the Ming dynasty, drama in the southern style reached its peak but differed from northern drama in language, form and music. Southern plays were much longer, and bamboo flutes accompanied songs. Ming playwrights were often sophisticated literary men. Most of the plays are about love affairs. The most famous romance-drama is *The Peony Pavilion* (《牡丹亭》) by

Tang Xianzu（汤显祖）from the Ming. This is a long play of fifty-five scenes centering on a love so strong that it is able to bring the dead back to life. One of the last southern masterpieces is *The Peach Blossom Fan*（《桃花扇》），which was completed by Kong Shangren（孔尚任）in 1699 and depicted the end of the Ming. The Southern drama continued to be performed, but toward the end of the eighteenth century, hundreds of new forms of opera emerged throughout the country. These new forms followed regional types and combined local dialects, folk songs, music and dancing. Among the best-known forms staged nationwide are Beijing Opera, *Pingjü*（found mainly in North China，评剧）, and *Yuju*（Henan Clapper Opera，豫剧）. Strictly speaking, all forms of traditional opera, including Beijing Opera, are based on the music and dialects of specific areas, so their popularity is largely confined to that area. The birth of Beijing Opera and the blossom of varied operas across the country indicate traditional Chinese opera has reached a high level of maturity.

In the middle Ming Dynasty, the most important center for painting was Suzhou, where the *Wu* School（吴派）flourished（1460 – 1560）, and the literati could pursue their interests in peace. Centers like the *Zhe* School（浙派）and *Wu* School were separated based on the artists' residence, style, and social status. Shen

Zhou(沈周) stands at the beginning of the Wu tradition by developing a style of his own that conveyed genial warmth and natural ease. Wen Zhengming (文徵明) studied painting under Shen Zhou. He was a versatile scholar, and followed the model of Zhao Mengfu. Some of his paintings contain references to painting styles going back to the Tang styles that revived during the Southern Song and the Yuan. Qing painters generally perceived themselves as latecomers in a tradition. In early Qing period, the most original work was done by men who refused to serve the Qing government. Among those who found tranquility in a Buddhist monastery was Hong Ren(弘仁). His masterpiece, *The Picture of Forest in Autumn*(《秋林图》), displays a marvelous sense of structural depth. One of the most eccentric was Zhu Da (朱耷), also called Bada Shanren (八大山人). His painting was unusual: surging landscape, huge lotuses, and birds and fish with the eyes of a *Zen* patriarch. Daoji (道济), a descendant of the Ming imperial house, became a Buddhist monk. In addition to his painting, he is known for his *Notes on Painting*(《搜尽奇峰打草稿图》). He writes of a single line from which the whole painting grows. There were also more orthodox painters like the four artists whose family names were all Wang (Wang Shimin,王时敏; Wang Jian,王鉴; Wang Hui, 王翚; Wang Yuanqi, 王原祁). In

1691, Wang Hui received an imperial commission to supervise a series of scroll paintings that commemorated Emperor Kangxi's southern tour. Wang Yuanqi became Kangxi's chief artist adviser.

In the Ming period, porcelain was produced in factories, notably at Jingdezhen(景德镇) in Jiangxi Province. The imperial factories produced exquisite ware, not only for the palace but also for purchase by the wealthy and for export. The fine china clay known as *gaoling*(高岭土) could be heated to a high temperature to become extremely hard. Vessels could thus be made with walls thin enough to be almost translucent. The art of porcelain has a long history. In the Tang Dynasty, the color-glazed figures of horses and camels, as well as bowls and vases are in yellow, green, brown, blue, black, and white. Yellow, green and brown are the major colors. The delicate pale green celadon of the Song is sometimes plain and sometimes lightly incised. The porcelain vessels of the Yuan had already had varied patterns of scrolls, leaves, sunflowers, weaves peony, fruits, dragon, phoenix, and flowing streams, but a rich variety of painted designs opened great prospects for painting on Ming porcelain. The well-known patterns of painted porcelain include Blue-and-white porcelain(青花瓷), under-glaze red porcelain(釉里红), polychrome over-glaze décor porcelain(五彩瓷), and soft-colored over-glaze décor porcelain(粉彩瓷). A special type of porcelain known as trade porcelain arose during the Qing to meet the demand of European aristocrats and wealthy merchants in the seventeenth and eighteenth centuries. Chinese artists would paint western designs according to the customer's wishes.

Notes: ①nationalist 民族主义者 ②anti-feudal 反封建的 ③thematic 主题的 ④outlaw 反叛者 ⑤pilgrimage 朝圣之行 ⑥scripture 经文 ⑦imaginative 富于想象力的 ⑧humorous 幽默的 ⑨decline 下降 ⑩playwright 剧作家 ⑪sophisticated 富有经验的;精通的 ⑫popularity 流行;大众化 ⑬maturity 成熟;完善 ⑭genial 温和的 ⑮perceive 察觉 ⑯latecomer 迟到者;新来者 ⑰tranquility 平静 ⑱exquisite 精致的 ⑲translucent 半透明的 ⑳celadon 青瓷 ㉑porcelain 瓷器 ㉒polychrome 多色的

古建筑风格
Ancient Chinese Architecture

1 中国原始社会房屋建筑的概况是怎样的?
How did primitive dwellings evolve?

In primitive times, man resided in caves to protect himself from animals and the elements. As people began to live in tribes, they also started to build their dwellings. An ancient book says, "In the remote ancient times, people built their nests with wood in order to avoid being hurt by animals(上古之世……构木为巢，以避群害)." They also dug the ground on hills to build caves for dwelling. According to archaeological studies, there were two kinds of dwellings built in the Neolithic Age in China, one of which was a cave type dwelling (半地穴式建筑)and the other a house on stakes(桩上建筑).

The shape and depth of cave dwelling varied greatly. There were some piles or posts inside these buildings that were propped up in the middle of a house or between walls to support the roof. Rammed mud was added around the main posts to strengthen the base. Some mud was mixed with fragments of pottery and burned soil in red; some post bases were made of natural stone.

The roof was coated with mud mixed with grass. Beneath the mud was firewood or straw that were spread on crossbeams and rafters placed on piles or posts. Some caves were deep inside, with no piles or posts. People simply placed eaves on walls. In addition, people plastered walls with lime or mud mixed with grass in order to make their dwellings durable. Some walls had been fire-burnt for the same purpose. Some dwelling entranceways were a slope; some others had steps. Inside the dwellings was a cooking pit in the ground, facing the entrance gate. This pit could be used to cook food, warm the family, and light the dwelling.

A house on stakes was prevalent across and to the south of the Yangtze River. Even till now this type of housing is still inhabited by people in Southwest China and by some ethnic minorities in Taiwan. This house is made of bamboo and couch grass(茅草). Beneath the house is a low framework made of erected stakes or bamboo, which hold the house above the ground. In the primitive society, people could even process the thick trees into suitable square stakes, planks, tenons (榫)

and mortise(卯).

In the later stages of primitive society, with the rise of the patriarchy family life, the family housing structure also developed. First the inner space shrunk. The dwelling might be a single room or a pair of interlinked rooms. Some buildings had upright wooden posts, forming walls around the dwelling on the ground. A house beam was erected in the centre of the dwelling structure, and two sloping sides on the roof covered the whole dwelling. Some large dwellings, which were built on the ground, appeared rectangle. Inside might be one room alone or two interlinked rooms partitioned by a wall and a shared kitchen range. Some walls had already been built with sun-dried mud bricks. In the primitive society appeared the wooden post network structure and the technology of tenon and mortise. These facts had laid the foundation for further development of the unique frame-work type housing construction in the country.

Notes: ①primitive 原始的 ②dwelling 居住 ③archaeological 考古学的 ④stake 桩;棍子 ⑤fragment 碎片 ⑥crossbeam 横梁 ⑦plaster 在……上涂灰泥 ⑧plank 厚板 ⑨tenons 凸榫 ⑩mortise 接合;卯 ⑪interlink 连接 ⑫partition 划分

2 中国进入阶级社会时的房屋建筑有什么变化?

What were the housing changes as classes emerged in Chinese society?

During the feudal society, people of different social levels lived in different dwellings. According to archeological discovery from village ruins dating from the Shang Dynasty, most of the dwellings were cave dwellings. These round or square dwellings appeared extremely simple and crude and did not have any underground foundation or rammed mud walls.

Dwellings owned by slave owners or nobles were constructed on the ground with sun-dried mud walls and wooden-post roofed frames. Most of these roofs sloped down on two sides or four sides. There were three types of dwellings: a single room, double rooms, or triple rooms. The indoor ground was smooth, and some of the ground, after being burnt twice by fire, was even smoother and harder. The palace ruins dating from the early Shang Dynasty were unearthed in Erlitou Village(二里头), Yanshi area(偃师) in Henan. Based on its original form, the palace was a wooden building constructed on a rammed soil terrace. Corridors surrounded the palace, and the roof had double-eaves and sloped down on four sides.

During the Western Zhou Dynasty, the technology of housing architectures greatly developed: tiles covered roofs; walls were built with rammed soil and wooden boards; indoor ground and walls were plastered with mud mixed with yellow-colored soil, gravel, sand, and lime; drainage systems were placed in and out of an architectural complex. The whole dwelling resembled the current northern styled compound with houses on four sides.

Notes: ①ram 夯实(土等) ②triple 三倍的 ③doubleeaves 双屋檐 ④drainage 排水系统 ⑤compound 有围墙（或篱笆等的）住宅群

3 汉朝末年中国建筑有什么特征?

What were the features of ancient Chinese architecture by the end of the Han Dynasty?

Wooden housing had already existed by the Han Dynasty(206 BC – 25 AD). The framework consisted mainly of wooden pillars and crossbeams perfectly interlocked with brackets so that the whole weight on the roof and eaves was transferred to its foundations through the pillars, beams, lintels, and joists. Walls bore no load; they only separated indoor space. Windows, doors, and walls were not restricted to certain locations on the house. Crossbeams were supported by the system of wooden brackets on the top of columns, which is one of the characteristics of ancient Chinese wooden architecture.

During the Han Dynasty, the construction had extensive sets of brackets on top of the columns. These brackets not only served as an attractive ornament, but also firmly strengthened the structure and helped the eaves extend further; this innovation came from the Shang Dynasty.

A Han dwelling House usually consisted of covered verandas, courtyards and multi-floor buildings. The main roof patterns in ancient Chinese architecture appeared at that time. These included the Wudian Roof (庑殿顶), Xieshan Roof (歇山顶), Yingshan Roof (硬山顶) and Xuanshan Roof (悬山顶). The Wudian Roof has five ridges; one is horizontal and the other four have slightly sloping downward ridges(垂脊)on the four roofed sides. The Xieshan Roof includes one horizontal ridge, four slightly sloping downward ridges and still another four supporting ridges(戗脊). Both the Yingshan and Xuanshan Roofs slope down on two sides in a simple fashion. The difference between Xuanshan and Yingshan Roofs is that eaves on the Xuanshan roof overextend beyond the tall walls located at the sides of a building, and eaves on the Yingshan roof stay within the tall walls.

In addition, there were wooden-board doors, jointly patterned windows (交棂窗), and curtains behind windows. In the Han Dynasty, bricks were not in full use yet so rammed soil wall still remained the norm.

Toward the end of the Western Han Dynasty, a fortress-type manor house appeared which had high walls enclosed this housing residence with a gate-room and an arch over the gate in the centre of the residence. The residence layout was similar to a courtyard with main rooms, kitchen, warehouse, lavatory, and pigsty. Some courtyards had a screen wall facing the main entrance gate, and even had the second entrance door in the court which was usually called the front yard and the back yard; in the back yard were large rooms.

Notes: ①interlock 使连扣 ②lintel 楣 ③joist 栏栅;托梁;桁 ④bracket 撑架;托座 ⑤column 圆柱 ⑥veranda 走廊 ⑦horizontal 水平的 ⑧overextend 过分延伸 ⑨fortress 要塞 ⑩pigsty 猪圈

4 从唐朝到清朝房屋建筑的概况是怎样的呢？

How did architecture evolve from the Tang to the Qing Dynasty?

By the Tang Dynasty (618 – 907), the ancient architecture thrived. Palaces, temples, and towers appeared in a large number across the country. Color glazed materials and carved stones were more common as well. Strong brackets in the architecture linked with the roof beams, pillars, lintels and joists; bricks for walls were available for large constructions.

During the Song Dynasty (960 – 1279), the building models tended to be more beautiful using multiple plane surfaces and three-dimensions instead of dull and totally symmetrical patterns. Brick and stone constructions continued to develop and led to the birth of beamless brick and stone halls. By the Ming Dynasty, more beamless halls had been constructed both in the North and South of China.

During the Ming and Qing dynasties (1368 – 1911), some new changes took place in the wooden framework construction. Roof-beam architecture had been simplified, and a slanting roof-beam structure also came to be used. Some large buildings still used brackets that functioned as ornaments. Woodcut, stone or brick engravings, and decorative paintings were hung in residents' houses. During this period, an official or landlord's residence was a closed housing complex big enough for a big family of four to five generations. Generally the room assignment reflected the feudal ethical codes and patriarchal system of that time. The elder members of a family lived in the main rooms, the younger generation in the side rooms, and servants in the inferior rooms. Women could not freely walk into the front yard, and visitors were not allowed to enter the back yard.

Notes: ①three-dimension 有立体感 ②symmetrical 匀称的 ③beamless 无梁 ④roof-beam 屋顶梁 ⑤slanting 倾斜的 ⑥ornament 装饰 ⑦assignment 任务 ⑧inferior 低等的

5 古建筑如何反映了封建社会里的等级制？

How did ancient buildings reflect the social system of feudal China?

In ancient China, emperors, empresses, and princesses lived in imperial palaces. Undoubtedly the palaces rank as the highest class of building according to the ancient social system. The same class goes to the Majestic Buddha Hall(大雄宝殿)in a Buddhist monastery and the Three Purity Hall(三清殿)in a Daoist Temple. These buildings appear typically magnificent because they have yellow glazed tiles, multi-layer eaves, the Wudian Roof, decorative paintings, painted dragons, phoenix patterns, and giant red gates. The residence owned by government officials and rich businessmen is called the Large-Type Housing Building (大式). These buildings have no glazed tiles, and brackets on top of the columns reflect the social system. The third grade residence is called the Small-Type Housing Building(小式)used frequently by common people.

The raised base of the ancient architecture also reflects the social system of the feudal society. The ordinary base is simple and flat to support the small or Large-Type Housing Buildings. Another kind of the raised base is called the *Xumi* Seat Patterned Base (须弥座) which originally came from the pattern of the bottom base for a statue of Buddha. This Buddhist pattern came into the traditional Chinese architecture after Buddhism entered China. This structure supports important halls in the imperial palace complex as well as buildings in a monastery or temple. The purpose is to show the resident's noble status and rank. In addition, this base has white marble railings. The third kind of raised base is the superfine base that consists of multi-stone-floors; each floor is the *Xumi* Seat Patterned Base circled by jade stone railings. The multi-floor base is only used to support key halls in the imperial palace complex and some key buildings in a monastery or a temple like the Hall of Supreme Harmony (太和殿) in the Forbidden City and the Dacheng Hall in the Qufu Confucian Temple(曲阜孔庙的大成殿). According to *The Canon Collection of the Qing Dynasty* (《大清会典》), the raised base is limited to 0. 67 meter in height for the residence owned by high officials of the third rank and above, and 0. 33 meters in height is for the residence owned by officials of the fourth rank and below.

A *jian*(间) or bay is the area within 4 pillars; one *jian* is approximately 15 square meters. According to the ancient social estate system, a main hall in the imperial palace usually is a 9-*jian* hall. During the Qing Dynasty, the Hall of Supreme Harmony in the Forbidden City was expanded from 9 *jian* to 11 *jian* in dimension to show imperial power. Under the Ming Dynasty, a top ranking duke's front, middle and rear halls were permitted to extend to 7 *jian*, and his front gate was limited to 3-*jian* in space. Officials of the first to fifth ranks could have 7-*jian* major and minor halls. Officials of the sixth and seventh ranks had 3-*jian* major and minor halls. Ordinary citizens were not permitted to have rooms of more than 3 *jian* in size although they were not limited to any specific number of rooms they could build. The Qing period saw many changes in these rules, but the system laid down by the Ming remained basically intact.

At the end of the sloping and branch ridges on ancient buildings, there are often a group of small animals called *wenshou* (zoomorphic ornaments, 吻兽). Their size and number are determined by the status of the owner of the building in the feudal hierarchy. The largest number of zoomorphic ornaments is found on the Hall of Supreme Harmony (太和殿) in the Forbidden City. A god riding a rooster, the first animal, leads the flock. Behind the god, comes a dragon, a phoenix, a lion, a heavenly horse, a sea horse and five other mythological animals. The Palace of Heavenly Purity (乾清宫) has nine animal figures; the Palace of Earthly Tranquility (坤宁宫) has seven; the other twelve halls used to house the imperial concubines each have five.

Notes: ①undoubtedly 无疑地 ②majestic 尊严的 ③multilayer 多层 ④glazed tile 琉璃瓦 ⑤railing 栏杆 ⑥approximately 大约地 ⑦intact 完整无缺的 ⑧zoomorphic 兽形的 ⑨mythological 神话的 ⑩concubine 妾

6 古建筑的色彩有什么特点?

What role did color play in ancient Chinese architecture?

The painting on ancient buildings functions as an

ornament. Ancient architects applied decorative painting and color patterns to the roof beams and ridges in order to obtain the result of splendid ornament and display the status of the owner of the building accordingly. During the Warring States Period(475 BC - 221 BC), decorative paintings on roof beams had already existed in official buildings. In the Han Dynasty(206 BC - 25 AD), the popular painted images included floating clouds, celestial fairies, plants, and animals. Lotus petals were the most popular during the period of the Six Dynasties. After the Tang and Song dynasties(618 - 1279), there were more and more geometry and plant patterns; dark green replaced red.

In the Qing Dynasty (1616 - 1911), decorative painting and color patterns commonly fell into several categories. The *Hexi* Five-color Decoration (合细五彩画) only decorated the key buildings in imperial palaces and altars. Usually, a dragon or a phoenix was painted on a green background, and paint lines were gilded with gold powder or gold foil. Circular Color Decoration (旋子彩画) decorated government buildings, key buildings in temples, attached buildings of imperial palaces and altars. Suzhou Decoration developed into two schools: the southern and northern. Southern Suzhou Decoration focused on bright designs, and the Northern on landscapes, figures, flowers, and pavilions.

Notes: ①decorative 装饰的 ②splendid 壮观的 ③geometry 几何学 ④foil 金属薄片 ⑤altar 祭坛

7 你能讲讲亭台楼榭吗?

Could you tell me something about towers and pavilions?

An ancient tower or pavilion is mainly built with wood. In some examples of their construction, not a single nail is used. Sets of brackets link up the joints of the wooden structures. Wooden teeth bite into points where wooden pieces or stuff meet.

In ancient times, a tower(楼)functioned as a storage house for books, scriptures, and portraits of famous people. A tower can beautify a garden or a scenic spot, offering visitors a space where they are able to look far into the distance. Famous towers include Yueyang Tower(岳阳楼) in Hunan Province and the Yellow Crane Tower(黄鹤楼) in Hubei Province.

A pavilion(亭) usually has a roof but no walls. Most pavilions have gently upturned eaves, splendid glazed tiles, and bright red pavilion posts. Green trees, grass, and water often encircle the pavilion, forming a beautiful landscape. The Chinese often say that a pavilion represents humankind's place in the universe. During the Qin and Han dynasties, a pavilion was set up every 5 kilometers for the convenience of people walking by who might stop in for a rest or lodging. The pavilion functioned as a sentry box in border districts. Later on, the pavilion turned into a small-scale building in which a visitor could have a rest or overlook the scenery all around. In the Tang Dynasty (618 - 907), it was common to build pavilions in scenic places and gardens. The design of pavilions varies. The most common design is the square shaped pavilion. A common feature of Chinese gardens is the waterside pavilion (台榭) which is half built on land and half raised on stilts above a body of water to offer a view from all sides. Through a combination of natural and artificial elements, designers seek balance and harmony between man and nature in their design.

Notes: ①storage 贮存 ②humankind 人类 ③stilt 支撑物

道教与佛教
Daoism and Buddhism

1 老子和庄子是谁?

Who are Lao Zi and Zhuang Zi?

When Sima Qian came to write the biography of Lao Zi, he found so few facts that he had difficulty even with Lao Zi's identity. All he could do was to collect together traditions about the man current in his time. According to *Records of The Historian*, Lao Zi was a native of the Li Village (历乡) of Ku Xian County (苦县) in the State of Chu. His surname was Li(李), his personal name was Er (耳), and his posthumous title was Dan (聃). He was the historian in charge of the archives in Zhou. He lived in Zhou for a long time, but seeing its decline he departed. Before he passed through the gate of the frontier, the guard asked him to leave a short account of his philosophy, and Lao Zi obliged with the work *Dao De Jing*(*The Classic of the Way and Its Vir-*

tue,《道德经》).

Lao Zi cultivated the way and virtue, and his teachings aimed at self-effacement. The school of thought supposed to have been founded by Lao Zi is known as Daoism. It can be seen that the *Dao* was considered the central concept in the thought. Unlike Confucianism, Daoism is preoccupied with man's place in the natural world. In this form, the secret for man is simply to abandon self-effort and ease himself into the rhythm of the universe, the cycle of the seasons, and the inevitable progression of day and night, life and death.

The most famous successor of Lao Zi was Zhuang Zi (庄子), who lived and wrote in the fourth century BC. He went even further than his predecessor in stressing the relativity of the attributes of all things. Zhuang Zi said that efforts to regulate life and improve the world are not only useless and absurd but positively harmful. By Daoist prescription of *wu wei* (non-action, 无为), Zhuang Zi apparently did not mean total inaction, laziness, or defeatism. Rather he describes the approach to government led by an ideal sage. This sage is fully alert, aware of the processes of nature, and the needs of men; he is prepared to keep the life force in himself and others going, but wary of interfering in any way with what is "natural." The *Dao* is everywhere and in everything. To understand is to be like Cook Ding (庖丁) who is so familiar with every turn and twist in the anatomy of an ox. Over 19 years, he cut up thousands of oxen without ever having to sharpen his knife. He simply slid his knife through the spaces between the joints. One of Zhuang Zi's favorite themes is the relativity of ordinary distinctions. He tells a story of waking up from a nap and being unable to tell whether he dreamed of the butterfly or the butterfly dreamed of him. Which is dream and which is "real?" For him, true comprehension leads to ecstatic acceptance of whatever life may bring.

Notes: ①identity 身份 ②posthumous 死后的 ③self-effacement 自我谦逊 ④preoccupy 使全神贯注 ⑤self-effort 自我努力 ⑥inevitable 不可避免的 ⑦predecessor 前任;前辈 ⑧attribute 把……归因于 ⑨prescription 规定 ⑩alert 警惕 ⑪anatomy 解剖学 ⑫comprehension 理解力

2 什么是《道德经》?

What is *Dao De Jing*?

Dao De Jing or *The Book of the Way and Its Virtue* is the first great Daoist classic. The scholarly evidence suggests that the book took shape over a long period of time before the Han Dynasty (206 BC – 220 AD). The book circulated in several versions until it was standardized shortly after the Han Dynasty. The book has two parts—*Dao* and *De*. The *Dao* part traditionally has 37 chapters; the *De* part comprises the other 44 chapters of the book. This classic, much of which is in verse, is paradoxical and highly suggestive.

The work begins by saying that the *Dao* is inexpressible but then suggests some similes which hint at its nature. The Way is humble like water which flows downward and seeks the lowest place. The Way is like empty space, but emptiness has been undervalued. The hollow in the center of a bowl, the space in a wheel between rim and hub, or the empty space of a window or door in a room are the very things which give these objects their point and their usefulness. Thus Nonbeing as well as Being has a positive value. The mutuality of this pair of opposites in the universe, matter and space, being and nonbeing, must be recognized. The Way is like the *yin* or female because it is passive, yielding, receptive, not active and dominating.

The book is the most frequently translated Chinese book, for its language invites a multitude of interpretations perhaps because the *Dao* cannot be named or defined but has to be experienced.

Notes: ①scholarly 博学的 ②version 版本 ③verse 诗；韵文 ④paradoxical 自相矛盾的 ⑤suggestive 引起联想的 ⑥hint at 示意 ⑦hub(轮)毂 ⑧mutuality 相互关系 ⑨passive 被动的 ⑩receptive 易于接受的 ⑪dominate 支配 ⑫multitude(+ of) 许多

3 你对道教了解多少？

How much do you know about Daoism?

Daoism is a polytheistic religion that contains *shen* (deity,神), *xian* (Immortal or transcendent being,仙) and *gui* (ghost,鬼) who reside in their designated circles. The Heaven Jade Emperor takes charge of the group of *shen*, Dong Wanggong(Eastern Senior King,东王公) and Xi Wangmu (Western Senior Prince,西王母) take charge of the realm of *xian*, and Shidian Yanluo(Ten Hall King of Hell,十殿阎罗) takes charge of the realm of *gui*. The fundamental belief of the religion is the *dao*(道) that represents the creation and maintenance of the universe in being. According to Daoism, when a man attains the *dao*, he will turn into an immortal (得道成仙). Daoism believes that the human beings' supreme pursuit is to be an immortal through *dao*'s cultivation and energy practice.

Daoist followers worshiped Lao Zi (老子) as their great teacher who founded the Daoist School dating back from pre-Qin period (before 221 BC). According to an old story, Lao Zi traveled west and disappeared into the vast desert there. Five hundred years later, a man named Zhang Daoling (张道陵) in the Eastern Han Dynasty founded the Five *Dous* of Rice Sect (五斗米教) in the name of Lao Zi and took *Dao De Jing* (《道德经》) as their accepted standard doctrine.

In the early years, Daoist priests mainly spread Daoism among common people. It is said that an ordinary person could turn into an immortal throughout *dao*'s energy practice and cultivation. Accordingly Daoism spread far and wide among common people, then entered the literati and official circle, and finally gained admission into the imperial court where emperors resided.

Emperor Tuoba Tao of the Northern Wei Dynasty (386 – 534) (北魏太武帝拓跋焘) thought highly of Daoist Priest Kou Qianzhi (寇谦之); Emperor Ming Di of the Southern Dynasties (宋明帝) offered a special patronage to Daoist priest Lu Xiujing (陆修静). Both Lu and Kou came from the literati and official families. As Daoist priests, they gave Daoism the ideas, imagination, and wisdom of the literati and official circle, thus gradually enriching Daoist scriptures, doctrines, rituals, *shen* and *xian* system as well as methods of Daoist cultivation and energy practice.

In early Tang Dynasty (618 – 907), the Tang emperor, in order to dignify his own social status, proclaimed himself to be a descendant of Lao Zi. As we know, *Li* was the Tang emperor's surname, and Lao Zi's proper name was Li Er (李耳). During the Xuan Zong (唐玄宗)'s reign of the Tang Dynasty, *Dao De Jing* was honored as *Dao De Zhen Jing* (*The Essential Book of the Way and Its Virtue*,《道德真经》). At the same time, the title of the Daoist sage was given to a number of pre-Qin Daoist personages, including Zhuang Zi (庄子), Wen Zi (文子), Lie Zi (列子) and others. Emperor Xuan Zong himself annotated *Dao De Jing*, and ordered all the scholars, officials and common people to keep a copy of the book at home. Examination questions related to *Dao De Jing* had also been added to imperial examinations.

In the Song Dynasty (960 – 1279), Emperor Wei Zong (宋徽宗) proclaimed himself *daojun huangdi* (Dao Supreme Emperor, 道君皇帝). He also set up a *dao's* post ranking system based on traditional imperial official ranking patterns. This system included 26 ranks for *dao* officials, of which the supreme grade was named called *jinmen yuke* (金门羽客). The *jinmen yuke* literally means "A Guest with a Feather at the Golden Gate." Those who had this title could walk in and out of the imperial palace any time without any restrictions.

A multitude of Daoist sects and *dao* official posts mushroomed during the period of the Jin, Yuan and Ming dynasties. Based on the information from a book called *zhu zhen zong pai zong bo* (*The General Book of All Daoist Sects*,《诸真宗派总薄》), there were 86 Daoist sects in all throughout the course of history.

Since the Tang Dynasty, imperial governments of the dynasties consumed a huge sum of money to have scholars compile *The Collection of Daoist Scriptures* (《道藏》) in an attempt to keep and disseminate these scriptures. The imperial patronage lasted until the Qing Dynasty, in which the court government began to neglect Daoism. However, Daoist temples still remained popular with numerous believers from all walks of life.

Notes: ①polytheistic 多神崇拜的 ②immortal 不朽的 ③transcendent 卓越的 ④take charge of 负责 ⑤fundamental 基本的 ⑥maintenance 维修 ⑦supreme 最高的 ⑧literati (literatus 的复数) 文人;学者 ⑨patronage 恩惠;恩赐态度 ⑩imagination 想象 ⑪proclaim 宣告;公布 ⑫essential 必要的 ⑬restriction 限制 ⑭mushroom 雨后春笋般地涌现 ⑮disseminate 传播

4 什么是神仙?

What are *shen* and *xian*?

Shen and *xian* have different interpretations. *Shen* literally means "deity", and *xian* "transcendent being." *Shen* refers to the naturally born true sage, and *xian* to a man who has become immortal through his Daoist practice and cultivation; *xian* also has various magic power. During the later period of Daoism, on many occasions, people couldn't tell who was *shen* or *xian* because these supernatural beings appear indistinct. Therefore people simply called them *shenxian* together despite of their respective interpretation.

Tao Hongjing(陶宏景), a Daoist priest of the Liang Dynasty, listed about 700 *shenxian* supernatural beings in a book called *The Picture of True Spiritual Figures' Positions*(《真灵位业图》). Since then, the number of *shenxian* supernatural beings continued to increase as dynasties went by. In the Tang and Song dynasties, Daoist supernatural beings amounted to more than 10,000. This extensive sources of these beings basically came from the following three categories. The first category was a list of deities originated with Daoism like the Heaven Jade Emperor; the second was supernatural beings transformed into Daoism from Chinese ancient mythology and popular legendary tales like Dong Wanggong (东王公) and Xi Wangmu (西王母); the third was deities or ghosts originated from Buddhism.

In the Eastern Jin Dynasty (317 – 420), Yuanshi Heaven Emperor (元始天尊) appeared. Yuanshi literally means "primary or original." Yuanshi Heaven Emperor is esteemed as the supreme deity who is also called the Jade Heaven Emperor responsible for the realm of *shen*. In the realm of *xian* (gods), Dong Wanggong (东王公) takes charge of male *xian*; Xi Wangmu (西王母) takes charge of female *xian*. Shidian Yanluo (十殿阎罗) in Fengdu (丰都) takes charge of the realm of *gui* (ghost).

Notes: ①indistinct 不清楚的 ②amount to 等于 ③extensive 大量的 庞大的

5 什么是佛教?

What is Buddhism?

Buddhism was founded in India around the 6th century BC. It is said that the founder was Sakyamuni (释迦牟尼). The essence of Buddhism's early teaching was summarized in the Four Noble Truths (四谛): Life is suffering; the cause of suffering is desire; the answer is to extinguish desire; the way to this end is by the Eightfold Path(八正道), a pattern of right living and thinking. Specifically, his followers vowed not to kill, steal, lie, drink, or lose their chastity. Monastic orders for men and women were soon set up. The Three Precious Things(三宝) were said to be the Buddha (佛), the Dharma(the teaching or Way, 法) and the Sangha(the Monastic Order, 僧).

Buddhism became established in China in its Mahayana form(Greater Vehicle, 大乘). The split between Hinayana(Lesser Vehicle, 小乘) and Mahayana had already taken place some centuries earlier in India. Buddhism is practiced today as Hinayana in Sri Lanka, Burma, Thailand and elsewhere in Southeast Asia, while various sects of Mahayana are in China, Japan, Korea, Mongolia and Tibet.

The worship of a whole series of Buddhist deities include Bodhisattvas(Enlightened Existences, 菩萨) in various manifestations. One of the popular Bodhisattvas are Amitabha (阿弥陀佛), the compassionate savior of the Western Paradise. Another is Maitreya (弥勒佛), the Buddha who is to descend to the world to replace Sakyamuni and continue the spread of Buddhism. A third is Avalokitesvara(观音菩萨), literally, depicted as the Goddess of Mercy. These Bodhisattva figures were ready for entry into Nirvana, a release from the cycle of rebirth; but they vowed to turn back to the world and not accept their own salvation until all sentient beings, humans and animals, were saved.

Notes: ①summarize 总结 ②extinguish 熄灭 ③Mahayana 大乘佛教 ④Hinayana 小乘佛教 ⑤manifestation 表现形式 ⑥compassionate 有同情心 ⑦savior 救星 ⑧salvation 拯救 ⑨sentient 有感情的

6 你能简要介绍一下佛教在古代中国的早期发展吗？

Could you give me a brief introduction of Buddhism in the early years of ancient China?

In the later Han Dynasty (206 BC – 220 AD), Buddhism was introduced into China from Persia, Central Asia, and India by way of the Silk Road. There is a legend that the Han emperor Ming Di, in response to a dream, sent for images and scriptures from India. Two monks by the names of Matanga(摄摩腾) and Dharmaraksa(竺法兰) established the White Horse Temple (白马寺) close to the imperial capital at Luoyang. The Northern Wei Dynasty is perhaps best known for its legacy of Buddhist art, particularly the sculpture found in caves at Yungang in Shanxi Province and Longmen near Luoyang. These works of art are but one of the visual signs that mark the beginning of the complex process by which a foreign religion took hold in ancient China and was, in turn, influenced by Chinese styles and viewpoint.

When Buddhism first reached China, it was introduced as the religion of foreign merchants. During this time, Buddhism was at first considered an insignificant cult. Most of the Chinese gentry were indifferent to Buddhism, which was unknown and seemed alien and amoral to Chinese sensibilities. However, Buddhism both acclimatized itself to Chinese circumstances and became more appealing to those who were disillusioned with the old ways. Political patronage was important, but Buddhism had to win a wide following among the Chinese people in order to survive and prosper.

The early Buddhism was spread entirely orally, but in about the first century BC a large body of scriptures began to accumulate. So the early pilgrims therefore devoted a great deal of their time to the difficult task of translation. In this endeavor, words and ideas, as well as artistic forms, had to be translated into Chinese terms. The first Buddhist scripture to be written in Chinese was probably *Sutra of Forty-two Sections* (《四十二

章经》), although its authenticity is a matter of debate. An Shigao(安世高), a Buddhist priest, arrived at the Han capital in 148 and was the first to initiate a systematic translation of Buddhist texts into Chinese.

Notes: ①visual 视觉的 ②insignificant 无足轻重的 ③cult异教;教派 ④amoral 不属道德范围的 ⑤sensibility 感觉能力 ⑥accumulate 积累 ⑦endeavor 努力

7 佛教在古代中国的什么时候处于旺盛时期?

When did Buddhism flourish in ancient China?

During the Tang Dynasty (618 – 709), the state employed Confucian forms and learning, and Tang emperors often favored Daoism. The early Tang state could restrict the number of monks and regulate monasteries. However, monasteries gradually flourished; they fulfilled important roles; and the most outstanding monks had sufficient self-confidence to make their own formulation of doctrine and develop the teaching in new ways. For Buddhist art, it was an age of classic achievement.

There were eight Buddhist sects that appeared between 581 and 755. Of them, four only enjoyed temporary or limited success: the Disciplinary Sect(律宗),

the Dharma Image (法相宗), the Sect of the Three Stages (三论宗) and the Esoteric Sect (密宗). The growth of sects not only illustrated the inner vigor of Buddhist religion, but also manifested the strength of Buddhist monasteries. In the countryside, Buddhist monasteries performed important economic functions operating mills and oil presses. The monasteries also held much land that was cultivated by semi-servile labor. Much of their wealth was channeled into building and the arts.

Notes: ①monastery 僧院 ②flourish 昌盛 ③sufficient 足够的 ④self-confidence 自信 ⑤formulation 规划;构想 ⑥temporary 临时的 ⑦disciplinary 纪律的;惩戒的 ⑧esoteric 秘传的;难理解的

8 什么是净土宗?

What is the Pure Land Buddhism?

Pure Land Buddhism is a sect of Mahayana Buddhism which derives its name from the paradise in the West over which Amitabha(阿弥陀佛), the Buddha of Infinite Light, presides. Pure Land Sect first became prominent when a monastery was set up by Hui Yuan

(慧远)on the top of Mt. Lushan (庐山) in 402. Then it spread throughout China quickly, and currently it is one of the most dominant sects of Buddhism in Asia.

Pure Land Buddhism is based upon the Pure Land sutras first brought to China by Shi Dao'an (释道安) during the Jin Dynasty(265 – 420). Drawing on a long Mahayana tradition, this sect emphasizes faith as the means for gaining rebirth in the land of bliss. The main idea behind this sect is that Nirvana is sometimes hard to obtain by ourselves, so we need help from the Buddha. Instead of solitary meditative work toward enlightenment, the Pure Land Buddhism teaches that devotion to Amitabha will lead us to the Pure Land from which Nirvana will be easier to attain. A special practice of Pure Land Buddhism is that a devotee should devoutly chant the name of Amitabha to reinforce a proper and sincere state of mind in order to be reborn in Amitabha's Pure land in the West.

Notes: ①paradise(通常大写)天堂 ②infinite 无限的 ③prominent 突出的 ④dominant 占优势的 ⑤nirvana 涅槃 ⑥solitary 隐居的;孤独的 ⑦meditative 冥想的 ⑧enlightenment 启蒙;教化 ⑨devoutly 热诚地

9 什么是禅宗？
What is the Zen Sect of Buddhism?

The word "*Zen*" means "dhyana" in Sanskrit language, meaning "concentrated meditation." The Chan Buddhism is a major sect of Chinese Mahayana Buddhism. According to traditional accounts, the sect was founded by an Indian monk whose name was Bodhidharma(菩提达摩). He traveled to China by ship, arriving in South China in around 475. Legend has it that he spent nine years in meditation, facing the rock wall of a cave about a mile from the Shaolin Temple(少林寺).

The Zen Buddhism taught meditation as the way for one to pierce through the world of illusion, to recognize the Buddha nature within oneself and to obtain enlightenment. Zen rejected all other practices, such as the performance of meritorious deeds or study of scriptures. The Zen Buddhism underwent a schism during the 7th century resulting in the formation of two branches: the Southern Branch and the Northern Branch. The Northern branch of Zen emphasized sitting in silent meditation and attaining enlightenment gradually; the Southern Zen, founded by the man known as the Six Patriarch, Hui Neng (慧能), maintained that illumination came in a sudden flash, although only after long search. The

Southern Zen teachers often employed unorthodox methods to probe their disciples on the road of illumination. The Northern Branch disappeared over a period of time, but the Southern Branch, after the time of Hui Neng, began to branch off into numerous different schools, each having its own special emphasis, but all of them kept the same basic focus on meditation practice and personal instruction.

Notes: ①Sanskrit 梵语 ②illusion 幻想 ③undergo 经历 ④schism 分裂 ⑤illumination 解释;启发 ⑥unorthodox 非正统的

10. 什么是天台宗?

What is the Tiantai Sect of Buddhism?

The Tiantai Buddhism or the Lotus Sutra School was a sect of Mahayana Buddhism founded by Zhi Yi (智颜, 538 – 597) on Mt. Tiantai(天台山) during the Sui Dynasty. This sect enjoyed the most official support under the Sui and developed doctrinal and metaphysical syncretism by combining elements of various doctrines and practices into the Five Periods and Eight Types of Teachings(五时八教). The complete truth was contained in the *Lotus Sutra*(《妙法莲华经》).

Tiantai doctrine centers on three truths: ①thetruth that all phenomena are empty, and products of causation are without a nature of their own; ②the truth that they, however, exist temporarily; ③the truth that encompasses but transcends emptiness and temporariness. These three truths all involve and require each other—— throughout the Tiantai. A rich and unified cosmology is built on temporariness which consists of ten realms. Since each realm includes the other, there will be a total of 1,000 results. Besides, each realm in turn has three aspects(圆融三谛), including the aspect of living beings, the one of aggregation and the one of space. The result is a single idea at the moment embraces 3, 000 realms(一念三千). Since truth is immanent in everything, it follows that all beings contain the Buddha nature and can be saved.

Notes: ①doctrinal 教义的;学说的 ②metaphysical 形而上学的 ③syncretism 融合 ④phenomena 现象 ⑤encompass 包含 ⑥cosmology 宇宙学 ⑦aggregation 聚集 ⑧immanent 内在的

11 什么是华严宗?

What is the Huayan Sect of Buddhism?

The word "*huayan*" means "*avatamsaka*" in Sanskrit language, or "flower garland." The Huayan Sect was a sect of Mahayana Buddhism, which flourished in China during the Tang Dynasty. A monk, Fa Zang(法藏) of the Tang Dynasty(618 – 907), established this sect. The other important patriarchs who contributed to the establishment of the sect were Du Shun(杜顺), Zhi Yan(智严)and Cheng Guan(澄观).

The *Avatamsaka Sutra* (《严华经》) contains the most complex teachings of the Buddha. The sutra teaches the doctrine of emptiness and interpretation of all phenomena; all phenomena arise simultaneously in reciprocal causation(法界缘起). Huayan Buddhists distinguish between *li* (principle,理) and *shi* (phenomena,事), an approach which resembles in some ways the concept of *purusha* (spiritual) and *prakriti* (physical) of Hinduism. These *li* and *shi* was independent and interact; one thing contains all things in existence, and that all things are one.

Notes: ①garland 花冠 ②sutra 佛经 ③simultaneously 同时地 ④reciprocal 相互的 ⑤causation 引起 ⑥Hinduism 印度教

附　录
Appendices

购　物
Shopping

1 去购物的路上
On the Way to Stores

While touring China, you will never feel it a problem in finding opportunities to shop. All city tour guides will take you to visit different kinds of stores as part of your tour. Tourists' interests while shopping are a lot different from local residents'. Local residents buy their daily necessities. Tourists on the other hand want to pick up unusual things like antiques or mementos as souvenirs and gifts for relatives or friends back home.

Shopping however is more than a simple act of buying artifacts or souvenirs. Tourists can learn to appreciate and admire Chinese history and art found in such stores.

Well, this type of experience begins before you reach the shops or market. While touring China, you will observe the people on the streets, consider the inscriptions and carvings on the ever-present walls and gates, and notice the traditional architecture that casts the hint of history over modern apartment buildings.

With an open mind as you shop, I recommend that you take particular notice of each item. Notice the size, shape and color, and you will often be surprised. In such antiques, you may find the legacy of 5,000 years of culture, a legacy on which China so endlessly prides herself. As you gaze at the traditional artistic objects with wonder, their distinctiveness will fascinate you, and you will gain an insight into the aspirations of the Chinese and a better understanding of the Chinese society. It is for this reason that most tourists, after having their interest aroused in the culture, want to come back again.

Many tourists often ask themselves, "Where can I buy high quality Chinese souvenirs?" Friendship stores used to stock goods either imported from the West or in short supply in the ordinary stores. This type of stores is primarily meant for foreigners. However, now local Chinese department stores sell much more than friendship stores did before. A visit to a major city department store is a must, not simply to compare prices, but to get a feel of everyday Chinese life. Usually there is no bargaining to be done. Tours of handicraft factories end up at a small shop selling articles produced there. Small souvenir shops have sprung up at all the main tourist spots and in hotel lobbies. Goods sold there range from the shoddy to some attractive and unique.

In China, commodity prices can be state-fixed prices, regulating prices and market prices. Most of the tourist commodities fall in the category of the market prices. Therefore, you may go to several shops where you may stumble on some reasonable priced goods. In addition, local guides will offer you the right information related to shopping in the local area.

Notes: ①daily necessities 日用品 ②antique 古董 ③memento 纪念品 ④artifact 手工艺品 ⑤ever-present 始终存在 ⑥aspiration 愿望 ⑦bargain 讨价还价 ⑧commodity 商品 ⑨category 种类;部属 ⑩stumble (+ on/upon/across) 偶然碰见

2 在丝绸店

In a Silk Store

Travelers, here we are at the store where silk brocade and embroidery products are on sale. Silk and silk fabrics emerged at least 5,500 years ago in China. As early as the 4th century BC, local people in Sichuan were able to produce a kind of plain silk cloth. From 138 to 126 BC, sericulture and silk production techniques gradually spread into many other countries along the Silk Road.

In some stores, the store assistant will show you silkworms that spin raw silk cocoons. The assistant may throw cocoons into boiling water and then unravel silk from them; this operation has been done for thousands of years. An experienced worker is able to unwind about 1,000 meters long silk from one cocoon.

In this store, silk brocade and embroidery products are on sale. They include four famous local brocades, including Shu Brocade (蜀锦) from Sichuan Province, Yun Brocade (云锦) from Nanjing, Song Brocade (宋锦) from Suzhou, and Zhuang Brocade (壮锦) from Guangxi Zhuang Autonomous Region.

Brocade is a soft and colorful silk product, which has developed for over twenty centuries. There are several hundred types of brocade. Some patterns are so popular that they may be considered pattern models. The present brocade fabrics include the front of a quilt, the materials of clothes, brocade aprons, headscarves, and materials for other decorative purposes.

At present, handmaking brocade has been replaced by modern textile industry. Factories specialize in mechanically manufacturing brocade fabric with an electronically equipped jacquard loom. However, this silk store keeps a traditional jacquard wooden looms and employs some experienced weavers to demonstrate to tourists how to hand-weave brocade. Please come and view this big wooden loom—six meters long, five meters high, and 1.5 meters wide. Usually there are two weavers to operate one wooden loom. One weaver sits on the top of the loom, using his/her fingers to pick out the end of each single-dyed silk thread. At the same time, the other weaver, seated in the front, weaves the other end of the silk tapestry. These two will usually take one week to weave a piece of brocade the size of a handkerchief.

Well, let us move to the embroidery section where some young ladies are stitching patterns on silk fabrics. Please come and look at this product. One side of the fabric displays a cat, and the other a fish. Figures on the both sides have been done on a single piece of transparent fabric and both are completed at the same time. They're set in a frame, and notice how there are no ugly knots on the back. Long ago, women in China started to learn how to stitch flowers when they were young. Girls made embroidered birds, flowers, fish, incense bags, or a pair of mandarin ducks. The purpose of their ornamental needlework was either for their own use, or to be sold in the market.

The embroidery products are made of soft satin and colored threads. All of them are stitched by hand, and the varied stitching methods create unique local styles. There are four kinds of famous embroidery: Sichuan embroidery (蜀绣), Suzhou embroidery (苏绣) from Suzhou area, Xiang embroidery (湘绣) from Hunan Province and Yue embroidery (粤绣) from Guangdong Province. What are their main differences? Sichuan embroidery patterns are chosen from local folk art; Suzhou embroidery is famous for its extremely delicate stitches; Xiang embroidery for its rich colors; Yue embroidery, by contrast, tends to have rather complicated patterns.

Embroidery has a strong artistic effect, which focuses on the needlework method relating to minute details and perfect stitched patterns. Stitch lines appear smooth, and embroidery patterns look elegant and delicate. The traditional Chinese painting also provides favorite subjects for embroidery patterns that include flowers, birds, landscapes, fish, worms, and human figures.

Well, that is all for my brief introduction of brocade and embroidery. You may go and pick up any silk products you want to buy like embroidered quilt covers, bed sheets, pillow covers, and cushions. In addition, this store sells embroidered pictures framed in wooden cases or screens. These works represent the preservation and continuity of traditional Chinese arts.

Notes: ①brocade 锦缎 ②embroidery 刺绣 ③fabric 织品；布料 ④sericulture 养蚕(业) ⑤spin 纺 ⑥cocoon 茧 ⑦unravel 解开 ⑧autonomous 自治的 ⑨quilt 被子 ⑩apron 围裙 ⑪mechanically 机械地 ⑫manufacture 制造 ⑬jacquard 提花机 ⑭weaver 纺织工 ⑮tapestry 花毯 ⑯handkerchief 手绢 ⑰transparent 透明的 ⑱mandarin duck 鸳鸯 ⑲stitch 缝；绣 ⑳complicated 错综复杂的 ㉑preservation 保存 ㉒continuity 连续性

3 在书画市场

At a Painting and Calligraphy Market

Travelers, here we are at a market where Chinese paintings and calligraphy are on sale. I know that some of you are interested in purchasing artifacts here. At this market, each shop specializes in painting, calligraphy, or seal carving, and so I' d like to suggest that you go from shop to shop, examining and appreciating as if you were in a Chinese fine arts museum. Hopefully you may come across in this shop an artist who can demonstrate to you how to make Chinese painting step by step and practice calligraphy stroke by stroke. They will also explain in detail the use of these strokes to represent trees, flowers, boats, rocks, insects, and other subjects.

Please come and take a look at a group of Chinese brush paintings. As you know, Chinese painting is an important part of the country's cultural heritage. Chinese painting can be classified into three main categories: landscape painting, bird and flower painting, and figure painting. Traditional Chinese painting is done on *xuan* paper(宣纸)or silk. When Chinese artists paint landscape paintings, they express their awe of nature by recreating a panorama of a thousand miles onto a mere foot of paper. The landscape painting is a more intense and private thing to be shared with like-minded men. Artists take it for granted that behind every painting lies a moral or philosophical message. Chinese artists may paint individual rocks and trees, but they are not concerned in their finished works with the scenery, or with accidents of time and place; they are making a general statement about nature in its eternal aspect. Western techniques focus on shading and one-point perspective, which fixes the time of day, direction of the sun, and position of the viewer.

Ink occupies an exceedingly important position in traditional Chinese painting, with black being the main color. Brush and ink depict images; colors enrich them. Traditional painting stresses varying the shades of colors on the basis of different images. A piece of painting normally consists of the painting itself, calligraphic writing, and seal stamps. The principal forms include hanging scrolls, albums of paintings, fan surfaces, and long horizontal scrolls. Hanging scrolls are both horizontal and vertical. They are mounted and hung on the wall. Paintings by famous painters are usually mounted on scrolls which can be hung or rolled up.

Now please move to the next shop where Chinese calligraphy is on display. Chinese calligraphy was a separate art form in ancient China. The medium of this art is line—straight or curved. Chinese people value calligraphy for the sake of the harmonious nature of its lines, and strokes are deliberately formed in direct imitation of a natural object. To the artist, calligraphy is a mental exercise that coordinates the mind and the body to choose the best styled form in expressing the content of the passage. Calligraphy is a highly relaxing yet extremely disciplined exercise for one's own physical and spiritual well-being. Many Western scholars, while visiting China, have developed a keen interest in Chinese calligraphy and end up studying Chinese characters to better understand calligraphy. Westerners who study calligraphy are usually drawn to the beautiful flower-like characters, and the abstract nature of this historical art.

Chinese writing originated approximately 4, 500 years ago. At present, there are several popular writing styles like the Standard Script (楷书), the Running Script (行书), the Clerical Script(隶书)and the Cursive Script (草书). Principles of beauty in calligraphy include asymmetrical balance, momentum, dynamic posture, simplicity, imagination, and universality. These aesthetic principles govern the composition of Chinese characters and reflect the most basic ideals of the Chinese mind in the fine arts.

As we talk about Chinese calligraphy and painting, we have to mention the "four treasures of the study(文房四宝)." Traditionally the four treasures consist of a brush pen, an ink-stick, *xuan* paper, and an ink-slab. Chinese painters or calligraphists use these items to create Chinese art.

Well, please come and view these items here. The head of the brush pen may be made of the hair of a goat, wolf, rat, or rabbit. Rabbit-hair brushes are soft, flexible and absorbent and produce bold lines. Sometimes a brush uses mixed hair in order to obtain a balance between heavy and light lines. The handle of the Chinese brush can be made of bamboo, wood, or porcelain.

The ink-stick is the ink of Chinese traditional painting and calligraphy. The most well-known ink-stick is *huimo*(徽墨), made of burnt pine soot which is as hard as stone and does not fade for at least ten years.

Chinese painters and calligraphists use *xuan*-paper. This kind of paper absorbs ink well and shows clearly the lines and strokes. Artists prefer using this type of paper because of the paper's tensile strength and long lasting quality.

Chinese ink-slabs are flat, hard, and can be shaped into beautiful objects. While writing, calligraphists put some water in the ink-slab, and then grind an ink-stick against it. Gradually the water becomes black with enough ink for writing or painting.

Now please come to the seal store where you will see some Chinese engraved seals on sale. This art of seal engraving can be traced back to more than 3,000 years when people engraved inscriptions on tortoise shells. This art developed rapidly in the Qin Dynasty when people engraved their names on utensils and documents to claim ownership. After the invention of paper, people started to stamp the paper with an engraved seal. The surface of the seal that touches the paper is usually moistened with red ink paste.

The seal engraving requires both strength of the wrist and movement of the fingers. At present, seal materials include jade, gold, brass, stone, and wood. People in China traditionally use Chinese name seal as a personal signature. Chinese artists like to stamp their personal seals on their paintings rather than sign their names in the western way. So I'd like to encourage you to purchase a seal stone in the store and invite an experienced seal engraver to have your name engraved on it for a memory of your tour in China. The engraver can write Chinese scripts in different styles and arrange styled characters in a perfect balance. Sometimes, he may exaggerate strokes to be very thin or thick, or he may deliberately straighten or curve them in an attempt to create an artistic effect.

Notes: ①calligraphy 书法 ②specialize (+ in) 专门从事 ③appreciate 欣赏 ④insect 昆虫 ⑤awe 敬畏; 畏怯 ⑥philosophical 哲学的 ⑦eternal 永久的 ⑧perspective 透视图法 ⑨exceedingly 非常; 极度 ⑩vertical 垂直的 ⑪stroke (写字、绘画的)一笔 ⑫deliberately 有意地 ⑬coordinate 协调一致 ⑭asymmetrical 不对称的 ⑮momentum 动力 ⑯dynamic 有生气的; 强有力的 ⑰posture 姿势 ⑱simplicity 简单 ⑲universality 普遍性 ⑳absorbent 能吸收(水、光等)的 ㉑tensile 抗拉 ㉒grind 磨碎 ㉓moisten 使湿润

4 在陶瓷市场

At a Pottery and Porcelain Market

Travelers, here we are at a store of pottery and porcelain art objects. In this store, you may buy specialty products, but you should do some research and find out what you are truly interested in, and of course try to get a good bargain.

Pottery and porcelain are two easily confused terms used to describe Chinese ceramics. So I'd like to offer you some information to help see the difference in these two arts.

Now please come and view these porcelain wares. China has been recognized as the "home of porcelain." China clay is used to form the basic material, including pure white *gaoling*（高岭土）, feldspar, and quartz. Porcelain has a coating of vitreous glaze, and well-fired porcelain is non-porous and translucent. Throughout the ages, China's porcelain has been admired and valued for its usefulness and beauty. Primitive porcelain first appeared during the Shang and Zhou dynasties (1600 BC – 256 BC). Real porcelain wares appeared in the Han Dynasty (206 BC – 220 AD). From the Han Dynasty, celadon porcelain and black porcelain were mainly produced. During the Tang Dynasty(618 – 907), celadon manufacture reached a high degree of artistic expression. During the Northern and Southern Dynasties (420 – 589), the kilns in Southern China manufactured celadon porcelain; in North China, white porcelain was produced. The porcelain vessels of the Yuan (1206 – 1368) already had varied patterns. At that time, "blue-and-white" porcelain (青花瓷) first appeared. Other forms of painted porcelain include under-glazd red porcelain (釉里红), polychrome over-glazed décor porcelain(五彩瓷), and soft-colored over-glazed décor porcelain(粉彩瓷). In the Ming Dynasty (1368 – 1644), blue and white porcelain wares became the main porcelain production. In the Qing Dynasty (1616 – 1911), blue and white porcelain continued to develop, and its influence went far beyond China. Among the Qing porcelain wares, those produced during the reigns of Kangxi, Yongzheng and Qianlong are the most famous. A piece of porcelain is judged by the shape, painting, whiteness, glaze and finesse of the material. The colors are of actual metals and should not carelessly overlap the outlines of the design. The celadon porcelain is highly prized and costly.

Now let's move to pottery section. Pottery is made from a mixture of clay, feldspar, and quartz, and is shaped by drying and firing. Pottery began during the

Neolithic Age. The earliest earthenware was molded by hand. Painted pottery began in the period of Yangshao and Longshan cultures (仰韶和龙山文化), and was entirely hand-made and fired at a fairly low temperature. In the Shang and Zhou dynasties, pottery was mainly grey—either grey clay pottery or grey sandy pottery. The structures and types of vessels were practically identical with those made of bronze. A great innovation of the Zhou pottery was the production of pottery plate, tube tiles, and bricks for housing construction. The colors of pottery during the Warring States Periods were grey, red, dull brown or black. The dull brown pottery was painted with colored patterns, and many were used for funerary or sacrificial rites. Painted pottery of highly artistic quality has existed since the Han Dynasty.

The Han Dynasty also produced lacquer-coated pottery. What is lacquer-coated pottery? Lacquer is a natural substance obtained from lacquer trees. Raw lacquer is the liquid in lacquer trees, which hardens when exposed to air. Therefore, before sunrise, a lacquer collector has to collect the lacquer from the trees. The main reason is that when the sun goes up, there is less moisture in the air, which stops the raw lacquer flow. Lacquer ware can resist moisture and heat as well as acid and alkali. The color and luster are also highly durable. A layer of lacquer is applied to vessels to give the surface a lustrous shine. For instance, Beijing lacquer wares usually have dozens to hundreds layers of lacquer coatings, reaching 5 to 18 millimeters of thickness. Afterwards, an engraver chases on the hardened lacquer surface, creating "carved paintings" related to landscapes, human figures, flowers, and birds. In Yangzhou, you can also find excellent lacquer ware whose typical features are carvings in relief and patterns inlaid with gems, gold, ivory, and mother-of-pearl. Products include screens, cabinets, tables, chairs, vases, trays, cups, boxes, and ashtrays.

Now let's move to another store of tri-color pottery items. This pottery style dates back to the Tang Dynasty. The Tang tri-color includes yellow, green, brown blue, black, and white glazed pottery; the major colors are yellow, green and brown, and the body is made from white clay. After the clay mold is fired into a fixed shape, a mineral frit is applied. These minerals contain elements of copper, iron, cobalt, and manganese. The body is then fired again at a temperature of around 900 degrees centigrade, allowing the different colors to permeate. In ancient times, tri-color pottery was used mainly for burial utensils, and rarely used for daily items. The tri-color art objects on sale here include human figures, horses, and camels. These tri-color human figures wear fashionable costumes with full figures and round faces; tri-color horses appear robust and handsome. The union of glazed colors and sculpture has boosted the appreciation of this traditional pottery through the ages.

Here is another store where cloisonné products are on sale. Cloisonné is a kind of enamelware that was introduced from the Middle East in the 14th or 15th century, but reached its zenith in design, craftsmanship and beauty in China. The word, cloisonné, comes from French, meaning "to partition." The enamel is poured into *cloisons* or compartments formed by copper wire fillets, baked under several firings, polished, and gilded. The finished product is a splendid sight with gleaming gilded copper wire fillets separating each segment of brilliant enamel color. The metal most often used in China is copper. Here are some cloisonné bracelets and earrings in the typical colour of blue, and glittering thin copper strips you should take a look at. You may buy cloisonné vases or figures of various colors to enhance your décor. Other products include table lamp bases, food containers, fruit bowls, incense burners, jewelry boxes, and mirror frames. Some designs are worked in relief and marvelously intricate.

Notes: ①specialty 特产 ②feldspar 长石 ③quartz 石英 ④non-porous 非多孔的 ⑤overlap 重叠 ⑥funerary 殡葬的 ⑦sacrificial 献祭的 ⑧durable 耐用的 ⑨lustrous 有光泽的 ⑩ashtray 烟灰缸 ⑪frit（用以制造瓷器或釉料的）玻璃质 ⑫cobalt 钴 ⑬manganese 锰 ⑭permeate 渗透 ⑮cloisonné 景泰蓝瓷器 ⑯zenith 最高点；顶点 ⑰craftsmanship 手艺 ⑱gild 把……镀金 ⑲marvelously 奇异地 ⑳intricate 错综复杂的

5 在玉器店

At a Jade Store

Travelers, here we are at a jade store with items like jade jewelry, figurines, chopsticks and combs. Well, I'd like to give you some information about Chinese jade.

Jade(玉)is a beautiful stone that comes in green, white, grey, black, yellow, or violet. Generally jade in China is classified into either soft jade(nephrite,软玉) or hard jade (jadeite,硬玉). In ancient times, China only had soft jade; hard jade was imported from Burma in the Qing Dynasty. Therefore, the word jade usually refers to soft jade, or "traditional jade." Hard jade is called *fei cui*(翡翠)in Chinese.

Both jadestones tend to be white or colorless, while

colors such as red, green, and gray indicate the presence of iron, chromium, or manganese impurities. Some colors are peculiar to one stone or another. In both types of jade, the microscopic crystals not only are tightly compressed, but also have wide levels of translucency.

In the beginning of the 19th century, experts highlighted the difference between these two jade stones finding that they differ in both chemical composition and crystalline structure. The two different types of jade, when worked and polished, can usually be distinguished by their appearance alone. The fine luster of polished soft stone is oily rather than vitreous (glassy), while hard jade has the opposite appearance.

In China, the most reputable jade production area is Hetian(和田) in Xinjiang Uygur Autonomous Region (新疆). Soapstone or serpentine jade(岫玉) is mainly from Xiuyan County(岫岩县) in Liaoning Province(辽宁). Lantian jade (蓝田玉) is produced in Lantian County(蓝田县) of Shaanxi Province(陕西). Dushan Hill(独山) in Nanyang County(南阳县) in Henan Province(河南) is famous for its abundant Nanyang jade(南阳玉) or Dushan jade(独山玉).

In the late Paleolithic Age, cavemen had already begun to appreciate the decorative quality of jade and other kinds of stones. Cave dwellers selected attractive pebbles and bones and wore them as necklaces. In the late Neolithic Age, ornaments made of jade began to appear, such as *bi* (pierced discs, 璧), *huang* (pendant, 璜) and beads. During the Shang Dynasty (1600 BC – 1046 BC), people began making small ornamental plaques with decorative designs of animals. From the later part of the Zhou Dynasty (1046 BC – 256 BC), jade began to be made into a wide variety of utilitarian and luxury objects, such as belt hooks, ornaments, swords, and scabbards. The craft of jade carving in China attained maturity toward the close of the Zhou Dynasty, and the tradition continued for the next 2,000 years. In the periods of the Qin and Han dynasties (221 BC – 220 AD), jade-ware became more practical. At that time, people began to believe that jade increased longevity, and therefore by wearing jade they would live forever. Henceforth the practice of burying the dead with jade-wares became common. Invaluable jade figures and clothes sewn with gold threads have been found in tombs dating back to the Han Dynasty. During the periods of the Three Kingdoms to Song and Yuan dynasties (220 – 1368), there was no great development in the jade-carving technique. However, white jade vessels with gold holders and white jade bowls with gold covers were unearthed in the Ming tombs. These discoveries indicate the high level of jade carving during that period. The jade-ware technique advanced in the Qing Dynasty especially during the reign of Qian Long(1736 – 1795) when thousands of carved jades were added to the imperial collections, and jade objects were used for countless decorative, ceremonial, and religious purposes in public and in the homes of nobles and officials. In the same dynasty, greater quantities of jade entered China than ever before, especially the highly appreciated emerald-green jadeite from Burma. People paid large sums of money for high-quality carvings of figures, animals, plants, bottles, urns, vases, and other vessels. As a popular Chinese saying says, "Gold is valuable while jade is invaluable(黄金有价玉无价)," emphasizing that jade has a special appeal to Chinese people.

Well, I'd like to tell you a story called Heshibi (和氏璧). A man named He Shi (和氏) in the state of Chu found a piece of unpolished jade in Mountain Chu and presented it to King Li. The king summoned a jadesmith to examine it. "It is only a rock," said the jadesmith. The king thought that He Shi was trying to cheat him, so he ordered He Shi's left foot be cut off. After the king died, King Wu came to the throne. He Shi presented the jade to King Wu and the king summoned an expert on jade to examine it. "It is only a rock," said the expert. King Wu also thought that He Shi was trying to cheat him, so he ordered He Shi's right foot be cut off. After King Wu died, the rule of King Wen began. He Shi tightly held the jade in his arms crying at the foot of Mountain Chu. He cried for three days and nights until his tears ran dry and his eyes bled. When King Wen heard of this, he sent someone to ask He Shi why he was so upset. "Many people have had their feet cut off," said the visitor. "And why are you crying so sorrowfully?" He Shi replied, "I am so sorrowful not because my feet have been cut off, but because this valuable jade has been regarded as a mere rock and the loyal subject as a swindler." King Wen then ordered a jadesmith to polish the jade. As expected, it was a piece of precious jade. So the king named it "Heshi's Jade."

In Chinese culture, jade symbolizes beauty, nobility, perfection, power and immortality. Jade may be carved into many shapes to enhance its luxurious value. Typical subjects are peaches, mandarin duck, deer, bat, fish, double phoenixes, bottle, lotus, bamboo, and fans. People may wear these shaped jade objects or use them to decorate their houses.

Travelers, now I'd like to let you learn how to appreciate jade. There are four ways to judge the quality of jade. First are tone and color; the best jade's colors are penetrating, and they should be pure and evenly distributed. The second are translucency and clarity;

the best jade has a consistent clarity. The third is texture; the best jade is clear and free of impurities. The fourth is cutting; the shape of the jade is of great importance. Soft jade creates an oily luster and hard jade a vitreous luster; tiny cracks will lower the value of jade; air bubbles should be invisible in a real jade object.

When you have purchased your favorite jade objects, you should take great care of it.

(1) Jade is delicate, and thus easily cracks. The interior structure is also sensitive and can get invisible cracks. As time goes on, these cracks may become visible and thus reduce its value.

(2) Keep your jade object away from dust or greasy dirt. You may clean the object with a soft brush or wash it with clean water.

(3) Store the jade object in a case or box.

(4) Keep jade away from perfume, perspiration, and chemicals.

(5) Do not expose your jade object to sunlight for a long time because it may cause the jade to swell, and thus lower the quality of the object.

(6) Keep jade in a humid or moist environment.

Well, so much for my introduction. Please go and view the items sold in the store. Here are necklaces of jade beads in various hues; beaded or solid carved bracelets; earrings; pendants, and rings. Here are sets of symbolic animals for the twelve Earthly Branches: Mouse, Ox, Tiger, Hare, Dragon, Snake, Horse, Goat, Monkey, Cock, Dog and Pig. Over there are some other items, such as jade napkin rings and jade combs.

Notes: ①jewelry 珠宝 ②figurine 小人像 ③nephrite 软玉 ④jadeite 硬玉 ⑤chromium 铬 ⑥impurity 杂质 ⑦crystalline 透明的;清晰的 ⑧soapstone 滑石 ⑨serpentine 蛇纹石 ⑩pebble 卵石 ⑪scabbard 鞘 ⑫longevity 长寿 ⑬invaluable 无价的 ⑭emerald 翠绿色的 ⑮sorrowfully 悲哀地;忧愁地 ⑯swindler 骗子 ⑰immortality 不朽 ⑱consistent 一致 ⑲clarity 清澈 ⑳invisible 看不见的 ㉑sensitive 敏感的 ㉒perfume 香水 ㉓perspiration 汗水 ㉔bracelet 手镯 ㉕napkin 餐巾

6 在中药店

At a Herb Store

Travelers, here we are at an herb store where you can purchase some local herbs. Please come into the store with me. In the store, you will see hundreds of herbs on sale, including roots, bark, flowers, seeds, fruits, leaves, and branches.

In China, there are over 3,000 different herbs of

which 300 to 500 are commonly used. Chinese herbs can be divided into various types depending on their functions. A patient usually receives small packages at a pharmacy of traditional medicine in accordance with the prescription of his/her doctor. Each package contains various dry herbs. The patient usually puts them in a pot, adds water until they are completely soaked, and then heats them in the pot over a fire. When the water begins to boil, the temperature is immediately reduced, but the herbal water is kept simmering for another 30 or 40 minutes. Then the herbal water is poured out into a bowl; and the herbs themselves remain in the pot, which is refilled with water and again placed over the fire. The whole process is repeated three times until enough concentrated herbal water is produced. When herbs are combined, they can increase or promote the effectiveness of each other.

Herbal therapy has three main functions: ①to treat the immediate problems such as bacteria or viruses; ②to strengthen the body and help it recover; ③ to maintain the body's health. Chinese herbs have a low risk of adverse reaction or side effects, and some Chinese herbs even function as stimulants. The herbs are mixed in a way to keep completely safe because they keep the balance in the body and improve the function of all bodily organs.

You may be interested in knowing the different attitudes between Chinese and Western medical practitioners towards disease. One of the major assumptions inherent in traditional Chinese medicine is that disease comes from an internal imbalance of *yin* (阴) and *yang* (阳). So disease can be treated by correcting the *yin* and *yang* imbalance. Western medicine tends to approach disease by assuming that it is due to an external force, such as viruses or bacteria, or a slow degeneration of the body. Western medicine is based on the Cartesian philosophy that the body represents one functioning system and the mind another. One system may affect the other, but essentially it sees disease as either physical or mental. The Chinese assume that the body is a whole, and all its parts are intimately connected. Each organ has a mental as well as a physical function. Western drugs often control symptoms, but do not cure the source of the disease whereas Chinese herbal medicine treats the underlying disease defined by traditional diagnosis.

The theory of the *yin* and *yang* holds that all things have two opposite aspects, which are at the same time interdependent. The ancient Chinese used water and fire to symbolize *yin* and *yang*; anything moving, hot, bright and hyperactive is part of the *yang*, and anything quiet, cold, dim and inactive is part of the *yin*. In the application of *yin* and *yang* to the human body in Chinese medicine, the upper part is *yang*, the lower part *yin*; the exterior is *yang*, the interior *yin*; the back is *yang*, the abdomen *yin*. With regard to internal organs, the heart, liver, spleen, lung, and kidney are *yin*, also called the *zang*(脏)organs, while the six intestinal organs are *yang*, also called *fu*(腑)organs. These organs are the gallbladder, the stomach, the large intestine, the small intestine, the urinary bladder, and the triple warmer. The Chinese believe that by maintaining the body in a balanced state, health can be achieved and disease prevented.

The body however is a delicate balance of *yin* and *yang*, and its balance is not always exact. Sometimes a person's mood may be more fiery, or *yang*, while at other times he may be quieter and therefore more *yin*. Normally the balance changes from hour to hour and day to day, but if the balance is permanently disordered, for instance, if *yin* consistently outweighs *yang*, then the body is unhealthy and sick. Therefore, traditional Chinese doctors use acupuncture, herbs, and food to help correct the *yin-yang* imbalance so that the body returns to a healthy state.

Apart from the *yin* and *yang* theory, *qi* (气), blood and body fluid are important substances that sustain the vital activities and nourish the body. *Qi* is a complex concept that relates to both substance and function. The formation and circulation of blood depends on *qi*, whereas the distribution of *qi*, as well as the health of the various organs of the body, is dependent on adequate nourishment from the blood. Body fluid is formed from food and drink, and it exists in the blood, the tissues, and all the body openings and cavities. One basic notion of Chinese medicine is that *qi* must circulate through living organs, and when this circulation is blocked, disease results. So many treatments are to get *qi* to flow properly through the body without being interrupted.

Qi channels and pathways (经络) vitalize the organs of the body. They are responsible for conducting the flow of *qi* and blood through the body. The central principle of traditional Chinese medicine is to diagnose the cause of the internal disease (the *yin* and *yang* imbalance within the body) and by using the relevant acupuncture points, to correct the flow of *qi* in the channels and thus rid the body of disease.

Chinese doctors mainly use pulse diagnosis. According to classical Chinese medicine, there are six pulses at each wrist. These pulses occupy three positions at each wrist over the radial artery, and each position has a deep and superficial pulse. Each of these pulses represents a different organ, and in this way each of the twelve *zangfu*(脏腑) organs is represented by a wrist pulse. The character of the pulse indicates the state of health and the balance between organs. However, pulse diagnosis is not used in isolation. The other methods include inspection of facial complexion, examination of the tongue (the tongue proper and the tongue coating), listening to the speech, listening to the respiration, listening to the cough, and an interview. The standard ten questions(十问) include: "One, chill and fever; two, perspiration; three, head and trunk; four, stool and urine; five, food intake; six, chest; deafness and thirst are seven and eight; nine, past history and ten, causes."

Some patients receive acupuncture treatment. The traditional explanation says that there exists a network of pathways called channels that link all parts of the body, and in these channels more than 360 acupuncture points are located. *Qi*, or vitality, flows through these channels and acupuncture points to support tissues, muscles, and organs. When the *qi* is blocked or clogged at certain critical acupuncture point, the strength of tissues, muscles, and organs is weakened. An acupuncturist therefore usually inserts acupuncture needles into certain points to help *qi* flow. At the same time the needlework helps correct *qi* imbalances and improve energy and internal processing.

When receiving acupuncture treatment, people may feel different sensations: sore, numb, warm, swelling, or even relaxed. Six to eight needles are used during acupuncture treatment at most of the time. Ten or more needles may be used if two or more symptoms need acupuncture treatment at a time. Normally, each acupuncture treatment takes 20 to 30 minutes, but doctors must also keep in mind the sensitivity of each individual.

Well, I have offered you some basic information about traditional Chinese medicine. Now please come and look at some of the herbs here. All the clerks in the store are very helpful and ready to answer any questions you have.

Look, this is the *Chuan Bulb of Fritillary* (川贝母). *Chuan* in the names of herbs symbolizes the origin of herbs and their high quality. The fritillary herb is slightly cold and affects the lungs by clearing heat and moistening dryness. The herb is used for hot-type bronchitis with dry cough. A patient suffering from a cough eats the steamed pear with fritillary powder and also drinks the juice formed during steaming.

This is Tianma (the Tuber of Elevated Gastrodia, 天麻). Literal English translation is "heavenly hemp." The plant has been used for medical treatment for more than 2,000 years, and is categorized in traditional Chinese medicine as a sweet and neutral herb. *Tianma* mainly cures patients of arms and legs' contraction, hemiplegia, headache, or dizziness.

This is *Chongcao* (Chinese Caterpillar Fungus, 虫草). The caterpillar fungus is a traditional medicine that has been widely used as a tonic and medicine by the Chinese for hundreds of years. It is either ground to powder, or mixed with other tonics to increase strength or to recover from a long serious injury. The most common way to prepare it is to stuff a duck with caterpillar fungus and then boil the duck in hot water. Patients then drink the liquid which has a pleasant aroma and tastes sweet.

This is *Duzhong* (the Bark of Eucommia, 杜仲). The outer surface is light brown or grayish-brown. The inner surface is smooth and dark violet in color. The bark is used to nourish the liver and kidney and to strengthen the bones and muscles. In addition, it may be used to treat a deficiency of the liver-*yin* and kidney-*yin* commonly seen as soreness and weakness of the loins and knees.

Well, after purchasing our herbs, we will go for a traditional Chinese medicine meal. These meals are unique in the Chinese food culture as they are prepared with selected food ingredients and herbs aimed to treat specific health conditions. I hope that the traditional Chinese medicine meal will help you better understand how healthy Chinese herbal medicine can be.

Notes: ①package(香烟等的)一包 ②pharmacy 药房 ③in accordance with 一致;符合 ④prescription 处方 ⑤concentrated 浓缩的 ⑥herbal 草本的 ⑦bacteria 细菌 ⑧virus 病毒 ⑨stimulant 刺激物 ⑩nurture 滋养 ⑪practitioner 开业医生 ⑫assumption 设想 ⑬inherent 固有的 ⑭internal 内部的 ⑮imbalance 不平衡 ⑯external 外部的 ⑰intimately 亲密地 ⑱underlying 基本的 ⑲diagnosis 诊断 ⑳interdependent 互相依存 ㉑hyperactive 活动过度的 ㉒exterior 外表 ㉓interior 内部 ㉔intestinal 肠的 ㉕gallbladder 胆囊 ㉖stomach 胃 ㉗urinary 泌尿的 ㉘bladder 膀胱 ㉙maintain 维持;保持 ㉚permanently 永久地 ㉛acupuncture 针刺疗法 ㉜fluid 流质;液 ㉝substance 物质 ㉞circulation循环;运行 ㉟nourishment 营养品 ㊱tissue(动植物的)组织 ㊲pulse 脉搏 ㊳superficial 表面的 ㊴complexion 气色 ㊵coating 被覆;外层 ㊶respiration 呼吸 ㊷vitality 生命力 ㊸fritillary 贝母 ㊹bronchitis 支气管炎 ㊺neutral 不确定的 ㊻contraction 挛缩 ㊼hemiplegia 半身不遂 ㊽dizziness 头晕 ㊾caterpillar 毛虫 ㊿fungus 菌类植物 51tonic 补药 52grayish-brown 浅灰棕色 53deficiency 缺乏 54ingredient 成分

部分景点细节描述范例
Highlights of Some Famous Scenic Spots

1 天安门广场
Tian'anmen Square

Tian'anmen, the Gate of Heavenly Peace on the north side of the square, dominates the entrance to the Forbidden City. Two marble lions and two ornamental pillars stand in front of the five marble bridges spanning the Golden Stream and leading to the five openings in the gate. Chairman Mao's portrait hangs over the entrance; to the left of the portrait is the slogan "Long live the People's Republic of China" and to the right "Long Live the Unity of the Peoples of the World."

Tian'anmen Square was built in modern times. The Great Hall of the People(人民大会堂), on the west side of the square, was built in 1959 and is the home of the National People's Congress. On the east side of the Tian'anmen Square is the National Museum of China(中国国家博物馆), which is a comprehensive museum focusing on history and arts, systematically showing the long history of China. The Monument to the People's Heroes(人民英雄纪念碑) is an obelisk in memory of all the revolutionary martyrs of the 19th and 20th centuries and stands directly south of Tian'anmen. Chairman Mao's Memorial Hall (毛主席纪念堂), on the south side of the square, was started in November 1976 and completed in nine months. On October 1, 1949, Chairman Mao proclaimed the founding of the People's Republic of China on the rostrum of the gate, and the national flag was hoisted for the first time on the flagpole to the south of the gate.

Notes: ①portrait 肖像 ②hang over 把……挂起 ③exhibit 展览 ④obelisk 方尖石碑 ⑤martyr 烈士 ⑥hoist 举起 ⑦flagpole 旗杆

2 故宫部分大殿

Some Main Halls in the Palace Museum

The Forbidden City is divided into two main sections: the Outer Palace (外朝) and the Inner Palace(内廷). The Outer Palace is dominated by the three great halls formerly used for official and public purposes. The

Taihedian(太和殿, Hall of Supreme Harmony) presides over the vast and empty courtyard and is where thousands of kneeling officials would wait for the arrival of the emperor. The Taihedian, with its eleven-bay-wide facade and its double roof, is the largest building in the Forbidden City and is the formal throne hall used on the emperor's birthday and major festivals. Behind the Taihedian is the Zhonghedian(Hall of Complete Harmony, 中和殿), which was used by the emperor while he prepared to receive audiences. The third hall is the Baohedian(Hall of Preserving Harmony, 保和殿) where the emperor received tribute-bearing envoys from vassal countries and also scholars who had passed the official examinations. The stepping-stone at the back of the Baohedian, carved with clouds and dragons, is the largest monolithic carving in the palace.

Another three halls dominate the Inner Palace. The Qianqinggong(Hall of Heavenly Purity, 乾清宫) is an imposing nine-bay-wide hall reached by a marble causeway. Two famous banquets were given here, by Kang Xi (康熙) in 1711 and by Qian Long(乾隆) in 1785, for men over sixty-five. The next hall behind the Qianqinggong is the Jiaotaidian (Hall of Heavenly and Earthly Contact, 交泰殿), a place where the empress held her birthday party as well as any important ceremony such as New Year or winter solstice. The last of the three smaller halls, the Kunninggong(Palace of Earthly Tranquility,坤宁宫), was the private apartment of the empress during the Ming Dynasty, but during the Qing Dynasty became the bedroom of the emperor on his wedding night. The two bridal chambers in the east wing are decorated in red, the color of happiness.

Notes: ①preside over 俯临 ②facade 正面 ③tribute 进贡;贡物 ④vassal (封建时代的)诸侯;封臣 ⑤monolithic 独块巨石的 ⑥imposing 气势宏伟的 ⑦tranquility 平静 ⑧chamber 寝室

3 天坛 The Temple of Heaven

As one passes through the double gate buildings, one enters a rectangular courtyard. The enclosure of the alter is round at the north but square at the south. At the southern end is a three-tiered marble terrace representing Heaven at the top level—following an ancient Chinese belief that the Sky is circular—then Earth, and Man at the lowest level. Immediately beside this terrace is the Imperial Vault of Heaven(皇穹宇), an octagonal building made entirely of wood with a roof of dark blue glazed tiles. At the end of a long raised walkway is the Hall of Prayer for Good Harvest (祈年殿). The roof is topped with a gilded knob. Inside are four pillars ,each being made of a single tree trunk,that support the vault of the roof, decorated with a central motif of a dragon within a circle of clouds. Twelve outer pillars support the outer wall.

Retracing our steps south on the causeway, we should see to the west the Palace of Abstinence (斋宫), where the emperor fasted as a sacrifice offered to Heaven during the summer solstice. In addition, the causeway ends at a wall enclosing the Imperial Vault of Heaven. The wall is circular, with one gate to the south, and is known as the Echo Wall (回音壁) because two people facing it at the opposite points can hear each other whisper.

Notes: ①rectangular 矩形的 ②enclosure 围栏;围墙 ③terrace(庭院中的)露台 ④circular 圆形的 ⑤vault 拱顶;穹窿 ⑥motif 中心思想 ⑦abstinence 节制 ⑧whisper 耳语

4 颐和园的部分描述

Description of Some Parts in the Summer Palace

Half-way along the Long Corridor（长廊）, we come to a large open space with wooden *pailou*（triumphal arch，牌楼）and on the north side the Wanshoushan（Hill of Longevity，万寿山）. On the lower level is the Paiyundian（排云殿）which means "Cloud Dispelling Palace." The Foxiangge（佛香阁）, Tower of Buddha's Fragrance, is a four-storied tower, which dominates the lake and has a view of the hills to the west. From the tower, you can also see the Bronze Pavilion（铜亭）, also called Baoyunge（Pavilion of Precious Clouds，宝云阁）, on the western slope of the Hill of Longevity. A steep path leads further up outside the enclosure to a temple made entirely of glazed tiles called the Zhihuihai（the Sea of Wisdom Temple，智慧海）that stands at the peak of the hill.

Climbing down the Hill of Longevity again, you will find yourself back on the terrace outside the Paiyundian and soon on the western half of the Long Corridor which ends in sight of the Marble Boat（石舫）. If you have the energy, you can start walking around the lake from there and enjoy looking at the palaces and temples from a distance in a quiet setting.

Notes: ①triumphal 胜利的 ②arch 拱 ③in sight of 看得见

5 云冈的部分石窟

Parts of Yungang Grottoes

Cave No. 5 is well preserved and protected by a four-storey structure. The main figure in the middle is a 17-metre-tall Buddha, the largest statue at Yungang. A heavy dress falls symmetrically over both shoulders. Like many Chinese stone sculptures, it is plastered over and gilded to protect from erosion; the eyeballs are made of glazed ceramic. The attendant figures have their sweeping robes and crossed sashes hung low. On the east side of the northern wall in the front room of this cave is a statue of Buddha with a lowered head, long eye-brows, a protruding nose and thin lips. The flying apsarah (angels) high on both sides of the entrance have peaceful smile on their faces, and can even be seen from the second floor.

Cave No. 6 contains the 33 bas-reliefs on the four sides of the pillar that depict the life story of Sakyamuni. The entrance is flanked by fierce guardians. In the center of the rear chamber stands a square two-storey pagoda-pillar. On the lower part of the pagoda-pillar against each side are four big niches filled with carved images, including the Maitreya Buddha. The walls of the cave are covered with sculptures of Bodhisattvas, Buddhas, flying apsarahs and so on. A relief on the east wall of the rear chamber shows Prince Gautama's(悉达多)encounter with a sick man; the prince rides a horse while his attendants protect him with an umbrella but cannot prevent him from seeing human suffering.

Cave No. 12 is decorated with little statues of Buddhas and Bodhisattvas carved in niches. The carved musicians play musical instruments on the north wall. Some play the flutes, some beat drums, and others play the pipa, a four-stringed lute. These sculptures shed much light on ancient Chinese musical instruments and their use. Every figure appears alive and vigorous, with all their attention on the music. There are some sculptures of flying celestial beings dancing on the ceiling and walls.

Notes: ①erosion 侵蚀;腐蚀 ②eyeball 眼球 ③ceramic 陶器 ④protrude 使伸出 ⑤flying apsarah 飞天 ⑥bas-relief 浅浮雕 ⑦encounter with 偶然碰见

6 西安郊外 Environs of Xi'an

The region around Xi'an and especially the hills on the north bank of the Wei River(渭河)are of great interest to archaeologists due to the dozens of imperial tombs and the remains of imperial capitals and palaces in the area. A number of sites have not yet been excavated and thus are not open to visitors.

The Neolithic Banpo Village(半坡遗址), 10 km east of Xi'an, which was first excavated in 1954, gives a remarkably complete picture of the life of men 6,000 years ago who cultivated the land, made pottery, stored food in pits, raised cattle, fished, and hunted. The Banpo Museum has a hall showing reconstructions of the life of Banpo people, and another hall which displays some of the objects unearthed.

The Huaqing Hot Springs(华清池)are some 30 km east of Xi'an below Lishan(骊山). During the Tang Dynasty, these natural hot baths were a favored retreat of emperors, who often came to enjoy the scenery and the springs. The Precious Concubine Yang Guifei(杨贵妃) of Tang emperor Xuan Zong (唐玄宗) used to bathe there, thus one of the pools still bears her name.

Not far from the Huaqing Hot Springs is the far

more interesting Mausoleum of Qin Shihuang(秦始皇陵), who died in 211 BC after having established a united Chinese empire for the first time in history. The Army of Terracotta Soldiers and Horses(兵马俑)stands in battle line. There are over 6,000 of these life-sized figures, all with individually molded features, hairstyles, and clothing. They are displayed in a museum built on the site, 500 m north of the tomb.

Notes: ①archaeologist 考古学家 ②excavate 挖掘 ③unearth 发掘 ④scenery 风景 ⑤precious 宝贵的 ⑥life-sized 实物大小的 ⑦hairstyle 发型

7 登泰山 Ascending Mt. Taishan

The ascent to Mt. Taishan can be made in three to four hours at a brisk pace, but most people will spend the day climbing. They usually have their lunch and rest at the half-way point. The visitor who has overestimated his or her strength can be carried in a chair, on the way up and down. However, I'd like to recommend that visitors take as little as possible while climbing. Drinks and snacks can be bought along the way. The higher one gets, the more expensive the things cost.

Two paths lead to the top: the main path, which was used by the emperor, and the western path. The beginning of the main path is marked by the Daizongfang (岱宗坊), a monumental stone portal, or Portal of the Great Ancestor, which was built in the Ming Dynasty and rebuilt in 1730. The first Heavenly Portal, Yitianmen (一天门), awaits visitors at the bottom of the first series of steps. Just behind it, another stone archway commemorates the place where Confucius rested before the ascent. The next stone archway bears the characters *tian jie* (Stairs to the Sky, 天阶). The Red Gate Palace (红门宫), named after some red stones nearby, is beside that path. The Tower of the Ten Thousand Immortals (万仙楼), built over the path, dates from the Ming Dynasty.

Still further up the steps, on the right lies the Doumugong (Temple of the Goddess of the Big Dipper, 斗母宫), once called the Monastery of the Dragon Spring (龙泉观). Shortly after the Doumugong, one should leave the main path and go to the right, across the stream, to visit the Valley of the Stone Sutra (经石峪), where the stream flows over large smooth rocks engraved with giant characters of the Diamond Sutra. The main path eventually leads across to the other side of the torrent, where one enters an area shaded by cypress trees called the Cypress Arbor(柏洞). At the end of this section is the Hutiange(Heavenly Kettle Pavilion, 壶天阁), a place marked by an archway, where the mountain forms the shape of a kettle. After the temple, the path becomes very steep and an archway indicates the Point Where the Horses are Turned Back(回马岭坊).

Notes: ①overestimate 过高估计 ②monumental 纪念性的 ③portal 入口 ④archway 拱道 ⑤commemorate 纪念 ⑥dipper (大写)北斗七星 ⑦engrave 雕刻 ⑧eventually 最终地 ⑨cypress 柏

8 洛阳白马寺

The White Horse Temple in Luoyang

The White Horse Temple, about 15 km east of town, is one of the oldest Buddhist temples in China. In the Western Han Dynasty(206 BC – 25 AD), two Indian monks, Matanga(摄摩腾) and Dharmaraksa(竺法兰), arrived in Luoyang riding white horses and carrying the Buddhist sutras; they founded the temple and their remains are said to be buried there as well. Two short stone white horses and two lions stand outside the gates. Most buildings in the courtyards date from the Ming or Qing dynasties(1368 – 1911).

The first hall, Hall of the Heavenly Kings, has, apart from the four guardians, a main figure of Maitreya Buddha(弥勒佛), and a statue of Wei Tuo Bodhisattva (韦驮菩萨) at the back, holding a mountain in his hand. The next hall is the Dafudian(Big Buddha Hall, 大佛殿), with a gilded clay statue of Sakyamuni Buddha(释迦牟尼佛) in the center and Wenshu Bodhisattva(文殊菩萨) on the right and Puxian Bodhisattva(普贤菩萨) on the left. In the back of the hall Guanyin Bodhisattva(观世音菩萨) sits on a throne which floats in the clouds. The Daxiongdian(大雄殿, Hall of the Great Heroes), has a very ornate main altar with a gallery above supporting another altar. The most interesting statues in this hall are the eighteen Luohans or "Arhat" (罗汉) made of *tuotai* and dry lacquer(夹纻干漆), of the Yuan Dynasty. Each of them is presented in a vivid manner. The Jieyindian(接引殿) or Reception Hall is smaller than the others. The Qingliangtai(清凉台) or the Cooling Terrace is said to have been built under Emperor Ming Di of the Han Dynasty(汉明帝). The terrace is shaded by a one-thousand-year-old cypress and also contains the sutra library.

Notes: ①statue 雕像 ②ornate 装饰华丽的

9 南京明孝陵和中山陵

The Mingxiaoling Tomb and Sun Yatsen Mausoleum out of Nanjing City

A few miles east of the city, on the Purple Mountains(紫金山), are a number of places worth a visit. If you leave by the Zhongshan Gate(中山门) and follow a road to the left, you will arrive at the Mingxiaoling Tomb(明孝陵). The tomb can be approached by the traditional Spirit Way(神道), which starts at Dahongmen(the Great Red Gate, 大红门). Near the gate lies a tortoise bearing a stone slab. After a turn of the path to the west and a marble bridge, begins the stone carved guard of honor which has pairs of standing and crouching animals followed by pairs of officials. A gate leads into the first courtyard with a terrace in the center. On the terrace is a building holding stone slabs. In the second courtyard, the main hall stands on the old marble base. A newly rebuilt gate leads to the third courtyard and is bordered on the north by a canal spanned by a marble bridge. The entrance to the tomb is through a passage sloping up under a stone tower and leading to a terrace.

Further to the east, on the southern slope of the Purple Mountains(紫金山), is the Sun Yatsen Mausoleum. The mausoleum covers an area of 8 hectares (19.75 acres), and a flight of 392 steps leads from the triple gateway at the entrance to the memorial hall at the top. A second gateway is inscribed with the words *tian xia wei gong*(天下为公), which means "The world belongs to everyone." A path paved with white stones leads to the stele pavilion, built of white stone and covered with blue-glazed tiles. In the mausoleum a seated statue of Sun Yatsen, carved in white marble occupies the center of the hall. Behind the statue is the entrance to the vault holding the coffin, on top of which is a reclining figure of Sun Yatsen.

Notes: ①crouch 蹲伏 ②passage 走廊 ③inscribe 题写;印 ④recline 使躺下

10 部分苏州园林

Some Gardens in Suzhou

Wangshiyuan (Garden of the Master of the Nets, 网师园) was laid out in 1140 by a retired official. The garden has a main pond in the center and an artificial hill. Just over half the grounds is the residential area which lies on the East and North-originally with side rooms for sedan-chair lackeys, guest reception and living quarters. The western part is an inner garden where a courtyard contains the Spring-Rear Cottage(殿春簃) and the Master's Study(书房). This garden shows a particularly good use of walls to create a multiple perspectives and an illusion of space. Despite the size, the scale of the building is large and it does not appear cramped.

ShizilinGarden (Lion-Rock Forest, 狮子林) was designed by a monk named Tian Ru(天如) in 1350 with the help of artists and painters. This garden was originally part of a monastery and named after the place — where the abbot of the temple had lived. Many of its rocks in the area are shaped like lions, which can also explain the temple's name. The former residential buildings are to the east and north, and four lakes divided by causeways and islands occupy the greatest part of the garden.

The Zhuozhengyuan (Humble Administrator's Garden, 拙政园) was laid out in the Ming Dynasty (1522) by a retired censor. There is a five-hectare water park that includes streams, ponds, bridges and islands of bamboo. The garden seems to be built entirely on water. The Central Garden(中园)'s main feature is a large lake with two islands that give an impression of spaciousness. On the south shore is the Hall of Distant Fragrance(远香堂)which has a sober and classical design. From the hall, you can get a view of everything through lattice windows. A wall, which has a rising top and the head of a dragon at the end, separates the Central Garden from the West Garden(西园).

The Liuyuan (Tarrying Garden, 留园) was made during the Ming Dynasty, and rebuilt and renamed in 1876. The garden consists of courts and buildings in the east, woods and hills in the west, pond and hills in the center, and cottages, bamboo fences, and idyllic scenes in the north. The space is partitioned by chambers and halls, corridors, whitewashed walls, and gateways. The central garden is laid out around a pond surrounded by covered walks; exotic rocks and artificial hills attract visitors.

Notes: ①artificial 人造的 ②residential 居住 ③lackey 仆人 ④multiple 复合的;多样的 ⑤illusion 幻想 ⑥cramped 狭窄的 ⑦spacious 宽敞的 ⑧lattice 格子 ⑨idyllic 田园诗的;牧歌的 ⑩whitewash 涂白 ⑪exotic 奇特

11 九寨沟部分景点

Some Scenic Attractions in Jiuzhaigou Valley

Nuorilang Waterfall(诺日郎瀑布)is one of China's largest waterfalls. During the rainy season, the waterfall produces a tremendous sound that echoes repeatedly in the gully. As the water hits the ground, the liquid immediately splashes high up into the air in the form of fine drops. The drops form a splendid water curtain. Visitors often view a rainbow that appears in the curtain while the sun shines upon it. In autumn, the water level is lower. The waterfall presents another wonder; the hanging cliff looks like a colorful silk cloth with matching multi-colored bushes.

In the dense primeval forest(原始森林), we will find ourselves deep in the boundless expansion of trees and plants, feeling as if we had gone to Heaven. The forest has an abundance of trees that are so tall that we can hardly see the sunlight when looking up. When you walk through the forest, cool greenery rests your eyes, a gentle breeze soothes your ears, and the utter quietness refreshes your heart.

The Long Lake(长海)is known for its boundless natural beauty. The lake lies calm as clouds float and water birds frolic below across the lake. Green forests surround the lake and cast shadows on the water. This sight will make you feel that there must surely be a god.

Notes: ①waterfall 瀑布 ②tremendous 惊人的 ③echo 回声 ④liquid 液体 ⑤splendid 壮观的 ⑥boundless 无穷的 ⑦expansion 扩大 ⑧abundance 丰富 ⑨greenery 绿色植物；绿叶 ⑩refresh 使清新

家训集览
Traditional Family Instructions

夫妇之际，人道之大伦

1 The Relationship Between Husband and Wife Is the Great Moral Relationship of Human Ethics

太史公曰："夏之兴也以涂山，而桀之放也以妹喜，殷之兴也以有娀，而纣之杀也嬖妲己，周之兴也以姜螈及大任，而幽王之擒之淫于褒姒。故《易》基乾坤，《诗》始《关雎》，夫妇之际，人道之大伦也。礼之用，唯婚姻为兢兢，夫乐调而四时和，阴阳之变，万物之统也，可不慎欤？"

（北宋）司马光《家范·妻》

Sima Qian says: "The rise of the Xia Dynasty was contributed by the woman Tu Shan; Jie was forced into exile because of the immoral behavior of Mei Xi; the rise of the Shang Dynasty was due to a woman named Song; Zhou, the last king of the Shang Dynasty was killed because of a special favor he offered to his concubine Da Ji; the dynamic growth of the Zhou Dynasty was due to the assistance of Jiang Yuan and Tai Ren; King You of the Zhou Dynasty was caught because of wasting time with Bao Si. Therefore, *The Book of Changes* begins with Heaven and Earth, two divinatory symbols; *The Book of Songs* begins with ' Guan! Guan! Go the Doves.' The relationship between husband and wife is the great moral relationship of human ethics. With regards to the system of rites, marriage should be done cautiously. When music sounds harmoniously, the four seasons pass smoothly. The change of *yin* and *yang*, the negative and positive, is the key to all things. Therefore, we must behave cautiously."

2 纳少者，谓之淫

Remarrying a Young Woman Reflects a Lack of Morality

田无宇见晏子独立于闺山内，有妇人出于室者，发斑白，衣缁布之衣而无里裘。田无宇讥之曰："出于室为何者也？"晏子曰："婴之家也。"无宇曰："位为中卿，田七十万，何以老为妻？"对曰："婴闻之，去老者，谓之乱；纳少者，谓之淫。且夫见色而忘义，处富贵而失沦，谓之逆遭。婴可以有淫乱之行，不顾于伦，逆古之道乎？"

《晏子春秋·外篇》

Tian Wuyu saw Yan Zi standing alone at door when a woman walked out of the house. Her hair was gray, and her garment black and white in color. She didn't wear a fur jacket inside. Tian Wuyu said with contempt, "Who is the woman who just came out of that house?" Yan Zi answered, "She is my wife." Tian Wuyu said, "You are up in the position as the central minister. In addition, you own as many as 700,000 *mu* of fields. Why do you still have such an old wife?" Yan Zi answered, "I am told that divorcing an aged wife causes disorder; remarrying a young woman reflects a lack of morality. A man has forgotten justice once he is enchanted by a woman's charm; he has betrayed the natural human relationship in traditional Chinese ethics when he indulges in wealth and social position. How can I behave promiscuously, ignore ethics, and violate the morality and justice that have been practiced since ancient times?"

3 兄弟相处之日最长

Brothers Spend the Longest Time Together

法昭禅师偈云:"同气连枝各自荣,些些言语莫伤情。一回相见一回老,能得几时为兄弟。"词意蔼然,足以启人友于之爱。然予尝谓人伦有五,而兄弟相处之日最长。君臣之遇合,朋友之会聚,久速固难必也。父之生子,妻之配夫,其时早者皆以二十岁为率。惟兄弟或一二年,或三四年,相继而生,自竹马游戏,以至鲐背鹤发,其相与周旋,多者至七八十年之久。若恩意浃洽,猜间不生,其乐岂有涯哉。近时有周益公,以太傅退休,其兄乘成先生,以将作监丞退休,年皆八十,诗酒相娱者终其身。章泉赵昌甫兄弟,亦俱隐于玉山之上,苍颜华发,相从于泉石之间,皆年近九十,真人间至乐事,亦人间希有之事也。

(清)张英《聪训斋语》

Fa Zhao, a Zen Buddhist master said, "Of the same breath and branches, each has his own development, and it is unnecessary to plunge into distress only because of a few words. We get older each time we meet with each other, and the time spent with brothers is especially valuable." What Fa Zhao said is so heart-stirring that it inspires people to value the feelings among brothers. As you know, there are five human relations, and the time which brothers spend being together is the longest. The monarch and his subjects may get along well, and friends often meet with one another, but it is very difficult to prolong their relationships. Parents should be at least 20 years old before they give birth to and bring up children. The same goes to the wife and her husband when they get married. However, brothers are born one by one, and one is older by one, two, three, or four years than another. As children, they play the bamboo stick-horse game and live together until they are humpbacked and their hair is grey. The longest time that they spend being together may be seventy or eighty years. Their happiness will be boundless if they get along well all the time and no misunderstanding occurs between them. In recent times, there was a man called Zhou Yigong. He retired as a senior Crown prince teacher. Mr. Cheng Cheng was his elder brother who retired as an assistant supervisal officer. They were both over 80 years old, and throughout their life, writing poems and drinking wine gave them much pleasure. Zhang Quan and Zhao Changfu are brothers who live together on Mt. Yushan. They are almost 90 years old, and their face is wrinkled and hair grey. In spite of that, they take strolls together along streams and on the mountain. How blissful and natural it is to live such a life!

4 四海皆兄弟

All Within the Four Seas are Brothers

汝辈稚小家贫，每役柴水之劳，何时可免？念之在心,若何可言?然你等虽不同生,当思四海皆兄弟之义。鲍叔管仲,分财无猜;归生伍举,班荆道旧。遂能以败为成,因丧立功。他人尚尔,况同父之人哉?颍川韩元长,汉末名士。身处卿佐,八十而终。兄弟同居,至于没齿。济北氾稚春,晋时操行人也。七世同财,家人无怨色。《诗》曰:“高山仰止,景行行止。”虽不能尔,至心尚之。汝其慎哉!吾复何言。

(晋)陶渊明《陶渊明集》

You are young, and your family is in poverty. When can we rest from working hard, gathering firewood, and carrying water? I often think about this matter, but what can I say? Though you are half brothers, you should ponder what Confucius said, "All within the Four Seas are brothers." In ancient times, no suspicions occurred between Bao Shu and Guan Zhong when they shared out their property. Gui Sheng and Wu Ju happened to meet each other when they were in difficulty; they unfolded bramble plants on the ground where they sat, chatting about the good old days. Guan Zhong eventually became a prime minister despite once being a prisoner; he helped Duke Heng of the Qi State settle his rule. Wu Ju returned from exile to the Chu state to accomplish great deeds. Friends can do all this, let alone half brothers. Towards the end of the Han Dynasty, Han Yuanchang of Yingchuan Prefecture was a celebrated scholar who was in charge of the Imperial Reception Department. During his life time, he lived together with his brothers until he passed away at the age of 80. In the Jin Dynasty, Si Zhichun of the Jibei state was a person with respectable morality. All his family members throughout seven generations did not divide up the family property and wealth, and they had no complaints at all. *The Book of Songs* says, "Look up to the lofty mountain and walk on the bright main road." Although you can't be like them, you should sincerely take them as models. You must be careful. What else can I say then?

5 奔死免父，孝也

It Is Filial Piety if by Returning I Will Exempt Our Father from Death

无极曰："奢之子材，若在吴，必忧楚国，盍以免其父召之。彼仁，必来。不然，将为患。"王使召之，曰："来，吾免而父。"棠君尚谓其弟员曰："尔适吴，我将归死。吾知不逮，我能死，尔能报。闻免父之命，不可以莫之奔也；亲戚为戮，不可以莫之报也。奔死免父，孝也；度功而行，仁也；择任而往，知也；知死不辟，勇也。父不可弃，名不可废，尔其勉之！相从为愈。"伍尚归。奢闻员不来，曰："楚君大夫其旰食乎!”楚人皆杀之。

《左传·昭公二十年》

Fei Wuji said, “Wu She’s sons are of great ability and talent. If they stay in the state of Wu, it will make the State of Chu uneasy. Why don’t we offer their father an official pardon to get them back? Their kind-heartedness will enable them to come back. Otherwise, it will bring disasters to the State of Chu.” So the king of Chu had someone bring them back, saying, “Come back. I will grant amnesty to your father.” Wu Shang, the eldest son of *she*, a senior official of the Tang County, said to his little brother Yuan, “You go to the State of Wu, and I plan to go back to the State of Chu and die there. My ability and talent are not as extraordinary as yours. I can die for our father and you can take revenge. We must return on hearing our return might exempt our father from death; we must have revenge for our family members who have been killed. It is a filial piety to return and be killed in the hope of saving our father; it is benevolent to take action in line with virtue; it is wise to assign tasks based on ability; it is brave that we won’t dodge death even if we are fully aware of death lying ahead. We can’t abandon our father, nor do we give up our reputation. So you’d better strive to take revenge on your own and this is much better than both of us die.”

On hearing that Yuan wouldn't come back, *She* said, "Perhaps the Chu monarch and senior officials will not have a meal on time." They were all killed by the people from the State of Chu.

6 不孝者有五

The Five Traits Unfit for Sons

孟子曰:"世俗所谓不孝者五,惰其四支,不顾父母之养,一不孝也;博弈好饮酒,不顾父母之养,二不孝也;好货财,私妻子,不顾父母之养,三不孝也;从耳目之欲,以为父母戮,四不孝也;好勇斗狠,以危父母,五不孝也。章子有一于是乎?夫章子,子父责善而不相遇也。责善,朋友之道也;父子责善,贼恩之大者。夫章子,岂不欲有夫妻子母之属哉?为得罪于父,不得近,出妻屏子,终身不养焉。其设心以为不若是,是则罪之大者,是则章子而已矣。"

《孟子·离娄下》

Mencius says, "There are five traits unfit for sons. The first trait is the son is lazy, ignoring his parents' livelihood. The second trait is the son likes playing chess and drinking, ignoring his parents' livelihood. The third trait is the son loves wealth and shows undue favor to his wife and children, ignoring his parents' livelihood. The forth trait is the son indulges himself and thus humiliates his parents. The fifth trait is the son acts aggressively and threatens his parents' safety. Is Zhang Zi involved with any of these five unfilial behaviors? Zhang Zi did nothing but act righteously to reproach his father to such an extent as to spoil the relation between his father and himself. Using righteousness to reproach is accepted among friends. However, this practice hurts the feelings most if it is used between the father and the son. Wouldn't Zhang Zi have no desire to reunite with his wife and sons? Because he displeased his father, and failed to be on good terms with him again, he therefore drove out his wife, became estranged from his sons and never let them serve him any more in his life. He thought that it would be his greatest mistake if he hadn't done this way. This is the behavior conducted by Zhang Zi in relations with other people."

7 骨肉之亲

The Flesh and Blood Relationship

周有申喜者，亡其母，闻乞人歌于门下而悲之，动于颜色，谓门者内乞人之歌者，自觉而问焉，曰："何故而乞？"与之语，盖其母也。故父母之于子也，子之于父母也，一体而两分，同气而异息。若草莽之有华实也，若树木之有根心也。虽异处而相通，隐志相及，痛疾相救，忧思相感，生则相欢，死则相哀，此之谓骨肉之亲。神出于忠而应乎心，两精相得，岂待言哉？

《吕氏春秋·季秋纪第九》

In the Zhou State was a man whose name was Shen Xi who had lost touch with his mother for a long time. One day he heard a beggar singing in front of his entrance gate. The songs grieved Shen Xi. He told his gate-keeper to let the beggar come in. Shen Xi received her in person, asking, "Why are you a beggar?" While talking, Shen Xi discovered that the beggar was his mother. Parents and children are one although they are separated into two parts. Parents and children share the same essence and vitality although they breathe differently, like wild grass fields where flowers and fruits grow; it is much like trees that have the same roots. They are mutually interlinked although they are in different places; their high hopes concern everyone; when someone is ill, all the other family members aid; when someone is unhappy, and the others comfort; while living, everyone is happy; when someone passes away, the others feel sorrowful. This is called the family relation. This natural instinct grows out of complete sincerity. When the mutual spirit is obtained, is it necessary to describe it with language?

8 为子之道
The Way of a Son

二十一年，骊姬谓太子曰："君梦见齐姜，太子速祭曲沃，归釐于君。"太子于是祭其母齐姜于曲沃，上其荐胙于献公。献公时出猎，置胙于宫中。骊姬使人置毒药胙中。居二日，献公从猎来还，宰人上胙献公，献公欲飨之。骊姬从旁止之，曰："胙所从来远，宜试之。"祭地，地坟；与犬，犬死；与小臣，小臣死。骊姬泣曰："太子何忍也！其父而欲弑代之，况他人乎？且君老矣，旦暮之人，曾不能待而欲弑之！"谓献公曰："太子所以然者，不过以妾及奚齐之故。妾愿子母辟之他国，若早自杀，毋徒使母子为太子所鱼肉也。始君欲废之，妾犹恨之；至于今，妾殊自失于此。"太子闻之，奔新城。献公怒，乃诛其傅杜原款。或谓太子曰："为此药者乃骊姬也，太子何不自辞明之？"太子曰："吾君老矣，非骊姬，寝不安，食不甘。即辞之，君且怒之。不可。"或谓太子曰："可奔他国。"太子曰："被此恶名以出，人谁内我？我自杀耳。"十二月戊申，申生自杀于新城。

《史记·晋世家》

In 656 BC King Xian's concubine Li Ji said to the

Crown prince, "The king saw Qi Jiang in his dream. You must go as soon as possible to Quwo to offer sacrifices and then present to the king the meat left after the sacrificial services." So the Crown prince offered sacrifices to Qi Jiang, his mother in Quwo, and he presented to King Xian the meat used for the sacrificial services. Right at that moment, King Xian had gone out hunting. So he placed the meat in the king's palace. Li Ji had someone put poison in the meat. The meat remained in the palace for two days before King Xian returned from his hunting. The cook presented the sacrificial meat, and King Xian was about to eat. Li Ji was by his side. She stopped him, saying, "The sacrificial meat came from a remote place. We should test it." They sacrificed the meat the ground. The ground bulged and formed the shape of a tomb. Then they gave the meat to a dog. The dog ate it and died. They gave it to a servant. The servant ate it and died. Li Ji cried, saying, "The Crown prince is very cruel. He wants to kill his father and take his place, let alone others. Moreover, you are getting old. He should respectfully serve the old man. Nevertheless, he attempts to kill you." Li Ji said to King Xian, "The Crown prince did this only because of Xi Qi and me. My son and I would rather find shelter in other states, or commit suicide more quickly than merely be victimized by the Crown prince. Initially you were thinking to move him away from the Crown prince status. At that time, I still felt sorry for him. Well, his current behavior made me regret not getting rid of him at that time." The Crown prince escaped to the Xin City upon hearing of the plot to kill him. King Xian got angry and ordered someone to kill Du Yuankuan, the Crown prince's teacher. Someone said to the Crown prince, "It was Li Ji who put poison in the meat. Why didn't you defend yourself and clarify the case?" The Crown prince said, "My father king is getting old. He can't sleep and eat well without Li Ji. My father king will get angry even if I clarify this case. No, I can't do it." Another person said to the Crown prince, "You can flee to other states." The Crown prince said, "Who dares to take me in when I flee and bear a bad name. I will commit suicide." In December, the Crown prince committed suicide in Xin City.

9 事事立个章程

Set Up Rules for Everything

夫人率儿妇辈在家,须事事立个一定的章程。居官不过偶然之事,居家乃长久之计,能从勤俭耕读上做出好规模,虽一旦罢官尚不失为兴旺气象。若贪图衙门之热闹,不立家乡之基业,则罢官之后便觉气象萧索。凡有盛必有衰,不可不预为之计。望夫人教训儿孙妇女,常常作家中无官之想,时时有谦恭省俭之意,则福泽悠久,余心大慰矣。

曾国藩《曾国藩全集·家书·致欧阳夫人》

My dear wife, while you stay at home, take care of our children and grandchildren. You should set up rules for everything. Being a government official only lasts for a while, but residence at home is permanent. Therefore, our family must prosper by means of hardwork, thrift, farming and schooling. so that if I am dismissed from office, our family can yet continue to be prosperous. If one seeks bustle and excitement in government offices, ignoring his family fundamental affairs in his hometown, he will experience a deserted and lonely atmosphere at home as soon as he is dismissed from office. Where there is prosperity, there is decline. We cannot but take it into account in advance. I wish you to educate children, grandchildren, and women at home to be modest and thrifty, and instill in them the idea that in our family there is no governmental official. In this way, a good fortune and comfort may last a long time, and I will also feel greatly relieved.

10 治家之法

Way of Household Management

初一日接尔十六日禀,澄叔已移寓新居,则黄金堂老宅,尔为一家之主矣。昔吾祖星冈公最讲求治家之法:第一起早;第二打扫洁净;第三诚修祭祀;第四善待亲族邻里,凡亲族邻里来家,无不恭敬款接,有急必周济之,有讼必排解之,有喜必庆贺之,有疾必问,有丧必吊。此四事之外,于读书种菜等事,尤为刻刻留心。故余近写家信,常常提及书蔬鱼猪,四端者,盖祖父相传之家法也。尔现读书无暇,此八事纵不能一一亲自经理,而不可不识得此意,请朱运四先生细心经理,八者缺一不可。其诚修祭祀一端,则必须尔母随时留心。凡器皿第一好者,留作祭祀之用。饮食第一等好者,亦备祭祀之需。凡人家不讲祭祀,纵然兴旺,亦不久长,至要,至要!

曾国藩《曾国藩全集·家书·谕纪泽》

On the first day of this month, I received your letter written on February 16 which said that Uncle Cheng has moved to the new residence and so you are now the head of the Huang Jin Tang old house. Xinggang Gong, my late grandfather, took particular care of the household management. He required everyone get up early, sweep and clean, offer respectful sacrifices, and treat relatives and neighbors well. You should respectfully host relatives or neighbors whenever they come and visit; give financial help to those who are in urgent need or difficulty; go and mediate a dispute whenever it occurs; go and congratulate a joyous event whenever it takes place; send regards to those who are sick; go to all funeral ceremonies. Apart from these four matters, you have to pay constant attention to reading and growing vegetables. In my recent letters to our family, I often mention four things: reading, growing vegetables, and raising fish and pigs. These things come from our family discipline that has been passed down from the grandfather. You are now in school, and have no free time. Even if you can't handle these eight things all in person, you should still understand their significance. Please ask Mr. Zhu Yunsi to manage these things with care. None of the eight things should be spared. As for sacrificial services, you must remind your mother that she should pay constant attention to handling them in a pious and respectful way. All the best utensils should be reserved for sacrificial services. The best food and drinks should be prepared also for the same purpose. If a family does not take much care of sacrificial services, its prosperity can't last a long time even if it may bloom for a short while. This is the most important!

11 节俭持家
Economical Housekeeping

我家入魏之始,即为上客。自尔至今,二千石方伯不绝,禄恤甚多。于亲姻知故吉凶之际,必厚加赠襚,来往宾僚,必以酒肉饮食,故六姻朋友无憾焉。国家初,丈夫好服彩色。吾虽不记上谷翁时事,然记清河翁时服饰。恒见翁着布衣韦带,常自约敕诸父曰:"汝等后世若富贵于今日者,慎勿积金一斤,彩帛百匹已上,用为富也。"不听兴生求利,又不听与势家作婚姻。至吾兄弟,不能遵奉。今汝等服乘渐华好,吾是以知恭俭之德,渐不如上也。……吾今日不为贫贱,然居住舍宅,不作庄丽华饰者,正虑汝等后世不贤,不能保守之,将为势家所夺。

(唐)李延寿《北史·杨椿传》

Since my family entered the State of Wei, each generation enjoys a high-ranking official status and receives a favorable official salary. Our family always presents full and rich gifts to our relatives and old friends when they have joyous events or funerals. Meanwhile we usually host guests with good food and drinks when they visit us so that our relatives and friends have nothing to complain. During the early period of the state, men from rich families preferred wearing splendid clothes. At that time, my grandfather worked as prefecture chief in Qinghe. He wore cloth gowns and a cowskin belt. He often admonished our elder family members by saying, "If you become wealthier and have a higher social position than you have now, you should never consider yourself rich, and in your family savings gold should not exceed 0.5 kilograms in weight and color silks should not be more than 100 rolls." You mustn't do commercial business or lend money at high interest rate, and you should not try to join an aristocratic family through marriage. Even we generation fail to abide by these rules. Now your clothes, carriages, and horses appear trendy and costly. This shows the virtue of modesty and thrift is not as strong as before... My family is no longer poor now, but we do not desire to buy a luxurious and splendid residence. This is because I am afraid that our descendants won't be virtuous and will fall prey to aristocratic families.

12 勤劳为本

Industry Is the Foundation

公父文伯退朝,朝其母,其母方绩。文伯曰:"以歜之家而主犹绩,惧忓季孙之怒也,其以歜为不能事主乎!"其母叹曰:"鲁其亡乎!使僮子备官而未之闻耶？居，吾语汝。昔圣王之处民也，择瘠土而处之，劳其民而用之，故长王天下。夫民劳则思，思则善心生；逸则淫，淫则忘善，忘善则恶心生。沃土之民不材，逸也；瘠土之民莫不向义，劳也。”

《国语·鲁语》

After Duke Father Wen Bo returned from the court, he paid a formal visit to his mother who was then making cord by twisting cord fibers between her palms. Wen Bo said, "In such as a family like mine, you have to twist cord fibers by hand, fearing Ji Sun's fury. Probably this is because I did not look after you properly!"

His mother sighed by saying: "The State of Lu will probably meet its doom! It allows children to work as officials, and this has never been heard of before. Have a seat and let me speak to you. In the past, a virtuous king arranged ordinary people to live on the deficient land, making them attentively engaged in working. In this way, his state could last a long time. If ordinary people keep working, it impels them to think of how to be frugal; then mercifulness grows out of this thinking. An easy life gives rise to scandalous behavior; scandalous behavior makes people forget to be merciful; evil intention rises once mercy is forgotten. Ordinary people living on the fertile land are difficult to be useful persons because they lead an easy life; ordinary people living on the barren land all have a sense of justice because they are hard working."

13 勤督训子女

Constantly Educate Children

吾见世间,无教而有爱,每不能然。饮食运为,恣其所欲。宜诫翻奖,应诃反笑。至有识知,谓法当尔。骄慢已习,方复制之,捶挞至死而无威,忿怒日隆而增怨,逮于成长,终为败德。孔子云:"少成若天性,习惯如自然",是也。俗谚曰:"教妇初来,教儿婴孩"。诚哉斯语!凡人不能教子女者,亦非欲陷其罪恶,但重于诃怒,伤其颜色,不忍楚挞惨其肌肤耳。当以疾病为谕,安得不用汤药针艾救之哉?又宜思勤督训者,可愿苛虐于骨肉乎?诚不得已也。

(北齐)颜之推《颜氏家训·教子》

Some parents in the world, I find, don't educate their children. Instead they spoil them. Usually these parents don't see any problem with what they do. They allow their children to indulge in any food, drinks, lodging, and travel. When parents ought to give a warning to their children, they give encouragement instead; when it is time to reprimand them, they praise them. They think that their children will naturally abide by laws this way when they become sensible. Well, at that moment, their arrogant habit has already been formed. By then, parents come to prevent their children's bad habit, but their authority does not work even if they beat their children half-dead. Anger increases day by day, and complaints also rise thereupon. As their children grow to manhood, their morals are lost at last. Confucius says, "A habit formed in childhood is much like a natural instinct; a habit formed throughout a long period is just like second nature." It is truly so. As the saying goes, "One should begin to educate his wife when she gets married and moves into his household; one should begin to educate children since their baby period." These words sound very true. Those who are not good at educating their children have no desire at all to let children move towards crimes. They simply don't want to reprimand their children loudly and make them lose face. Moreover, they hate to whip their children for fear that it would injury their skin. Let's take an illness as an example. Who can cure a disease without a necessary medical prescription, acupuncture, and moxibustion? Do you think those parents, who diligently supervise and educate their children, are willing to maltreat their own flesh and blood? There is really no other alternative.

14 爱之当教之

Those Who Love Their Children Should Educate Them

石蜡谏卫庄公曰:"臣闻爱子,教之以义方,弗纳于邪,骄奢淫泆,所自邪也,四者之来,宠禄过也。"自古知爱子不知教,使至于危辱乱亡者,可胜数哉?夫爱之当教之使成人,爱之而使陷于危辱乱亡,乌在其所爱子也。人之爱其子者,多曰儿幼未有知耳,俟其长而教之,是犹养恶木之萌芽,曰:俟其合抱而伐之,其用力顾不多哉?又如开笼放鸟而捕之,解缰放马而逐之,曷若勿纵勿解之为易也。

(北宋)司马光《家范》

Shi La advised King Zhuang of the Wei State, "I am told that parents who love their son should teach him morality and justice so that he will not to go onto evil ways. Arrogance, gluttony, debauchery and an idle life are the causes that induce a person to follow evil ways. These four evils come into being only because of excessive fondness." Parents have always loved their children since ancient times, but they don't know how to educate them. This results in danger or shame for their children; or they may cause chaos to society, which leads to the loss of their lives. Can we count one by one the number of the people like this? Those who love their children should educate them to grow up healthy and sound. How can one cherish his children if parents' love leads them into a dangerous and unhealthy situation and end up rebelling against society and possibly losing their lives? This totally leads children into a trap. Those who love their children often say that their children are still young and not sensible so that they won't start educating them until they grow up. If we do this way, it is much like a bad tree. When it is still a seedling, one says, We won't cut it down until it grows up so big that one can get one's arm around. Wouldn't it take much more efforts to bring it down by then? It is like a man who opens his birdcage and lets his bird fly away, and then he goes to catch it back. It is like a man unties his horse's reins and sets the horse free, and then he goes to chase it. In fact, it is better not to set the bird free and not to untie the reins. In this way, it will be much easier.

15 伯俞有过

Bo Yu Makes a Mistake

伯俞有过,其母笞之,泣,其母曰:“他日笞子,未尝见泣,今泣何也?”对曰:“他日俞得罪,笞尝痛。今母之力衰,不能使痛,是以泣也。”故曰,父母怒之,不作于意,不见于色,深受其罪,使可哀怜,上也;父母怒之,不作于意,不见于色,其次也;父母怒之,作于意,见于色,下也。

(西汉)刘向《说苑·建本》

One day when Bo Yu made a mistake, his mother whipped him, and so he wept. His mother asked, “You didn’t weep when I whipped you before. Why are you weeping now?” Bo Yu answered, “As I offended you before and you whipped me, your whipping was very painful. I am weeping today because mother’s physical strength is weaker now so that your whipping can’t hurt me.” Therefore, when parents get angry, children mustn’t care about that or reveal their emotions. Instead the best way is to endure the punishment and appear pitiful. When parents get angry, children neither care about that nor reveal on facial expression what they feel. This is the second best plan. When parents get angry, children care about that and reveal on facial expression what they feel. This is the most inadvisable.

16 君子之道,修身为上

The Gentleman's Way Is to Cultivate His Moral Character

昔杨介夫谓其子用修曰:"尔有一事不如我,尔知之乎?"曰:"大人为相,位冠群臣之上,此慎之所不如也。"曰:"非也。"曰:"大人为相,三归而为乡人创大利三焉,此慎之所不如也。"曰:"非也。"曰:"天子南征,大人居守,政事取决,如伊尹、周公之摄,此慎之所不如也。"曰:"非也。""敢问慎之所不如者何事?"杨公笑曰:"尔子不如我子也。"

唐子曰:"鄙哉!杨公之语其子也。多其子之为状元,而又有望于其孙,请为更之。谓其子曰:'慎乎,尔知尔之不如我乎?君子之道,修身为上,文学次之,富贵为下。苟能修身,不愧于古之人,虽终身为布衣,其贵于宰相也远矣。苟能修身,不愧于古之人,虽老于青衿,其荣于状元也远矣。我之教子,仅得其次;尔之教子,且不如我,我复何望哉!'"

(清)唐甄《潜书·诲子》

Yang Jiefu once said to his son Yong Xiu, "You are not as good as me in one respect. Do you know what that respect is?" Yong Xiu said, "You work as the prime minister, and your position is superior to all government officials. I am not as good as you in this respect." Yang Jiefu answered, "No." Yong Xiu said, "As the prime minister, you returned to your hometown three times and did three good things for your hometown. I am not as good as you in this respect." Yang Jiefu said again, "No." Yong Xiu said, "Once the emperor went away for a war expedition in the south, and you were appointed to stay behind in the capital, taking care of all kinds of governmental affairs. You acted as regent much like Yi Yi and Zhou Gong. I am not as good as you in this respect." Yang Jiefu said, "No." Yong Xiu said, "Could I ask in which respect I am not as good as you?" Yang Jiefu said with a smile, "Your sons are not as good as my sons."

Tang Zi says, "What Yang Jiefu said sounds really superficial! It is because most of his sons have won the number-one-scholar title in the imperial examinations. Therefore, he is expecting his grandsons to follow suit. Please let me correct his words by saying to his son, 'Yong Xiu, do you know why you are not as good as me? The gentleman's way is to cultivate his moral character first, take literature second, and seek wealth and social position at last. Suppose that he is able to cultivate his moral character and he won't feel qualms before the ancients, he will be more highly privileged than the prime minister even though he remains as an ordinary person. Suppose that he is able to cultivate his moral character and he won't feel qualms before the ancients, he will be more honorable than number-one-scholar title winners even though he remains all his life in non-governmental circles. I teach my sons who only have succeeded in the gentleman's second pursuit. You teach your sons, but you are not as good as me, so I have no hope any more!'"

17 人需要立志

People Need to Make a Resolution

吾非徒望尔辈但取青紫，荣身肥家，如世俗所尚，以夸市井小儿。尔辈须以仁礼存心，以孝弟为本，以圣贤自期。务在光前裕后，斯可矣。吾惟幼而失学无行，无师友之助，迨今中年，未有所成，尔辈当鉴吾既往，及时勉力，毋又以贻他日之悔，如吾今日也。习俗移人，如油渍面，虽贤者不免；况尔曹初学小子，能无溺乎？惟痛惩深创，乃为善变。昔人云，"脱去凡近，以游高明。"此言良足以警，小子识之！吾尝有《立志说》与尔十叔，尔辈可从抄录一通，置之几间，时一省览，亦足以发。方虽传于庸医，药可疗夫真病。尔曹勿谓尔伯父只寻常人尔，其言未必足法；又勿谓其言似有理，亦只是一场迂阔之谈，非我辈急务；苟如是，吾未如之何矣。

（明）王守仁《王阳明全集·赣州书示四侄正思等》

I do not hope that you study only to secure an official position and to make yourselves glorious and build up a family fortune so as to show off among ordinary people. You should bear in mind all the time benevolence and courtesy, take filial piety very seriously, and take the sages as models. Anyhow, it will be all right so long as you can win honor for predecessors and bring benefit to future generations. In my childhood, I discontinued my schooling, and I had misbehavior; there was no help from teachers and friends. Therefore, when I am in middle age now, I haven't had any achievement yet. You should learn my lesson and study hard all the time. Otherwise in the future you will feel sorry as I do today. Customs change people as oil sludge stains the face. Sometimes even a wise and able person can't be exempt from its influence, let alone you young people who just begin your schooling. Only when you earnestly and deeply reform your misdeeds, will you wake up and change for the better.

The ancient says, "Break away from ordinary and superficial persons and learn from wise men." What is said is good enough to be an epigram, and you should remember it. I wrote an essay called *On Making a Resolution*, and I gave it to your tenth uncle. You can copy it, put it on your desk and read it often. This essay will inspire you to some extent. Although the prescription is handed down by a quack physician, the medicine can cure the real sickness. Dont't think what I said is unnecessary to follow because I am an ordinary person. Nor should you think although what I said sounds reasonable, but impractical and not an urgent task for you to do. If you really do think like this, I don't know what is to be done.

18 求君子之道

Seek the Way of a Gentleman

今我告尔以老,归尔以事,将闲居以安性,覃思以终业。自非拜国君之命,问族亲之忧,展敬坟墓,观省野物,胡尝扶杖出门乎!家事大小,汝一承之。咨尔茕茕一夫,曾无同生相依。其勖求君子之道,研钻勿替,敬慎威仪,以近有德。显誉成于僚友,德行立于己志。若致声称,亦有荣于所生。可不深念邪,可不深念邪!

(南朝·宋)范晔《后汉书·郑玄传》

I am getting old now. I entrust you with my family business so that I will lead a quiet life, nourish my temperament, and think profoundly in order to complete my book. I wouldn't go out on my walking stick, unless for commission authorized by the emperor, to inquire about the major issues of the relatives, offer sacrifices to mausoleums, and watch the growth of crops. So you are totally responsible to handle family affairs, no matter whether these are major issues or trivial things. Well, you are alone without brothers and sisters to support you. However, you should seek principles of how persons with moral integrity behave in relation with other people. In addition, you should continue your academic research work and carefully keep solemn behavior in an attempt to have morality and dignity. Compliments come from colleagues and friends, but good morality will be established by one's own pursuit. If I could receive a good reputation presented by others, I would feel glorious all my life. You must remember all this well!

19 太宗谓皇属

Taizong's Words to His Imperial Family Members

太宗尝谓皇属曰:"朕即位十三年矣,外绝游观之乐,内却声色之娱。汝等生于富贵,长自深宫。夫帝子亲王,先须克己,每著一衣,则悯蚕妇;每餐一食,则念耕夫。至于听断之间,勿先恣其喜怒。朕每亲临庶政，岂敢惮于焦劳。汝等勿鄙人短，勿恃己长，乃可永久富贵，以保终吉，先贤有言：逆吾者是吾师，顺吾者是吾贼。不可不察也。”

（唐）李世民《戒皇属》

Taizong, one of the Tang emperors, once said to his imperial family members, "I have been emperor for 13 years. Throughout this period, I have never taken a pleasure trip outside the imperial palace, and I have resisted songs, dances, and woman's charm inside the palace. You were born into wealthy and high-status families and grew up within the palace. As the emperor's children and princes, you should be strict with yourselves first. Each time when you wear a garment, you should show sympathy for hardworking women who raise silkworms; each time when you eat a meal, you should think of farmers who plow hard in the fields. As for dealing with legal cases, you cannot act recklessly according to your moods. I always handle in person various kinds of governmental affairs, and I have never dared to shy away from this exhausting work. You cannot look down upon other people's shortcomings, nor can you rely on your own strong points. In this way, the wealth and high social positions shall last for a long time, and good fortune remains all your life. The sage of the past says, 'Those who dare to rake up my faults are my teachers; those who flatter me are thieves.' You must be wary of this ."

20 知足常乐

Contentment Brings Happiness

世欺不识字,我忝攻文笔。世欺不得官,我忝居班秩。人老多病苦。我今幸无疾。人老多忧累,我今婚嫁毕。心安不移转,身泰无牵率。所以十年来,形神闲且逸。况当垂老岁,所要无多物。一裘暖过冬,一饭饱终日。勿言舍宅小,不过寝一室。何用鞍马多,不能骑两匹。如我优幸身,人中十有七。如我知足心,人中百无一。傍观愚亦见,当己贤多失。不敢论他人,狂言示诸侄。

(唐)白居易《白香山集》

This world always humiliates the illiterate so I have made great efforts to improve my writing ability. This world always humiliates those who aren't officials so I have exerted myself to obtain an official position. When people get old, sickness follows them. Fortunately now I am healthy. When people get old, more worries follow them, but I have completed marital affairs of my children. My heart is quiet and I am in good shape, and free from worry. Therefore, in the past ten years, I have always been at leisure physically and spiritually. Moreover, as people get older, they need fewer things. One fur coat may keep me warm throughout the winter; one full meal may satisfy a whole day. Don't say that my house is too small, for one room is big enough for me to sleep in. What is the point in having so many horses and saddles? I can't ride two horses at the same time. Out of ten people, there are seven who are lucky and happy like me, but out of 100 people no one rests content like me. An onlooker can see it clearly even if he is unwise. However, those who are closely involved may have some faults even though they are able and virtuous. I do not dare to comment on others. This is just my crazy talk to my nephews.

古代寓言
Popular Chinese Fables

1 杞人忧天

Unnecessary Worry

杞国有人忧天地崩坠,身亡所寄,废寝食者。又有忧彼之所忧者,因往晓之,曰:"天,积气耳,亡处亡气。若屈伸呼吸,终日在天中行止,奈何忧崩坠乎?"其人曰:"天果积气,日月星宿,不当坠耶?"晓之者曰:"日月星宿,亦积气中之有光耀者,只使坠,亦不能有所中伤。"其人曰:"奈地坏何?"晓者曰:"地,积块耳,充塞四虚,亡处亡块。若躇步跐蹈,终日在地上行止,奈何忧其坏?"其人舍然大喜,晓之者亦舍然大喜。

——《列子·天端》

A man in the state of Qi frequently feared that one day the sky would fall down and the earth collapse, and he wouldn't have a place to shelter. He was so worried that he could not eat or sleep well. Another man learned about his fear and worried about him. He went to help the man from the Qi get rid of his fear.

He said to the man, "The sky is only air mass and is present everywhere. All day you move around in the air bending, stretching, inhaling and exhaling. Why are you worried that the sky might fall?"

"If the sky is a mass of air," said the man from the Qi, "the sun, the moon and the stars will surely fall down, won't they?"

The other man replied, "The sun, the moon and the stars are merely shiny air masses. If they did fall, they wouldn't hurt anyone. "

Then the man of the Qi asked, "What should I do if the earth collapses?"

"The earth is a mass of dust and soil. There is no place that isn't soil and dust. As you move about on the earth all day stepping and jumping, why do you worry about the earth collapsing?"

A smile of relief grew on the face of the man from the Qi. The other man was happy to see the smile. Both men relaxed.

2 狐假虎威

The Fox Borrows the Tiger's Terror

虎求百兽而食之,得狐。狐曰:"子无敢食我也!

天帝使我长百兽,今子食我,是逆天帝命也。子以我为不信,吾为子先行,子随我后,观百兽之见我而敢不走乎?”虎以为然,故遂与之行。兽见之皆走。虎不知兽畏己而走也,以为畏狐也。

——《战国策·楚策一》

Tigers always try to catch any preys. One day a tiger caught a fox.

"You dare not eat me," said the fox. "The emperor of Heaven has appointed me king of all the beasts. If you eat me, you will be disobeying the emperor's order. If you don't believe me, I can walk ahead and you follow close behind. In this way, we will see whether the beasts will flee or not at the sight of me."

The tiger thought what the fox said made sense, so he followed the fox. When the other beasts saw them, they fled for their lives. The tiger didn't know the real reason why all the beasts ran away was that they were afraid of him. Instead he thought that the beasts were afraid of the fox.

3 东施效颦

Dong Shi Imitates Eyebrows Knitting

西施病心而颦其里,其里之丑人见之而美之,归亦捧心而颦其里。其里之富人见之，坚闭门而不出；贫人见之，挈妻子而去之走。彼知颦美，而不知颦之所以美。

——《庄子·天运》

Xi Shi was well-known for her extreme beauty. Once Xi Shi walked through her village, knitting her eyebrows and with her hands on her chest because she had pains in her heart.

An ugly woman in the neighborhood saw Xi Shi walking through the village with her hands on her heart. She thought the gesture was graceful. So the ugly woman returned home and she imitated Xi Shi. When she walked in the village, she also knitted her eyebrows and put her hands on her chest. Seeing the ugly woman's movement, the rich people shut their doors and refused to come out while the poor people gathered up their families and quickly ran away.

The ugly woman thought the eyebrow knitting was graceful, but she didn't know why.

4 叶公好龙

Insincere Love of Dragons

叶公子高好龙，钩以写龙，凿以写龙，屋室雕文以写龙。于是天龙闻而下之,窥头于牖,施尾于堂。叶公见之,弃而还走,失其魂魄,五色无主。是叶公非好龙也,好夫似龙而非龙者也。

——《新序·杂事第五》

Lord Ye, whose name was Zi Gao, loved dragons so much that he had them painted on his belts and his wine containers. The roof beams, doors, windows and both inside and outside of his house were painted and carved with dragons.

The dragon in Heaven heard of this and descended to visit Lord Ye. When the dragons arrived at Lord Ye's home, it popped its head in at the window and swayed its tail into Lord Ye's house hall.

At the sight of the dragon, Lord Ye immediately turned and fled. The real dragon scared him out of his wits and he lost all the color in his face.

Lord Ye didn't truly love dragons. He loved something that looked like a dragon but actually wasn't a real dragon.

5 自相矛盾

Self Contradiction

楚人有鬻楯与矛者,誉之曰:"吾楯之坚,莫能陷也。"又誉其矛曰:"吾矛之利,于物无不陷也。"或曰:"以子之矛陷子之楯,何如?"其人弗能应也。夫不可陷之楯与无不陷之矛,不可同世而立。

——《韩非子·难一》

A man of the state of Chu was selling his spear and shield. He boasted his shield by saying, "My shield is the strongest. Nothing can pierce through it." Then he boasted his spear by saying, "My spear is very sharp. There is nothing it can't pierce through."

Someone said, "What will happen if you use your spear to pierce your own shield?"

The salesman could not answer because an impenetrable shield couldn't coexist with a spear which could pierce through anything.

6 守株待兔

Waiting by a Tree Stump for More Rabbits to Bump into the Tree

宋人有耕田者,田中有株,兔走,触株折颈而死。因释其耒而守株,冀复得兔。兔不可复得,而身为宋国笑。

——《韩非子·五蠹》

One day, a farmer in the state of Song was working in the field, where there was a tree stump. It was there that a rabbit ran very fast and accidentally bumped itself against the tree stump. It broke his neck and died there. The farmer laid down his farming tools and went to stand by the stump, hoping to pick up more rabbits this way.

Of course, not a single rabbit came any more, and the farmer became a laughing stock all over the state of Song.

7 纪昌学射

Ji Chang Learns How to Shoot an Arrow

甘蝇,古之善射者,彀弓而兽伏鸟下。弟子名飞卫,学射于甘蝇,而巧过其师。纪昌者,又学射于飞卫。飞卫曰:"尔先学不瞬,而后可言射矣。"纪昌归,偃卧其妻之机下,以目承牵挺。二年之后,虽锥末倒眦而不瞬也。以告飞卫。飞卫曰:"未也,必学视而后可,视小如大,视微如著,而后告我。"昌以氂悬虱于牖,南面而望之。旬日之间,浸大也。三年之后,如车轮焉。以睹余物,皆丘山也。乃以燕角之弧,朔蓬之簳射之,贯虱之心,而悬不绝。以告飞卫。飞卫高蹈拊膺曰:"汝得之矣!"

——《列子·汤问》

In ancient times, Gan Ying was an expert archer. When he drew his bow, beasts would lie on their backs and birds would fall from the sky. Gan Ying had a student by the name of Fei Wei who sought instruction on how to shoot an arrow. Fei Wei's skills grew and surpassed the level of his teacher.

There was another man by the name of Ji Chang who went to seek instruction from Fei Wei.

"If you want to learn how to shoot an arrow," said Fei Wei, "you must train your ability to set your eyes on a single object without blinking even once."

Ji Chang went home. He lay under his wife's loom and focused his concentration on the shuttle rushing back and forth while his wife was weaving. He practised that for two years, and afterwards during his concentration he wouldn't blink an eyelash even if someone jabbed his eyelid with a needle. Ji Chang reported it to Fei Wei.

"That's not enough," said the teacher. "Train the power of your eyes and then learn how to shoot an arrow. Practise until you are able to look at a tiny object and see it as a big one; and practice until the blurred image becomes distinct. Come and see me after you have achieved all of this."

Ji Chang returned home. He tied a louse to a strand of a yak's hair and hung it from his window sill. He stared at the louse and in ten days the tiny louse grew big in his eyes. After three years, the louse appeared as large as a cart wheel. Ji Chang then looked around and saw that everything seemed as large as hills. So Ji Chang shot the louse with a bow made of an ox from the state of Yan and an arrow made of a kind of bamboo from the north. The arrow pierced the heart of the louse while the hair, which hung the louse, remained unbroken. Ji Chang went to Fei Wei and reported on his practice.

On hearing this, Fei Wei happily jumped to his feet, patted himself on the chest and said, "You have really mastered the skills of archery!"

8 刻舟求剑

Marking Where the Sword Fell

楚人有涉江者,其剑自舟中坠于水,遽契其舟,曰:"是吾剑之所从坠。"舟止,从其所契者入水求之。舟已行矣,而剑不行,求剑若此,不亦惑乎!

——《吕氏春秋·察今》

One day a man in the state of Chu was crossing the river in a boat. His sword suddenly fell off the boat into the river. The man immediately cut a mark on the side of the boat. He said, "This is the place where my sword fell off."

Once the boat was anchored to the shore, the man jumped into the river and searched in the water for his sword beneath the mark on the boat.

The boat had kept moving, but his sword remained where it fell. Is it foolish to try to recover a sword from the depths in this manner?

9 鹬蚌相争

The Fight Between a Snipe and a Clam

蚌方出曝，而鹬啄其肉，蚌合而箝其喙。鹬曰："今日不雨，明日不雨，即有死蚌。"蚌亦谓鹬曰："今日不出，明日不出，即有死鹬。"两者不肯相舍，渔人得而并禽之。

——《战国策·燕策二》

Once, a clam opened its shell to let in sunshine when a snipe flew over and pecked at the clam inside its shell. Quickly the clam shut his shell, which closed on the snipe's beak.

The snipe said, "If it doesn't rain today or tomorrow, you will be a dead clam."

The clam retorted, "If I don't release your beak today or tomorrow, you will be a dead snipe, too."

The clam and the snipe kept struggling and neither side was ready to yield. It was at this time that a fisherman came and captured both of them.

10 鸡犬皆仙

When a Man Attains the Dao Way Even His Pets Ascend to Heaven

淮南王学道,招会天下有道之人,倾一国之尊,下道术之士。是以道术之士,并会淮南,奇方异术,莫不争出。王遂得道,举家升天,畜产皆仙,犬吠于天上,鸡鸣于云中。

——《论衡·道虚》

Once, there was a king in the state of Huainan who was a follower of the Daoist Way to immortality. He decided to learn from all the people in the world who were masters of the Dao, so he gave up his king's dignity and humbly made friends with practitioners of the Dao.

So many of the masters gathered in Huainan and did their utmost to teach the king their extraordinary skills. Eventually the king attained the Dao and became immortal. His whole family followed him as he ascended to Heaven and so did his domestic animals that also became immortal. His dogs barked in Heaven while his cocks crowed among the clouds.

11 塞翁失马

Loss Sometimes Spells Gain

近塞上之人，有善术者，马无故亡而入胡，人皆吊之。其父曰：“此何遽不为福乎？”居数月，其马将胡骏马而归，人皆贺之。其父曰：“此何遽不能为祸乎？”家富良马，其子好骑，堕而折其髀，人皆吊之，其父曰：“此何遽不为福乎？”居一年，胡人大入塞，丁壮者引弦而战，近塞之人，死者十九，此独以跛之故，父子相保。故福之为祸，祸之为福，化不可极，深不可测也。

——《淮南子·人间训》

Once, near the frontier lived a man who was good at foretelling.

For unknown reasons, one of his horses ran away to an area dominated by the Hu peoples. Everyone came to comfort him, but he said, “Who knows whether the loss may be a blessing? Was it actually a loss?”

Several months later, the lost horse returned with another fine horse of the Hu breed. Everyone came to congratulate him, but he said, “Who knows whether the blessing may be a loss? Was it actually a blessing?”

The man raised many fine horses at home. His son enjoyed riding. One day his son fell off a horse and broke his thigh bone. The people again came to comfort him, but he said, "Who knows whether the loss may be a blessing? Was it actually a loss?"

One year later, the Hu peoples stormed the adjoining area. The young or able-bodied people took up weapons and fought the Hu peoples; nine out of every ten men living near the border were killed. The son, who had broke his leg and became crippled, didn't go to fight. He himself and his father survived.

So a blessing can actually be a misfortune and a misfortune can actually be a blessing. Such a change can go on forever. The reason for this change is beyond our calculation.

12 画蛇添足

Adding Feet to a Sketch-snake

楚有祠者，赐其舍人卮酒。舍人相谓曰："数人饮之不足，一人饮之有余。请画地为蛇，先成者饮酒。"一人蛇先成，引酒且饮之，乃左手持卮，右手画蛇，曰："吾能为之足。"未成，一人之蛇成，夺其卮曰："蛇固无足，子安能为之足？"遂饮其酒。为蛇足者，终亡其酒。

——《战国策·齐策二》

In the state of Chu was a man who offered a small jug of the leftover ceremonial wine to his attendants after his sacrificial ceremony. Those attendants talked among themselves by saying, "The small jug of wine is more than enough for one person, but not enough for all of us. Therefore, each of us should draw a snake on the ground, and whoever finishes his drawing first will drink the wine."

A moment later, one of them finished his drawing first. He took the jug and held it in his hand, ready to drink while he kept drawing with his hand. "I have time to add some feet to my snake," he said to himself.

Just when he was adding the feet, another attendant completed his drawing.. Immediately this attendant grabbed the jug from the first attendant and said, "Snakes don't have feet. How can you add feet to a snake?" With these words, he drank up the wine.

In the end, the one who added the feet lost what should have belonged to him.

13 黔驴技穷

The Donkey in Guizhou Exhausted Its Tricks

黔无驴,有好事者船载以入。至则无可用,放之山下。虎见之,庞然大物也,以为神。蔽林间窥之,稍出近之,慭慭然莫相知。他日,驴一鸣,虎大骇,远遁,以为且噬己也,甚恐。然往来视之,觉无异能者,益习其声,又近出前后,终不敢搏。稍近益狎,荡倚冲冒,驴不胜怒,蹄之。虎因喜,计之曰:"技止此耳!"因跳踉大㘎,断其喉,尽其肉,乃去。噫,形之庞也类有德,声之宏也类有能,向不出其技,虎虽猛,疑畏卒不敢取。今若是焉,悲夫。

——《柳河东集·三戒》

A long time ago, there was no donkey in Guizhou. A man full of curiosity shipped one there in a boat. When the donkey arrived in Guizhou, the man found that the donkey was not of much use. He abandoned the donkey at the foot of a hill.

Then a tiger saw the donkey. Impressed by the donkey's huge size, he thought the donkey must be some kind of monster. Therefore, the tiger hid himself in the woods to peep at the donkey. A little while later, the tiger came out and tried with caution to get close to the donkey. He was not clear what kind of creature the donkey was.

One day the donkey brayed loudly and frightened the tiger that immediately ran away because he thought the donkey was going to bite him. But after the tiger paced back and forth watching the donkey, he realized that the beast had no extraordinary power. Gradually the tiger got used to the bray and moved closer to observe the donkey from both the front and the back. However, he still dare not attack the donkey.

Later on, the tiger moved even closer to the donkey. He tried to provoke the donkey by pushing him, leaning against him and butting him with his head. Finally the donkey lost his temper and kicked his back legs. The tiger became overjoyed because he thought that was all the donkey could do. Therefore, the tiger roared and sprang upon the donkey, and then bit the donkey's throat. The tiger ate the whole donkey and went away.

Well, the donkey was big and tall and seemed to have some virtues; his bray was loud and clear as if he was very powerful. If the donkey hadn't disclosed his limited power, the tiger wouldn't have dared to attack him. This was because at the first sight of the donkey, the tiger was filled with doubt and fear although he was ferocious. It was sad that the donkey suffered a fate like this.

14 拔苗助长

Trying to Make Shoots Grow by Pulling

宋人有闵其苗之不长而揠之者，芒芒然归，谓其人曰："今日病矣，予助苗长矣！"其子趋而往视之，苗则槁矣。

——《孟子·公孙丑上》

A man in the state of Song was always worried that his crops shoots might grow too slowly. So he went down into his fields and pulled every single one of his crops a bit upwards. After that, he returned home, tired and dazed. He said to his family, "I am exhausted today because I helped the shoots grow taller."

On hearing this, his son ran to the fields to look. He only saw that the shoots had all withered away.

15 愚公移山

The Foolish-Old Man Moves the Mountains

太行、王屋二山，方七百里，高万仞。本在冀州之南，河阳之北。北山愚公者，年且九十，面山而居。惩山北之塞，出入之迂也，聚室而谋曰："吾与汝毕力平险，指通豫南，达于汉阴，可乎?”杂然相许。其妻献疑曰:“以君之力，曾不能损魁父之丘，如太行、王屋何? 且焉置土石?”杂曰:“投诸渤海之尾，隐土之北。”遂率子孙荷担者三夫，叩石垦壤，箕畚运于渤海之尾。邻人京城氏之孀妻有遗男，始龀，跳往助之。寒暑易节，始一返焉。河曲智叟笑而止之曰:“甚矣，汝之不惠! 以残年余力，曾不能毁山之一毛，其如土石何?”北山愚公长息曰:“汝心之固，固不可彻，曾不若孀妻弱子。虽我之死，有子存焉;子又生孙，孙又生子;子又有子，子又有孙。子子孙孙，无穷匮也，而山不加增，何苦而不平?”河曲智叟无以应。操蛇之神闻之，惧其不已也，告之于帝。帝感其诚，命夸娥氏二子负二山，一厝朔东，一厝雍南。自此，冀之南，汉之阴，无陇断焉。

——《列子·汤问》

There were two big mountains by the name of Taihang and Wangwu, which had a circumstance of 700 *li* (*Li* is a Chinese measurement which is about 0.5 kilometer) and were 10,000 feet in height. Originally these two mountains were located south of Jizhou and north of Heyang.

There was an old man who was nearly ninety years old living north of the mountains and his name was Yu Gong, which means "foolish old man." Yu Gong's house faced the two mountains; The mountains blocked their access, so each time they left their house, they had to walk all the way around the mountains.

So one day Yu Gong called his family together to discuss his suggestions.

The old man said, "I suggest that you and I put our efforts together to level the mountains. We can remove obstacles and open a way until it reaches the area in the south of Yu Prefecture and the Han River; what do you think of my suggestion?"

Everyone discussed the matter and agreed with him.

His wife had her doubts, "With your limited strength, it is impossible to remove a hill like Kuifu. How can you think about moving the Taihang and Wangwu mountains? Besides, where will you place the earth and rocks?"

"We will carry them to the shores of the Bohai Sea and the places north of Yintu," said several people.

So Yu Gong took the lead and his three sons and grandsons who were strong enough to carry heavy rocks and earth followed him to the mountains, where they broke rocks, dug earth and carried them away in baskets to the shores of the Bohai Sea. A widow by the name of Jing Cheng, one of the old man's neighbors, had a son who was only seven. He came running to offer his help. Due to the long distance between the mountains and the shores, they left during the winter and returned in the summer.

In the Hequ lived another old man whose name was Zhi Sou, which means "wise old man." He stopped Yu Gong and said scornfully, "How foolish you are! At your old and ailing age, you can't even pull up a few blades of grass on these mountains, let alone try to move the earth and rocks to the sea shore!"

Yu Gong gave a deep sigh and replied, "Your old foolish ideas are obstinate, and you are unable to make changes. You are not even as smart as the widow and her son. After I die, my son will still be alive; my sons will have sons and their grandsons will continue to live and have sons of their own. Generation after generation of sons and grandsons there is no end to it. The two mountains won't grow any higher and our hoes will certainly conquer the mountains at last."

Zhi Sou had nothing to say. A god with snakes on his arms heard of what the foolish old man said, and he was afraid that the old man would keep digging, so he reported it to the God of Heaven. Impressed by the old man's determination, the God of Heaven ordered the two sons of Kua Ershi, a god of unusual strength, to carry away these two mountains on their backs and place one mountain in the east of Shou and the other south of the Yong Prefecture.

From then on, there were no more maintains between Jizhou Prefecture and places in the south of the Han River.

16 涸辙之鲋

A Carp on a Dry Rut of a Wheel

周昨来,有中道而呼者。周顾视,车辙中有鲋鱼焉。周问之曰:“鲋鱼来,子何为者耶?”对曰:“我,东海之波臣也。君岂有斗升之水而活我哉?”周曰:“诺。我且南游吴越之王,激西江之水而迎子,可乎?”鲋鱼忿然作色曰:“吾失我常与,我无所处。吾得斗升之水然活耳。君乃言此,曾不如早索我于枯鱼之肆!”

——《庄子·外物》

On my way here yesterday, I heard someone cry for help. I looked around and saw a small carp lying on a dry rut of the road.

1 said, “Why are you crying, my carp?”

“I am an official of the Dragon King from the East Sca,” said the carp. “Could you give me half a bucket of water to save my life?”

“All right,” I said. “I will go south to persuade the king in the states of Wu and Yue to divert some of the water from the Changjiang River to save your life. Is that all right?"

Upon hearing what I said, the carp turned red with anger. He said, "I have lost essential water I depend on. I can not live without it. Now only half a bucket of water can save my life, but unexpectedly you have made an empty talk. You'd better depart early to market to see me in the dry fish store."

17 小儿辩日

A Debate Between Two Children

孔子东游,见两小儿辩斗,问其故。一儿曰:"我以日始出时去人近,而日中时远也。"一儿曰:"我以日初出远,而日中时近也。"一儿曰:"日初出大如车盖,及日中,则如盘盂,此不为远者小而近者大乎?"一儿曰:"日初出沧沧凉凉,及其日中如探汤,此不为近者热而远者凉乎?"孔子不能决也。两小儿笑曰:"孰为汝多知乎?"

——《列子·汤问》

Once, as Confucius traveled to the east, he saw two children debating. He asked why they were arguing.

One child said, "I think the sun is close to us at

sunrise and more distant at noon."

The second child said, "I think that the sun is distant at sunrise and closer at noon."

The first child said, "At sunrise the sun appears as large as a carriage canopy; at noon it looks as small as a rice bowl. Is it not because things far away look small, whereas near things appear large?"

The second child said, "At sunrise the air is still chilly; at noon the weather becomes uncomfortably hot like placing your fingers in hot water. Is this not because it is warmer when close and colder when further away?"

Confucius couldn't judge which of the children was correct.

The two children laughed at Confucius saying, "Who said you possessed such a wide knowledge of things?"

18 鲁侯养鸟

The King of the Lu Feeds a Sea Bird

昔者,海鸟止于鲁郊。鲁侯御而觞之于庙,奏九韶以为乐,具太牢以为膳。鸟乃眩视忧悲,不敢食一脔,不敢饮一杯,三日而死。

——《庄子·达生》

A long time ago, a big sea bird flew to the state of Lu and stayed in the suburbs.

The state king warmly welcomed the sea bird. He held a feast to entertain the bird in the king's ancestral temple where musicians played ceremonious *jiushao* music to entertain the bird . Beef, lamb and pork were provided in the big plates to feed the bird.

The music, wonderful food and wine overwhelmed the bird. He became so confused that he grew depressed. He didn't dare to eat a piece of meat and drink a cup of wine. Three days later, he died.

19 望洋兴叹

Gazing at the Sea and Sighing at Its Infinitude

秋水时至,百川灌河;泾流之大,两涘渚崖之间,不辨牛马。于是焉河伯欣然自喜,以天下之美为尽在己,顺流而东行,至于北海。东面而视,不见水端。于是焉河伯始旋其面目,望洋向若而叹曰:"野语有之曰:'闻道百以为莫己若者',我之谓也。且夫我尝闻少仲尼之闻而轻伯夷之义者,始吾弗信。今我睹子之难穷也。吾非至于子之门则殆矣!吾长见笑于大方之家!"

——《庄子·秋水》

As autumn arrived, so did the rains. All the rivers rose and flowed to the Yellow River ,which expanded so widely that the cows and the horses on one bank of the Yellow River couldn't be seen from the other side. Hebo, a god in charge of the Yellow River, was excited. He thought that all the waters in the world flowed into his river, and his place had become the most splendid of all.

Hebo flowed eastward until he reached the North Sea where he looked further east and couldn't see the end of the sea. His complacent expression disappeared. Looking up, he sighed and emotionally said to the god in charge of the North Sea, "As the old saying goes, 'Those who know all the hows and whys often consider themselves much better than others.' This saying is directed at me. I heard that some people disrespected the knowledge of Confucius and scorned the righteous cause which Bo Yi preserved. At the beginning, I didn't believe it, but now I have discovered that the North Sea which you control is boundless. If I hadn't come here, great would be my sorrow, for those with great wisdom would laugh at me."

20 朝三暮四

Three in the Morning and Four in the Afternoon

宋有狙公者,爱狙,养之成群,能解狙之意,狙亦得公之心。损其家口,充狙之欲。俄而匮焉,将限其食,恐众狙之不驯于己也,先诳之曰:“与若茅,朝三而暮四,足乎?”众狙皆起而怒。俄而曰:“与若茅,朝四而暮三,足乎?”众狙皆伏而喜。

——《列子·皇帝》

There was a man who raised monkeys. He loved monkeys so much that they multiplied into a large group. He understood monkeys, and his monkeys knew how to please him. In order to satisfy his monkeys' desires, the old man took some of his family's food to feed them. But soon, the old man's food was running short. The old man needed to cut back on the amount of food he fed his monkeys, but he was afraid that his monkeys might become aggressive. So he tricked his monkeys by saying, "I am thinking of feeding you with acorns, three in the morning and four in the afternoon. Is that all right?"

The monkeys stamped their feet in anger when they heard his proposal. A moment later, the old man said,

"How about four in the morning and three in the afternoon? Is that all right?"

All his monkeys rolled on the ground in joy.

参考书目
Bibliography

Beth Bauer. *Enjoy China More*. Cain-Lockhart Press, 1985

Boye Lafayette De Mente. *Chinese Etiquette & Ethics in Business*. Lincolnwood: NTC Publishing Group, 1989

Coye, M. J., Livinggston, J., & Highland, J. *China Yesterday and Today* (third edition). Bantam Books, Inc., 1983

Evelyne, G. *China Companion*. London: Andre Deutsch Ltd., 1981

Lau, D. C. *Lao Tzu—Tao Te Ching*. Penguin Books, 1963

Schirokauer, C. *A Brief History of Chinese and Japanese Civilizations*. Harcourt Brace Jovanovich Publishers, 1989

Sinclair, K. *Culture Shock! A Guide to Customs and Etiquette*. Oregon: Graphic Arts Center Publishing Company, 1996

Terrill, R. *The China Difference*. New York: Harper & Row Publisher, Inc., 1972

W. Scott M. *China: its History and Culture*. Lippincott & Crowell Publishers, 1995

冯天瑜主编. 家训集览. 武汉:湖北教育出版社, 1994

苟承益著. 中国古代典籍一百种简介. 成都:成都电讯工程学院出版社, 1988

韩鉴堂编著. 中国文化. 北京:北京语言学院出版社,1999

齐雯编. 中国概貌(英文版, 修订本). 北京:外文出版社,1984

齐星编著. 中国传统节日民俗. 北京:外文出版社, 1988

汝信主编. 简明中国百科全书. 北京:中国社会科学出版社,1989

王建辉, 易学金. 中国文化知识精华. 武汉:湖北人民出版社,1989

谢谦编著. 国学词典. 成都:四川人民出版社,1998

许树安,郑春苗,王秀芳编著. 中国文化知识. 北京:北京语言学院出版社,1987

许树安, 郑春苗, 王秀芳编著. 中国文化知识(续编). 北京:北京语言学院出版社,1990

许渊冲选译. 唐宋一百首. 北京:中国对外翻译出版公司、商务印书馆(香港)有限公司,1991

业露华著. 佛教历史百问. 北京:中国建设出版社, 1989

策划：丁海秀

责编：王　艳

图书在版编目（CIP）数据

沿途导游掌中宝/杨天庆编著.—北京：旅游教育出版社，2007.1

ISBN 978-7-5637-1412-4

Ⅰ.沿…　Ⅱ.杨…　Ⅲ.导游-解说词-中国-英文　Ⅳ.K928.9

中国版本图书馆 CIP 数据核字(2006)第116951号

沿途导游掌中宝

杨天庆　编著

出版单位	旅游教育出版社
地　　址	北京市朝阳区定福庄南里1号
邮　　编	100024
发行电话	(010)65778403 65728372 65767462(传真)
本社网址	www.tepcb.com
E-mail	tepfx @ 163.com
排版单位	首都经济贸易大学出版社激光照排部
印刷单位	北京科普瑞印刷有限责任公司
经销单位	新华书店
开　　本	787×1092　1/32
印　　张	12.125
字　　数	164千字
版　　次	2007年1月第1版
印　　次	2007年11月第2次印刷
定　　价	20.00元

（图书如有装订差错请与发行部联系）